Business Dynamics in North America

Rajagopal · Vladimir Zlatev

Business Dynamics in North America

Analysis of Spatial and Temporal Trade Patterns

palgrave
macmillan

Rajagopal
EGADE Business School
Mexico City, Mexico

Vladimir Zlatev
Boston University
Boston, MA, USA

ISBN 978-3-319-57605-3 ISBN 978-3-319-57606-0 (eBook)
DOI 10.1007/978-3-319-57606-0

Library of Congress Control Number: 2017944609

Printed on acid-free paper

This Palgrave Macmillan imprint is published by Springer Nature
The registered company is Springer International Publishing AG
The registered company address is: Gewerbestrasse 11, 6330 Cham, Switzerland

Preface

Globalization and its impacts have profound implications for a broad range of issues important to the funding community. These issues range from the sustainable use of the worlds' resources and the protection and preservation of the environment, to the need to improve living standards, safeguard human rights, promote and protect cultures, and ensure democratic and responsive global governance. The multi-dimensional growth, in which a corporate firm manages relatively freestanding business units, was the most successful design of the marketing organizations of the twentieth century. However, some firms have evolved organizational designs that signal a new way of resolving the market competition and trade dynamics. The global competition is observed on both aggressive and defensive dimensions in the market. The companies are capable of managing appropriate diffusion of technology and adaptation process among the customer segments and are found to be highly successful. The North American Free Trade Agreement (NAFTA) was expected to primarily benefit the wealthier northern states of Mexico due to their proximity to the US market. Standard trade theory might predict that given Mexico's relative abundance of low-skilled labor, poorer regions with large pools of unskilled labor might benefit more from the trade agreement. The multi-dimensional growth of marketing organization is best understood as the next step in the evolution from a resource-centric business model to a customer-centric knowledge-sharing model. It is a way of managing competitive markets that are particularly well adapted to stimulating the market leadership that is necessary to create economic value in complex markets.

This book examines the growth of international trade in North America during the pre- and post-NAFTA and analyzes the complexities that occurred while the economic recession struck the global markets between 2007 and 2011. The trade and economy in North America have been woven around the market power of the USA since long. Globalization phenomenon has driven the emerging markets with several competitive advantages to rebuild their economy and contribute by sharing their business potential to cross-border destinations. Mexico, being a resource-rich country, has been at advantages to go global as it could cater to the upper and lower geo-demographic ends in the region. Emerging markets gained structural advantages embedded in the business operation within the global economy. This book presents new insights on developing competitive business and breakthroughs in managing them considering the time, territory, target, and tasks management assuring business gains and market competitiveness.

Globalization has opened many opportunities to explore trade development in the destination markets. However, global competition in business has created a critical chain of business functions to succeed in the competitive marketplace. Thus, most companies develop skills in carrying the work dynamics over the give time and space. The book extends discussions on the contemporary trade theories to the realm of international markets. Trade flows today encompass a broad diversity of endpoints, and no organization can aspire to cover the entire globe with adequate breadth and depth. Global banks' large yet often thin networks were typically designed to meet the needs of large corporate clients based in Europe or the USA, but now these networks are costly to maintain and inadequate in geographical reach. Regional and domestic banks typically enjoy strong relationships with SMEs, but they need access to an increasing number of foreign markets and want to defend against global players reaching down market. An integrated trade strategy captures the synergies between the dynamics of international economies and market competition that seek superior performance in the marketplace and non-market strategies that shape the trade environment across the regions. This book extends the conceptual and analytical foundations of international trade and economy in the North American region. While the impacts of cross-cultural business growth on international trade and foreign direct investment (FDI) have been much discussed, the influence of trade policy within a regional Free Trade Agreement has been underappreciated in international business. The discussions in the book address this paucity by integrating literature from international economics and international business by analyzing the international economic transactions in international trade and in foreign direct investment.

This book has been divided into 10 chapters spread over three sections comprising understanding North American trade and economy scenario, operationalizing business in destination markets, and rethinking future strategies. Chapter 1 discusses an overview of North American trade liberalization effects in reference to NAFTA and international trade policy perspectives to extend cooperation for rebuilding the trade and economy during the post-economic recession period. This chapter discusses several topics of interest that include international trade environment, global trade dynamics, recovery in regional economies, NAFTA trade regime, international competition and NAFTA responsiveness, and overall economic development measures. Chapter 2 critically examines various trade and economic development factor in the context of NAFTA partner countries. Among these, the shifts in industrial policy in Mexico, loose ends of industrial policy, US industrial policy, export trends in Mexico, financial integration and international trade, spending on research and development, and disruptive tendencies in markets have been deliberated in this chapter. Delineating the discussions on the market integration in NAFTA region, Chap. 3 analyzes the impact of market integration on the economy responding the pertinent questions that remain unresolved, whether the market integration through regional trade agreements delivers the desired benefits to the developing nations as compared to the one with the develop trade and economic conditions. Besides the market integration effects, this chapter also deliberates upon attributes of NAFTA, economic integration and growth, productivity and growth in the USA, market dynamics, franchising, direct marketing, and managing intellectual property rights in the North American countries. Chapter 4 discusses manufacturing performance among the North American countries during the post-NAFTA period across the product portfolios in the principal industries. Discussion on the other relevant subjects to doing business in North America such as revenue optimization strategies, export–import scenario, and international investment among the USA, Canada, and Mexico has also been discussed in this chapter. Various topics that make a significant contribution toward venture collaboration and management have been discussed in Chap. 5. This chapter broadly discusses the current scenarios of human resources management, talent search organizations, changing organization structures among the companies in the North American region, the status of innovation, technology, and research and development, attractions toward international investments, and the strategies of companies on arbitrage and hedging in international markets.

Market volatility and risk factors have been discussed in Chap. 6 with specific reference to the topics on product life cycle management, microeconomic technology drivers, NAFTA status in the decade of 2020, opportunities for business collaboration understanding the market competition, and probable international trade risks. Chapter 7 addresses international trade policy and development perspectives by critically examining the effects of changing political ideologies on international trade and economy in the North American region, international trade policies, NAFTA conflicts and settlements, globalization and business analytics, and new dimensions of competitive growth. Functional strategies in managing international trade are addressed in Chap. 8 from managerial perspectives with a focus on marketing-mix, distribution, operations and logistics, international branding, pricing in international markets, and bringing sustainable differentiation to stay competitive in the global marketplace. As the competition is growing continuously in the global market, the risk on traditional decision-making tools and techniques is also falling in jeopardy. This chapter discusses also investments and transfer of technology toward developing international trade in the North American marketplace. Chapter 9 discusses exploring opportunities in international trade development by emphasizing new strategies concerning modes of entry, strategic collaboration, and cross-border investment in the North American region. The concluding Chap. 10 addresses the challenges ahead in international trade in view of the current political thinking in the region, cross-cultural shifts in the global marketplace, business collaboration and market competition, and technology driver ahead in marketing at international destinations.

This book is an outcome of the continuum of the thought process from a classroom to a wider platform of the audience. Initially, we worked out a teaching agenda on international business management and business expansion models for North American companies and discussed them in length in the classroom encouraging timeless discussions on the subject that helped in developing new conceptual frameworks on the subject. This book reviews categorically the international trade theories, concepts, and previous researches, and discusses the applied tools and techniques for business projects. The book discusses contemporary trade dynamics for the companies to grow competitive along with the market players and consumers in the North American marketplace. This book significantly contributes to the existing literature and serves as a learning post and a think tank for students, researchers, and business managers. This book has been developed to serve as a status paper on the trade and economy of the North American region and a contemporary reference for the researchers in the area of international trade and economic growth. Besides serving as a reference book to the students within the subject area, this book would also inspire market analysts and business consultants engaged in business expansion in the international marketplace.

We hope this book will contribute to the existing literature and deliver new concepts to the students and researchers to pursue the subject further. Reading this book, researchers on international trade and economy may enrich their research base, hypotheses, and synthesis on the subject, while students would learn the new dimensions of marketing strategies.

Mexico City, Mexico — Rajagopal
Boston, USA — Vladimir Zlatev
March 2017

Acknowledgements

The thought process in evolving this book originated from the course on Doing Business in North America, which we have designed, developed, and began teaching online under the graduate program at Boston University since 2013. We have benefitted by the discussions of our colleagues within and outside the EGADE Business School and Boston University. We are thankful to Dr. Kip Becker and Dr. John Sullivan, co-chairs of Administrative Sciences Department of Boston University, and Dr. Maria de Lourdes Dieck Assad, Dean of EGADE Business School who have always encouraged me to take up new challenges in teaching graduate courses, develop new insights, and contribute to the existing literature prolifically. We had encouraging discussions with the students, online instructional course designers, and course facilitators on the subject while imparting the course, which helped in enriching the contents of this book.

We acknowledge the outstanding support of Liz Barlow, Senior Commissioning Editor of Palgrave Macmillan at Basingstoke, UK, who critically examined the proposal, guided the manuscript preparation, and took the publication process forward. The publication foreground of this book has been well supported by Marcus Ballenger, Commissioning Editor of scholarly business books at the New York office. We express our sincere thanks to Marcus and his team in providing all support during the production process. We also would like to thank Jazmine Robles for staying in touch with us all through the publication process and helping us with the adjustment on the deadlines of this book.

We are thankful to various anonymous referees of our previous research works on globalization, consumer behavior, and marketing strategy that helped in looking deeper into the conceptual gaps and improving the quality with their valuable comments. Finally, we express our deep gratitude to Arati Rajagopal who has been instrumental in completing this book. We acknowledge her help in copy editing the first draft of the manuscript and for staying in touch until the final proofs were cross-checked and the index was developed.

Contents

About the Authors

Rajagopal is Professor of Marketing at EGADE Business School of Monterrey Institute of Technology and Higher Education (ITESM), Mexico City Campus and Life Fellow of the Royal Society for Encouragement of Arts, Manufacture and Commerce, London. He is also Fellow of the Chartered Management Institute and Fellow of Institute of Operations Management, UK. Dr. Rajagopal is also Visiting Professor at Boston University, Boston, Massachusetts. He has been listed with biography in various international directories. He offers courses on Competitor Analysis, Marketing Strategy, Advance Selling Systems, International Marketing, Services Marketing, New Product Development, and other subjects of contemporary interest to the students of undergraduate, graduate, and doctoral programs. He has imparted training to senior executives and has conducted over 60 management and faculty development programs. Dr. Rajagopal holds post-graduate and doctoral degrees in Economics and Marketing, respectively, from Pandit Ravishankar Shukla University in India. His specialization is in the fields of Marketing Management, Rural Economic Linkages, and Development Economics. He has to his credit 50 books on marketing management and rural development themes and over 400 research contributions that include published research papers in national and international refereed journals. He is Editor-in-Chief of International *Journal of Leisure and Tourism Marketing*, *International Journal of Business Competition and Growth*, and *International Journal of Built Environment and Asset Management*. Dr. Rajagopal is also

Regional Editor of *Emerald Emerging Markets Case Studies*, published by Emerald Publishers, UK. He is on the editorial board of various journals of international repute. Currently, Dr. Rajagopal holds the honor of the highest level of National Researcher-SNI Level-III. He has been awarded UK–Mexico Visiting Chair 2016–2017 for collaborative research on "Global-Local Innovation Convergence" with the University of Sheffield, UK, instituted by the Consortium of Higher Education Institutes of Mexico and UK.

Vladimir Zlatev holds Ph.D. and MS degrees from Dresden University of Technology, Germany, and he is an experienced educator and entrepreneur, with an extensive background in industrial engineering and corporate management. He focuses on marketing research and competitive analysis based on specific industries and market segments, companies, and technologies. Zlatev's interests include applications of system dynamics in areas such as decision management, performance management, international trade, and international logistics; and researching and managing complex high-technology initiatives that involve international cooperation, intellectual property rights, and technology transfer. In addition to his work in developing and delivering professional education programs, he served as project leader in a European Union-financed initiative on the design, management, and implementation of educational programs and consulting projects as they relate to best business theories and practices in the management of international tourism companies and destinations. Zlatev is a member of the editorial board of the *International Journal of Business Competition and Growth* (InderScience Publishers, UK).

List of Tables

PART I

Understanding North American Trade and Economy Scenario

CHAPTER 1

Overview: North American Trade and Economy

North American trade and economy had suffered a severe setback after the financial downturn during 2007–2011 that crashed the international trade dynamics and reversed the booming business cycles. The trilateral agreement among the Canada, Mexico, and the USA had been driving the international trade faster in the region since its implementation in 1994. However, North American Free Trade Agreement (NAFTA) continues to be of interest to boost the regional balance of trade among the member countries as partners, and also because this agreement plays a significant role in the US trade policy. This chapter discusses an overview of North American trade liberalization effects in reference to NAFTA and international trade policy perspectives to extend cooperation for rebuilding the trade and economy during the post-economic recession period.

Globalization has become a functional dynamics of emerging firms in the business environment today. Most firms believe that globalization is a synonym to the business growth and invest perennial resources in developing a strategy for going global. It has become one of the most pertinent issues for managers of growing firms around the world. In the process of evolving global, many forces drive local enterprises to globalize by expanding their brand reach and participating in foreign markets through various modes of entry. In developed countries, domestic markets have turned mature and are demanding to seek international markets while in some countries like Brazil, Russia, India, and China,

Rajagopal and V. Zlatev, *Business Dynamics in North America*,
DOI 10.1007/978-3-319-57606-0_1

most companies in the present competitive marketplace are born global. A large number of companies in the USA are nourished by the huge domestic market but typically lag behind their European and Japanese rivals in internationalization. The born global firms hold dynamic growth in the competitive marketplace and achieve substantial international sales from an early stage in their development despite economic and technological constraints. They internationalize rapidly as the period from domestic establishment to initial foreign market entry is often 3 or less number of years. The born global firms are emerging in sizable numbers worldwide. Until recently, international business was mainly the domain of large, well-resourced multinational enterprises. The appearance of large numbers of born global firms is revolutionizing the traditional character of the international business and helping to reshape the global economy (Cavusgil and Knight 2009). Companies intending to go global exhibit two apparent objectives—to take advantage of opportunities for growth and expansion and survival in the business amidst growing competition. However, firms that fail to pursue global opportunities eventually lose their domestic markets and may be pushed aside by stronger and more competitive global firms. In the process of going global, firms need to adopt innovative marketing strategy to sustain against competing firms. Most firms follow a global perspective to expand their business across the destinations instead of adopting a country-by-country or region-by-region perspective in developing a marketing strategy (Rajagopal 2014).

International Trade Environment

The trade and economy in North America have been woven around the market power of the USA since long. Globalization phenomenon has driven the emerging markets with several competitive advantages to rebuild their economy and contribute by sharing their business potential to cross-border destinations. Mexico, being a resource-rich country, has been at advantage to go global as it could cater to the upper and lower geo-demographic ends in the region. Emerging markets gain structural advantages embedded in the business operation within the global economy. NAFTA has been a triangular convention between the USA, Canada, and Mexico toward the development of trade, economy, and factors of productions, which was promulgated by the trade authorities in 1994. Such regional agreement has also attracted the Western trade negotiators, in general, to focus their attention on mapping comparative advantages over the land, labor, capital, technology, and managerial know-how in going global. This strategy has also raised issues on stabilizing exchange rates of emerging countries like Mexico and improves its economy by making structural changes to streamline the advantages to reap in various sectors of international trade. But its roots run far deeper down to the fundamental issue that labor could not be freely traded on a single regional Free Trade Agreement, while capital and commodities could be paved into the other destinations. However, NAFTA encouraged contract manufacturing of products through the small and medium enterprises, commonly known as maquiladoras in Mexico taking advantage of cost of labor in a lower-wage emerging market country and save enormously on labor costs.

Major structural shifts in the global economy are creating new opportunities in transaction banking, particularly in trade finance. International trade is growing faster than global GDP, and Asia is now the center of global expansion, driving trade growth in other emerging markets and in developed economies as well. Where trade flows were once concentrated in a limited number of North–North corridors, trading relationships today extend to more geographical endpoints and encompass a broader range of companies. As small- and medium-size enterprises (SMEs) become more active in cross-border commerce, banks of all sizes comprising global, regional, and local face significant challenges to winning in trade finance. The stakes in the trade finance revenues approached $100 billion in 2012. To tap this important market, banks must first understand the increasingly complex nature of the trade finance landscape (IP et al. 2014).

An ongoing shift in global economic activity from developed to developing economies, accompanied by growth in the number of consumers in emerging markets, is the global development that executives around the world view as most important for business and most positive for their own companies' profits over the next 5 years. Executives also identify two other critical positive aspects of globalization: technologies that enable a free flow of information worldwide and, increasingly, global labor markets. The global economy faces significant challenges as it continues to integrate high levels of public debt in Europe and North America that are causing the fear of a negative impact on GDP growth. Emerging markets, with populations that are young and growing, will increasingly become not only the focus of rising consumption and production but also major providers of capital, talent, and innovation. This will make it imperative for most companies to succeed in emerging markets. In a pattern consistent across nearly all regions, executives view government's role in their companies' home markets over the next 5 years somewhat differently than do executives from other regions.

Global economic activities across the developed, developing, and transitional economies have broadly strengthened during the beginning of 2020s and expected to improve further by the end of the decade with much of the impetus for growth coming from advanced economies. Although downside risks have diminished overall, the lower-than-expected inflation poses risks for advanced economies. There is increased financial volatility in emerging market economies, and increases in the cost of capital will likely dampen investment and weigh on growth. Advanced economy policy makers need to avoid a premature withdrawal of monetary accommodation. Emerging market economy policy makers must adopt measures to change fundamentals, facilitate external adjustment, further monetary policy tightening, and carry out structural reforms (International Monetary Fund 2014). In emerging market and developing economies, growth picked up slightly in the second half of 2013. The weaker cyclical momentum in comparison with that in the advanced economies reflects the opposite effects of two forces on growth. On the one hand, the export growth increased, lifted by stronger activity in advanced economies and by currency depreciation. On the other hand, the investment weakness continued, and external funding and domestic financial conditions increasingly tightened. Supply-side and other structural constraints on investment and potential output (for example, infrastructure bottlenecks) are issues in some economies. These offsetting forces are expected to remain in effect through much of 2014. Table 1.1 exhibits the growth rates of the economy of USA, Canada, and Mexico alongside Latin America and Caribbean countries. The world export and import trend also has been shown in the table as reference indicator driving the economic growth of the countries.

The data exhibited in the above table reveal that the economic growth of Mexico has picked up again from 2013 and stands with the substantial share as against the Latin America and Caribbean region. Contrary to the economic growth of Mexico, the data show that the economic indicators of the USA and Canada are moving at a slower pace in the post-economic recession period. Overall, the emerging market and developing economies continue to contribute more than two-thirds of global

Table 1.1 Economic growth in NAFTA region (percent change)

Country/region	*2012*	*2013*	*2014*	*2015*	*2016 (P)*
USA	2.8	2.2	2.4	3.1	3.1
Canada	1.7	2.0	2.5	2.2	2.0
Mexico	3.9	1.4	2.1	3.0	3.3
Latin America and Caribbean	3.1	2.9	1.3	0.9	2.0

P Provisional

Source Calculated from the data of International Monetary Fund (2015), Uneven Growth: Short- and Long-Term Factors, *World Economic Report*, IMF Head Quarters, Washington, DC

growth, and their growth has shown an increase from 4.7% in 2013 to 4.9% in 2014 and further to 5.3% in 2015. In a recent evaluation of global economy, IMF estimates that global growth has increased slightly from 3.4% in 2014 to 3.5% in 2015 and further projected to pick up in 2016 to an annual rate of 3.8%. Growth in Latin America in the second half of 2014 was modest, reflecting lower-than-expected growth in Mexico, and weakening trend in other economies in the region. The data reveal that economic conditions in the USA remain in place for robust performance in 2015. Such sustainable economic growth in the country was supported by the lower energy prices, discrete inflation, reduced fiscal imbalance, strengthened banking and finance performance, and an improving housing market. These forces are expected to strengthen the dollar value in international markets through enhanced exports. As a result, growth is projected to reach 3.1% in 2015 as well as in 2016. However, despite the increased investment and services finance inflows from the NAFTA countries including the USA and Canada, Mexico's projected growth of 3% in 2015 appears to be 0.5% point lower than the previous year.

Only a modest acceleration in activity is expected for regional growth in Latin America, with growth rising from 2.5% in 2014 to 3% in 2015. Some economies have recently faced strong market pressure, and tighter financial conditions will weigh on growth. Important differences are evident across the major economies in the region. In Mexico, growth is expected to strengthen to 3% in 2014, resulting from a more expansionary macroeconomic policy stance, a reversal of the special factors behind the low growth in 2013, and spillovers from higher US growth. It is expected to increase to 3.5% in 2015, as the effect of major structural reforms takes hold. Activity in Brazil remains subdued. Demand is supported by the recent depreciation of the real and still buoyant wage and consumption growth, but private investment continues to be weak, partly reflecting low business confidence.

Downside risks to growth in emerging market economies have increased even though earlier risks have partly materialized and have already resulted in downward revisions to the baseline forecasts. Many of these economies are still adjusting to weaker-than-expected medium-term growth prospects. Foreign investors are also now more sensitive to risks in these economies, and financial conditions have tightened as a result. The higher cost of capital could lead to a larger-than-projected slowdown in investment and durables consumption, with recent monetary policy tightening in some economies adding to the risk. Risks could also come from unexpectedly rapid normalization of US monetary policy or from other bouts of risk aversion among investors. Either case could lead to financial turmoil, capital outflows, and difficult adjustments in some emerging market economies, with a risk of contagion and broad-based financial and balance of payments stress. These would lower growth.

Global Trade Dynamics

Commercial activity everywhere is increasingly dependent on international trade services. From 1990 to 2012, cross-border trade as a share of global economic output grew from one-fifth to one-third. This long-term growth can be attributed to a variety of factors, including the expansion of the middle class in emerging markets (especially in Asia) and trade liberalization. While recent protectionist measures and preference for regional over global trade agreements suggest that the pace of globalization may be slowing down, the cross-border trade as a share of total output will continue to expand, outpacing GDP growth by 20% over the medium term. The trade ecosystem not only comprises a more diverse set of internationally active companies but is also more geographically fragmented, with new corridors linking fast-growing emerging markets with Asia, the center of global trade growth. Growth is much slower in mature markets, but they still hold important opportunities. Europe remains the largest region for international trade, and North American trade with Latin America and emerging Asia (excluding Hong Kong, Japan, Singapore, South Korea, and Taiwan) grew by approximately 40% between 2007 and 2012.

Serving large corporates pose increasingly complex challenges as well. The expectation was that corporate needs would harmonize across countries and regions in a globalized world. However, the underlying motivation to use trade finance and the criteria used to select a service provider still differ significantly across regions. Trade services are vital to large corporates and a growing number of SMEs, and any bank unable to support its clients' increasingly diverse and geographically extensive trading demands puts their relationships with these institutions at risk.

Trade flows today encompass a broad diversity of endpoints, and no organization can aspire to cover the entire globe with adequate breadth and depth. Global banks' large yet often thin networks were typically designed to meet the needs of large corporate clients based in Europe or the USA, but now these networks are costly to maintain and inadequate in geographical reach. Regional and domestic banks typically enjoy strong relationships with SMEs, but they need access to an increasing number of foreign markets and want to defend against global players reaching down market. Correspondent banking and "white label" arrangements already address these gaps to some extent, but they usually provide only limited functionality within local markets, often do not cover new corridors adequately, and may expose a bank to client risks they do not understand and cannot evaluate thoroughly. Deeper technological integration among partners in various industries has opened access to underserved markets while streamlining processes and improving transparency. Technologically integrated alliances require broad client adoption of digital processes, either in parallel with the current documentary workflow or as an entirely new supply chain interface for sourcing, financing, and tracking. The economic recovery during the post-economic recession period (2011–2016) in the USA and Canada has been largely supported by the stability and gradual increase in the exports as indicated in Table 1.2.

The cross-border trade is growing relative to global output, making trade finance crucial to a wider cross section of cash management clients. This creates highly lucrative opportunities for banks of all sizes, but the geographical breadth and technological complexity pose significant challenges. While North corridors are still core to the business, the best opportunities for growth and future market leadership are in corridors linking Asia and other emerging markets. This expanded landscape, combined with wider participation of SMEs, is pushing global players to become more selective in whom they serve and where. In the past,

Table 1.2 Economic recovery indicators in the USA and Canada (percent change)

Country	*Period*	*GDP growth*	*Net exports*
USA	2011–2012	2.3	0.1
	2013–2014	2.3	0
	2015–2016	3.1	−0.4
Canada	2011–2012	2	−0.1
	2013–2014	2.3	0.7
	2015–2016	2.1	0.5

Source Calculated from the data of International Monetary Fund (2015), *Uneven Growth* Short- and Long-Term Factors, World Economic Report, IMF Head Quarters, Washington, DC

proprietary networks were adequate, but going forward, most banks will seek technologically innovative partnerships and alliances to achieve geographical reach and local depth in addition to the continued digitization of trade finance processes.

Clorox is a loose acronym formed from the names of its ingredients. It remained a one-product company until the 1970s, when it aggressively expanded into everything from cat litter to salad dressings. Yet, its geographic expansion has been much more modest: just $1.2 billion of its fiscal 2010 sales of $5.53 billion came from international markets, with the remaining 80% from Canada and the USA. Clorox's international presence is currently limited to Australia and Latin America. Yet, the incentive to expand geographically is obvious: Pretax earnings growth from international markets was 23% in fiscal 2010, compared with 7% for the core North American cleaning-products business. The executive charged with spearheading Clorox's expansion effort is Beth Springer, who joined the company in 1990 in brand management and is now executive vice president, international. In this interview with McKinsey's Amy Howe, she discusses how the history of Clorox has shaped its decision-making, and the way it evaluates potential growth markets (Howe 2010).

Delivering profitable sales growth requires using a combination of hard data and judgment. Companies start by looking for opportunities in categories, as they know well where growth is projected to remain above the company average, there is a profit pool or at least good indicators that the category can be profitable, and the competitive dynamics are attractive. It comes down to whether or not to see a way to achieve a number one or number two share position in our targeted categories and to command a price premium through the reapplication of category and brand insights, technology, and initiatives. Managing the volatility and the country risks and getting the right talent were difficult. Also, the US market was still growing faster than it is today. So, the companies have moved into developing markets more incrementally and primarily via acquisition and partnership.

Local market leaders aren't in that position by accident. If they have market share, they're doing something right, and we need to learn what's driving that. Some are also very low cost and scrappy, and especially effective in the traditional trade and outside urban centers, where multinational corporations tend to enter. Companies sometimes find that local players look good on the surface but don't deliver what we consider a decent return on investment. These guys can spoil a market, and we won't enter if we can't build a leadership share and earn a good return. It requires some bigger moves into new emerging markets, and we know the competition sees the same opportunities.

Business models in the twenty-first century are developed by the companies converging global–local strategies, and their design has become a key driver of the performance. In fact, the business model design is often associated with innovation. Many firms, though, fail to realize the full potential of their current business model simply because they are not aware of it. Nevertheless, Google succeeded in realizing its business model's full potential by offering its main service, Internet search, completely for free while capturing value from secondary opportunities such as Google AdWords. Especially for new ventures and SMEs, capturing value from secondary opportunities or business model sophistication is of critical importance toward increasing the pool of resources at hand and giving momentum to the firm's development. Of many companies, Google, Ryanair, the Super Girl Contest on Hunan TV, and Spreadshirt have found right opportunity in the right market segment. Some of these companies have employed business model sophistication strategies by uncovering additional functions of your product, identifying strategic benefits for customers and distributors, taking advantage of economies of scope, utilizing cross-selling opportunities, and involving mass users of the market. All these strategies lay a strong emphasis on stakeholder commitment (Kesting and Gunzel-Jensen 2015).

Increasing competition in the marketplace has driven innovation among firms, and most firms recognize that they should invest resources in building ideas and capabilities for innovation. Most firms attract tacit knowledge, diffuse on social media and within the organization, and develop trust among consumers and market players on innovations in the products and services of the firm. However, for most companies, innovation is an extensive collection of initiatives and growth stimulating changes but the lack of coordination, and is managed with vacillating strategies. Firms need a balanced innovation portfolio and the ability to approach for sustainable and expected returns for the long run. In order to manage innovations, it is necessary for the firms to develop the unique capacities needed for transformational innovation finding the talent required for the breakthrough of innovations and integration with the core business. Continuity in business innovation requires adequate financial and human resources as well as technology infrastructure. Innovations-related projects should be planned with a different priority in a pipeline management approach and developed through corporate growth metrics. Companies that learn how to manage for total innovation can fully harness innovation's energy and make it a reliable driver of growth (Nagji and Tuff 2012).

Recovery in Regional Economies

It has been observed that during the post-recession period (2012 onward) in the USA and Canada, the economy is growing robust. However, lower energy prices have boosted growth momentum in the USA as they lowered the risks to the Canadian economy owing to the relatively large size of its energy sector. In the USA, labor markets and business and consumer confidence have also shown sustainable improvements. The economic growth in the USA has shown upward trend revealing 3.9% growth on an average in 2014. Consumption index has been the main engine of growth during the above reference period. Besides, the economy also benefitted from steady job creation and income growth, lower oil prices, and improved consumer confidence. The indicators of economic recovery among the NAFTA countries are exhibited in Table 1.3.

The data reveal that the real GDP has grown among all NAFTA countries though the overall NATFA region indicates stagnation in real GDP growth during the project period of 2016 as compared to 2015. However, the consumer prices show an increasing trend in all NAFTA countries, which might lead to mild to medium inflation effects in the respective countries. Mexico's economy is projected to grow by 3.0%

Table 1.3 Trends in regional economies of real GDP and consumer prices (percent change)

Country/region	*2013*	*2014*	*2015*	*2016 (P)*
USA	1.9	2.4 (1.6)	3.1 (0.1)	3.1 (1.5)
Canada	2.0	2.5 (1,9)	2.2 (0.9)	2.0 (2.0)
Mexico	1.1	2.1 (4.0)	3.0 (3.2)	3.3 (3.0)
North America	1.8	2.4 (1.9)	3.0 (0.5)	3.0 (1.7)
Latin America and Caribbean	2.7	1.3	0.9	2.0

P Provisional
Figures in parentheses indicate consumer prices
Source Calculated from the data of International Monetary Fund (2015), Uneven Growth: Short- and Long-Term Factors, World Economic Report, IMF Head Quarters, Washington, DC

during 2015, which exhibits a strong prospect of positive economic shifts in the country, though the results might yield lower than projected. Such a low growth in the economy might be due to lingering sluggishness in domestic demand and a tighter fiscal stance over the positive spillovers from stronger growth in the US economy. Growth divergences among the developed countries contributing to the dynamics of global trade and economy in reference to investments, manufacturing, influencing interest rates, and currency adjustments also have shown varying effects across the NAFTA region. These factors have driven the foreign investment, services, and primary sector contributions in the trade and economic growth of USA, Canada, and Mexico in reference to the following trends:

- Decline in oil prices, which helped economies of these countries to lower the costs and consumer price indices, and augment the trade opportunities in the region,
- Growth in investments in the services and manufacturing sectors in Mexico, USA, and Canada, and
- The strengthening of the US dollar has driven the international trade and investments in manufacturing, services, and infrastructure development in Mexico and Canada during the post-recession period.

The housing bubble is one of the responsible factors in the USA to root the economic downturn in 2007. Some companies are also injecting new capital to take advantage of foreclosures, areas of limited housing supply and hotel demand with a spate of new funds raised in the past 3 years. After the unrestrained years of the US financial crisis and the stagnation over the recent past, the US consumers are buying and building homes again, and the private equity industry has taken notice. The persistent low interest rates and stronger job growth strategies have stimulated the home sales growth and contributed positively to the economic recovery.

It has been observed that between 2000 and 2007, about two-thirds of the US households nearly doubled their outstanding debt to $13.8 trillion making to an unprecedented amount in both nominal terms and as a ratio of liabilities to disposable income amounting to nearly 138%. But the global financial crisis worsened at the end of 2008, which induced a shift among the US households for the first time since World War II toward reducing their debt outstanding (Baily et al. 2009). The major causes including the boom and bust of the housing bubble, steep fall in consumption index, and investment pull overs that triggered the economic recession in the USA during 2007–2011 appeared to be restoring over the year 2012. During the post-recession period, the spending trend of consumers appeared to be increasing, and an 8.5% rate of growth of durable goods consumption by the end of 2014 suggests that the consumer markets are growing again. Besides, the investment on housing has also re-boomed in the post-recession period rising at a 14.4% annual pace during 2012–2013 periods. However, the cumulative growth rate on consumption indicators during the above referred period managed just a 0.33% point contribution to total growth due to low response of the economy to price stability. The overall scenario suggests that during the post-recession period, a recovering housing sector tended to continue to raise household confidence, and the price index for personal consumption expenditures rose against the low indices during 2007–2011.

In order to drive the economic recovery fast in the emerging economies like Mexico, there is a need to drive the productivity in manufacturing and services sectors. A number of factors propel productivity growth moving from low-productivity agriculture to market-driven productive manufacturing. Besides, it is necessary to drive up the service-sector markets and urban employment and automation to augment efficient operations leading to higher income and productivity. Such strategy toward economic recovery would drive and increase integration of the global and regional economy toward more productive modern businesses gaining higher share economic advantages. However, among developing economies, the variance in productivity performance has been much wider. There is no typical rate of productivity growth observed over 2007–2015 in these economies (McKinsey Global Institute 2015).

NAFTA Trade Regime

After the World War II, the developed and industrialized countries have been engaged in institution-building by opening the barriers on international trade particularly with a focus on gradual elimination of the cross-boarder tariffs. The World Trade Organization has reshaped the environment of world trade to such an extent that international trade flows have been boomed. The global trade has become more dynamic integrating regional trade partners through diplomatic agreements to boost regional trade and economy conditions. Consequently, the largest of the major regional institutions in the North American region, NAFTA, was signed on December 17, 1992, and took effect in early 1994. This agreement is in force for over a decade but its economic impact has not revealed measurable results for all partnering countries since the trade and investment trends are influenced by numerous economic variables including economic growth, inflation, and currency fluctuations. The agreement has accelerated the trade liberalization and negotiated several groundbreaking provisions. A legacy of the agreement is that it has served as a template or model for the new generation of FTAs that the USA later negotiated, and it also has served as a template for certain provisions in multilateral trade negotiations as part of the Uruguay Round. US trade with its NAFTA partners Canada and Mexico in October 2013 was $103.1 billion, which was higher than 4.5% from October 2012. Total surface transportation trade of the USA with its partner countries was as high as $81.7 billion in the first quarter of 2013. The previous high for truck was $60.0 billion in October 2012, and for rail, the previous high was $15.3 billion in May 2013. The US–Canada trade by vessel, of which 63.3% was imported by the USA and Canada, had the largest percentage increase of any mode during the above referred period and has grown by 40.2% (Bureau of Transportation Statistics 2014). The value of trade flows from the USA to partner NAFTA countries during 2012–2013 is exhibited in Table 1.4.

NAFTA has made a substantial impact on the integration of North America's agricultural markets. Market integration is aimed at facilitating the trilateral trade among the USA, Canada, and Mexico to the extent

Table 1.4 Values of US-NAFTA freight flows 2012–2013 (millions of current dollars)

Mode		*October 2012*	*October 2013*	*Percent change*
All modes	Imports	52,444	55,088	5.0
	Exports	46,188	48,001	3.9
	Total	98,632	103,089	4.5

Source Bureau of Transportation Statistics (2014), US-NAFTA Trade, USA Department of Transportation, Washington, DC. Retrieved online http://www.rita.dot.gov/bts/press_releases/bts001_14, July 05, 2015

that the markets of partner countries of NAFTA strengthen to form a single market. Integration of the market is visible in increased cross-border flows of goods, services, capital, and labor under the agreed terms of reference. Trade in goods consists of not only final consumer products but also intermediate inputs and raw materials, as firms reorganize their activities around regional markets for both inputs and outputs, spurred in part by greater foreign direct investment (FDI). Integration of agricultural markets, as fostered by NAFTA, offers many tangible benefits as it enables agricultural producers and consumers in the region to benefit standardized products with competitive prices as cross-border taxes on agricultural products are subject to gradual elimination under the NAFTA. As the producers have assured markets for their products in the trilateral countries, they take benefits of economies of scale though there remains the threat of domestic competition in the markets. In addition, the creation of a larger, single market offers comparative advantages of cheaper suppliers of inputs and creates new opportunities for FDI as firms tend to restructure their vertical and horizontal arrangements.[1] Table 1.5 exhibits the trade among the NAFTA partner country during the post-economic recession period (2010–2013).

The data exhibited in the above Table reveal that during the post-economic recession period, Canada and Mexico have shown a sustainable balance of trade by keeping the exports higher than imports. However, the US imports were higher than the exports during 2012 and 2013 as compared to the other two partner countries. Besides agricultural produce, the US manufacturing exports to NAFTA countries have increased manifold, and the USA maintains a growing manufacturing trade surplus with Canada and Mexico. American exports of computer and electronic

Table 1.5 Export–import performance within NAFTA countries (2010–2013) (in billion dollars)

Contributing sector	*Canada*			*Mexico*			*USA*		
	2010	*2012*	*2013*	*2010*	*2012*	*2013*	*2010*	*2012*	*2013*
Agricultural products	27 (20)	32 (25)	35 (25)	15 (19)	17 (22)	19 (23)	82 (81)	48 (49)	48 (53)
Fuels and mining	101 (20)	123 (27)	129 (33)	40 (23)	47 (34)	43 (33)	180 (181)	58 (169)	64 (170)
Manufactures	149 (180)	172 (209)	170 (208)	189 (114)	224 (139)	240 (138)	659 (600)	386 (362)	397 (369)
Total trade	295 (229)	343 (270)	351 (277)	250 (159)	299 (201)	310 (197)	956 (900)	508 (608)	528 (620)

Source Compiled from the published data of various year at World Trade Organization: International Trade Statistics, Geneva, Switzerland

products, furniture, paper, and fabricated metals all have more than tripled since 1994. In reference to the existing US–Canada FTA in place, most of the market opening measures resulted in the removal of US tariffs and quotas applied to imports from Mexico, and Mexican trade barriers applied to imports from the USA and Canada. In 1994, when the NAFTA went into effect, about 40% of US imports from Mexico entered duty-free and the remainder faced duties of up to 35% with a trade-weighted average rate of about 7% (Villarreal and Fergusson 2015).

The US trade with Canada more than doubled in the first decade of the Free Trade Agreement and NAFTA (combined) during 1989–1999 from \$166.5 to \$362.2 billion. The US exports to Canada increased from \$100.2 billion in 1993 to \$312.1 billion in 2014, which marked an increase of 211% over two decades. Simultaneously, the US imports from Canada increased from \$110.9 billion in 1993 to \$346.1 billion in 2014 showing an increase of 212% for the above reference period. However, The USA has run a trade deficit with Canada since the FTA/NAFTA era, increasing from \$9.9 billion in 1989 to \$74.6 billion in 2008, before falling back during the 2009 recession, and in 2014, the trade deficit was reduced to \$33.79 billion. In services, the USA had a surplus of \$32.8 billion in 2013 in trade with Canada. The US private services exports to Canada increased from \$17.0 billion in 1993 to \$63.3 billion in 2013. The US private services import from Canada has also augmented from \$9.1 billion in 1993 to \$30.5 billion in 2013 (Villarreal and Fergusson 2015).

After the implementation of NAFTA, the USA has become the leading partner of Mexico in merchandise trade. The exports to Mexico from the USA have increased rapidly since the onset of this trilateral agreement, which has driven the exports to Mexico from $41.6 billion in 1993 to $240.3 billion in 2014 revealing an increase of 478% in a period of over two decades. The US imports from Mexico have also increased from $39.9 billion in 1993 to $294.2 billion in 2014 driving a manifold increase of 637% since the beginning of the NAFTA. The trade balance with Mexico went from a surplus of $1.7 billion in 1993 to a deficit of $74.3 billion in 2007. Since then, the trade deficit with Mexico has fallen to $53.8 billion in 2014. In services, the USA had a surplus of $12.1 billion in 2013 in trade with Mexico. The US private services exports to Mexico increased from $10.4 billion in 1993 to $29.9 billion in 2013. The US private services imports from Mexico increased from $7.4 billion in 1993 to $17.8 billion in 2013 in a period of two decades of the agreement (Villarreal and Fergusson 2015).

International Competition and NAFTA Responsiveness

The pre-economic recession year 2006 witnessed robust growth in the world economy and vigorous trade expansion. The US economy maintained its overall expansion as weaker domestic demand was balanced by a reduction in the external deficit, mainly due to a faster export growth. In Japan, somewhat faster economic growth was achieved despite weaker domestic demand reflected in a widening of its external surplus. China and India continued to report outstandingly high economic and trade growth. The dynamic growth in global economic activity was the major factor in the vigorous expansion of global trade in 2006. The four regions with the highest share of fuels and other mining products in their merchandise exports (the Middle East, Africa, the Commonwealth of Independent States (CIS), and South and Central America) again recorded the strongest annual export rise in 2006. Real merchandise export growth was provisionally estimated to have grown by 8.0% in 2006 almost 2% points faster than in 2005 and well above the average expansion trade during 1996–2006. The expansion of real trade exceeded global output growth by more than 4%. Trade in less-developed countries grew by about 30%, fueled by higher prices for petroleum and other primary commodities. The developing and developed countries as a whole saw their shares of world merchandise trade reach record proportions. For some of the smaller suppliers, fear of a setback in textiles and clothing in the face of competition from China proved unfounded in 2006. In general, the trade expanded in real terms during 2006–2007, faster than production by a large margin.[2] The major economic drivers in the global trade are observed as:

- Reduction in trade and investment barriers
- Rapid growth and increase in size of the economies of developing countries and their impact on global production capacity
- Innovations in technologies involving transport and communications

The most prominent explanations, often interrelated, for the retardation in the global economic recovery included erosion of trust in institutional pillars such as public and corporate governance, weakening consumer and investor confidence, and rising geopolitical risks. The weakness of fixed investment expenditure particularly pronounced for non-residential investment contributed significantly to the sluggish overall growth in the industrial countries. Investment expenditures play a critical role in the business cycle. There were problems in sustaining the recovery once inventory levels had been re-established during the recent past. Investment activity generally picks up when prospects for profitable investment opportunities increase, and the utilization of existing production capacities reaches a level that calls for a further increase of these capacities. It has been observed that since 2005, the USA recorded its best annual merchandise export growth in more than a decade but its trade deficit continued to grow. However, China's trade growth continued to outstrip other major traders. China's merchandise exports grew by 27% in 2005. In the second half of 2006, its merchandise exports started to exceed those of the USA, but for the whole year, the US exports still exceeded those of China. Consumer confidence in the major industrial economies improved only temporarily in the first quarter of 2002 and declined or stagnated thereafter. Marginal employment gains in some countries and rising unemployment rates in others led to only moderate increases in wage incomes and depressed private consumption expenditure. In some countries, this led to an increase in precautionary savings.

Real merchandise exports of Asia remained the most encouraging of all regions at 13.5% in 2010. Asia's imports rose faster since 2004 and moved faster than world trade but continued to lag behind its export growth. Most of the excess of Asia's export over import growth can be attributed to the region's major traders, China and Japan. The expansion of China's exports was somewhat less dynamic in 2006 than in 2005, while Japan, the Republic of Korea, and Chinese Taipei recorded a faster growth (between 10 and 15%). Imports into Japan and Chinese Taipei, however, advanced by only 2–3% in 2006.[3] Also, merchandise exports in Africa rose by 21% in the same reference period, again faster than imports, which were estimated to have increased by nearly 16%. The share of Africa in world merchandise exports reached its highest level since 1990. The deterioration in the labor markets of industrial economies with rapidly aging populations rendered their already fragile social security systems even more precarious. The general public is increasingly aware that profound adjustments are needed to restore financial sustainability to social security systems, and that these adjustments can have a significant impact on future contributions and benefits. The clouded prospects of social security, and in particular pensions systems, contributed to the erosion of consumer confidence and exerted a negative impact on private consumption expenditure. Consumer confidence was also negatively affected by the wealth effect of continuing falls in stock prices, although in some countries (e.g., the USA and the UK), this was compensated for by the rising house prices.

Over the years during the post-economic recession period, emerging markets have gained more leverage in the global trade along with the developed nations. Mexico has shown leading exports of communication and distribution services within the North American region. Mexico has been identified as a potential growth destination for the manufacturing and services products among the NAFTA partners and European and Asian countries with preferential trade agreements with Mexico since 2007. The World Bank resources delineate that policies supported by efficient trade liberalization reform and export competitiveness transformed Hungary and Mexico from inward-looking to successful export-oriented economies in the second decade of twenty-first century (Reis and Farole 2012). In an unstable economic environment affected by the civil insecurity, it has been unlikely that the international trade and investments would turn favorable and prioritize support reform over macroeconomic stability. However, political will has been vital to the success of regulatory reform in Mexico during the period 2007–2014. In Mexico, the government created executive units in key ministries to overcome entrenched resistance to reform. Thus, Mexico is a good example of the efficient use of specific adjustment programs during privatization and trade liberalization, although it also highlights that these programs are fiscally expensive. The Mexican government embarked on an ambitious reform agenda to streamline its financial performance as part of a broader competitiveness agenda in the aftermath of the financial crises that hit Mexico in the 1980s and 1990s. Then, NAFTA provided a strong political anchor to a reform process by making reversion to protectionism politically impossible. The process was institutionalized through the creation of a regulatory-improvement agency. The Economic Deregulation Unit created as early as in 1989 was placed under the Secretariat of Trade's authority, but was given, by presidential decree, a broader authority than the Secretariat. It was then transformed into a formal federal agency, COFEMER, in 2000.

Mexico's major internationalization in the 1990s, mainly induced through NAFTA, has driven many large companies to become highly successful exporters. However, still, the small and medium enterprise sector is struggling with traditional barriers to growth and export participation. Most significantly, the access to finance has been linked to their lack of creditworthiness, which is pulling their competitiveness in the market, and NAFTA benefits are being filtered to large companies. In response to this, and partly as a strategic commercial move in its own right, *Nacional Financiera* (NAFIN), a state-owned development bank, developed a productive chains program in 2001 to link large creditworthy buyer firms with small risky firms unable to access formal finance to help them grow market competitive (Salas 2005).

Overall Economic Development Measures

The economic advancement of a country may be reviewed in reference to its fiscal, monetary, and exchange rate policies over time, and the effectiveness of the changing policy framework in promoting stability and growth. The contemporary concepts of economic advancement for developed countries include an entire range of governmental functions including sectoral policy reform, economic integration, privatization, public sector enhancement, labor market competitiveness, investment climate enhancement, e-governance, soft infrastructures for developing a knowledge economy, macroeconomic management, and effective long-range planning. The weight of the public sector constitutes a serious impediment to more rapid growth for many countries. Importantly, the large expenditure burden it requires does not always translate into an efficient and equitable distribution of services. Such performance is reflected by the public sector efficiency and governance in promoting the economic advancement of a country. The challenges of employment generation, economic growth, and societal advancement in changing demographic contexts can only be addressed through productive investment and value building. The climate for investment is therefore critical for the countries which need a strategic direction and an economic concentration on value building rather than value trading, which leads toward the higher degree of economic advancement in a country.

Economic advancement is directly proportional to the educational and training facilities available in the country. Human resources are not only producers of goods and services but they also play a multifold role in economic development. Economic advancement is characterized by the following factors:

- Allocation of labor force to agriculture
- Energy available in large amounts at low-cost per unit
- High level of GDP and income
- High levels of per capita consumption
- Relatively low rates of population growth
- Complex modern facilities for transportation, communication, and exchange
- Substantial amount of capital for investment
- Urbanization based on production as well as exchange
- Diversified manufacturing that accounts for an important share of the labor force, and technology that includes ample media and methods for the experiment

These factors may be utilized to examine economic standing of the host country, and analysis of a large variety of information on these variables may help to categorize the countries on an economic development scale. Besides, there are many historical, geographic, political, and cultural factors intimately related to the economic well-being of a nation.

Large nominal exchange rate changes affect the behavior of trade flows through their impact on the relative prices of tradable goods in the economy. A change in the nominal exchange rate affects the prices of export and import goods relative to domestically produced goods, which implies changes in the real exchange rate. There is a striking difference, as regards the behavior of the real exchange rate, between the two sets of countries indicated above. In Brazil, Peru, and Argentina, home currency goods became more expensive during this episode, due to an even higher domestic inflation rate. For the remaining countries, large nominal exchange rate devaluations were transmitted into real exchange rate devaluations. With the notable exception of Brazil and Argentina, all countries had experienced a relative convergence to their initial long-term real exchange rates, with rates of real depreciation much lower than those experienced only 2 years after the devaluation.

The macroeconomic policy refers to the top-down strategy developed and implemented in a country by the government and central banks, usually intended to maximize growth while keeping down inflation and unemployment. The growth factors determining the incentives toward investing in human capital for developing new products include government policies. The main instruments of macroeconomic policy are deviations in the interest rates and money supply, taxation, and public spending, known as fiscal policy. It has been observed that with the rise of rate of unemployment and inflation, the growth rate of the economy declines and the GDP of the country falls. This may be an evidence of poorly planned macroeconomic policy and implementation thereof. Higher public spending relative to GDP is generally associated with slower growth. The rise in the rate of inflation is contributed by the high social expenditure and political instability in a country. Business cycles may simply be an unavoidable fact of economic life that macroeconomic policy, however well-conducted, can never be sure of conquering. The long-run pattern of growth and recession in the business that may be explained as boom and bust of the economy of a country or a region may be described as a business cycle.

There has been continuous change in the economic indicators in Mexico after the new government took over in 2013. The improvements in the civil security situation and more liberalization of trade within the core industries have drawn some response on investment from global companies particularly from Europe, Asia, and NAFTA partner countries. However, global FDI flows were lowered by 7% in 2014, but flows to developing and developed economies differed significantly. Flows to the developed economies also fell by 14%, as FDI to North America plummeted by 54%, owing principally to a single divestment in the USA. Despite the strengthening of US–Mexico trade relations, Mexico recorded the steepest fall in FDI inflows, with a drop of 49% amounting to US$22.795 billion in 2013. This can be explained by a number of factors, including the fact that the 2013 FDI figures were inflated by the US$13.249 billion acquisition of beer maker Grupo Modelo by a European firm. Also significant was the divestment by US-based AT&T of its holdings in América Móvil, worth US$5.57 billion (ECLAC 2015). Beyond national policies, international agreements with a bearing on FDI from bilateral investment treaties to trade pacts such as the NAFTA may narrow the space in which governments are able to implement environmental policies (UNCTAD 2010).

A positive trend in the behavior of trade flows has been observed during the reforms period, resulting from the increased openness of these economies to international markets. There is a striking difference between the behavior of export and import volumes around the devaluation episodes. The credit restrictions have had a negative impact on consumption during the above referred period. However, after the country exercised appropriate economic measures to stabilize the economy of the country in the recent past, it has been observed that foreign business corporations consider Brazil to be Latin America's most attractive investment target. International marketers should examine the extent to which their business is vulnerable to economic conditions. For example, in a booming economy, consumers tend to buy durable goods; on the contrary in a recession, they avoid spending money. The prevailing economic environment is just an indicator to review the business fit in the given region or country. Even if the short-run economic environment is not conducive to profits, a company may decide to enter an overseas market in anticipation of favorable long-term economic prospects in the country such as growing political stability, declining inflation, or the low-wage rates. However, the long-run perspective is the most critical decision factor, which provides the firm sufficient resources to endure waiting for the future favorable environment. The market attractiveness of Mexico may be described from this point of view.

Despite the negative effects of NAFTA, the core philosophy of the trilateral agreement between Canada, Mexico, and the USA is encouraging trade liberalization and tariff reductions to increase the competitive pressures to which domestic firms are exposed to. This effect is expected to be stronger for import-competing firms and import-competing sectors than for export-oriented ones. However, in a world of differentiated products and intra-industry trade, firms can be simultaneously import or export competitive. However, NAFTA has not been analyzed by many economists as a win-win deal among the three countries. The two-way trade has expanded enormously, by a factor of five in current dollars. Just as the critics say, the US bilateral trade deficit with Mexico has also grown, going from a surplus of $5 billion in 1994 to a deficit of $45 billion in 2013 (Caldwell 2014).

Notes

1. The vertical integration may be defined as "the ownership or control by a firm of different stages of the production process," while a horizontally integrated enterprise is "one in which several different kinds of activities that produce different kinds of goods or services for sale on the market are carried out in parallel with each other" (OECD 2014).
2. World Trade Organization: Press Release # 472, 2007.
3. World Trade Organization: World Trade Report 2007.

References

Baily, M. N., Lund, S, and Atkins, C. (2009), *Will US consumer debt reduction cripple the recovery? The McKinsey quarterly*. New York: McKinsey & Co.

Bureau of Transportation Statistics. (2014). *US—NAFTA Trade*. Washington, DC: United States Department of Transportation. Retrieved online http://www.rita.dot.gov/bts/press_releases/bts001_14, July 05, 2015.

Caldwell, C. (2014). Popular sentiment is hardening against free trade, *Financial Times*, February 28.

Cavusgil, S. T., & Knight, G. (2009). *Born global firms: A new international enterprise*. New York: Business Expert Press.

ECLAC. (2015). *Foreign direct investment in Latin America and the caribbean*. Economic Commission on Latin America and Caribbean, Report (LC/G.2641-P), Santiago, Chile.

Howe, A. (2010). Making the leap into emerging markets: An interview with clorox's beth springer, McKinsey Insights, September.

International Monetary Fund. (2014). *World economic outlook: Recovery strengthen, remains uneven*. Washington, DC: International Monetary Fund.

International Monetary Fund. (2015). *World Economic Outlook*. Washington, DC: International Monetary Fund.

Ip, C., Istace, F., Lal, A., Masanam, P. K., Natale, T. & Tiwari, S. (2014). Insights into the dynamics of new trade flows. *McKinsey on Payments*, 19–26.

Kesting, P., & Gunzel-Jensen, F. (2015). SMEs and new ventures need business model sophistication. *Business Horizons, 58*(3), 285–293.

McKinsey Global Institute. (2015). *Global growth: Can productivity save the day in an aging world?* Report, McKinsey Global Institute. New York: McKinsey & Co.

Nagji, B., & Tuff, G. (2012). Managing your innovation portfolio. *Harvard Business Review, 90*(5), 66–74.

Organization of Economic Cooperation and Development (OECD). (2014). Glossary of Statistical Terms. http://stats.oecd.org/glossary/index.htm. Accessed July 05, 2014.

Rajagopal. (2014). *Architecting enterprise: Managing innovation, technology, and global competitiveness.* Palgrave Macmillan: Basingstoke, UK.

Reis, J. G., & Farole, T. (2012). *Trade competitiveness diagnostic toolkit.* Washington, DC: World Bank.

Salas, F. (2005). *Institution building: Lessons from Mexico, Public policy for the private sector.* Washington, DC: World Bank.

UNCTAD. (2010). *World investment report 2010: Investing in a low-carbon economy.* United Nations Conference on Trade and Development (BOPCOM-10/22).

Villarreal, M. A. & Fergusson, I. F. (2015). *North American Free Trade Agreement.* Congressional Research Service, Report #7-5700, Washington, DC.

CHAPTER 2

Industrial Policy and Trade Competitiveness in North America

Industrial policy and trade development are interrelated indicators that affect the economic growth of a country. In North America, the USA and Canada have a well-established symbiotic relationship in driving the national economic development. Mexico, being a country following the protectionism for a substantial period in the past and having several economic setbacks, has yet to overcome the black holes in low financial integration, industrial growth, and international trade competitiveness. This chapter critically examines the approach of Mexico and the USA on industrial policy, financial integration, and spending on research and development (R&D) as an impetus for augmenting the industrial production and trade competitiveness. However, the growing threat of disruptive innovation on the international business has also been discussed in this chapter.

Industrial policy of a country is considered to be the critical gateway to the internationalization of the trade and economy. The liberal trade policies attract substantial foreign investment in production and business operations of the country that contributes enormously to its GDP to drive the economic growth and international competitiveness. Most developing countries are reforming their industrial policies to overcome the conservative ideology laid with the protectionism maxims. In view of the globalization and industrial policy reforms, most developing countries are leaning toward outsourcing their requirements and purchasing goods that were originally manufactured internally. In another move, many countries are also intending to engage in offshoring activities

Rajagopal and V. Zlatev, *Business Dynamics in North America*,
DOI 10.1007/978-3-319-57606-0_2

to globally relocating manufacturing process and maintaining ownership control. Such policies helped companies to reduce their manufacturing costs and offer competitive prices in the international markets to stay in the global marketplace. Policy makers and business strategists alike are searching for theoretical frameworks to understand the underlying dynamics in industrial reforms in emerging countries that has driven global reshuffling of production activities innovations and market competitiveness (Andersen 2006).

Shifts in Industrial Policy in Mexico

The political and economic ideology of Mexican leaders tends to shift from protectionism to liberalism with the change in the political leadership and international moves on globalization since the mid-twentieth century. However, it is yet difficult to establish the clear inclination of the ideology growing in the country that supports globalization. Though NAFTA has influenced some drifts in the trade and economy liberalization, the country needs to reform its industrial policy to stay at part the emerging nations across the world in the twenty-first century. The Mexican economy has experienced slow economic growth per annum for nearly three decades prior to 2015. The economy of the country grew by only 2.1% during the period 1982–2010, which revealed much lower growth than the rate obtained during stabilizing the development period or the shared growth stage within the region. The economic situation of the country was on the brink when the GDP per capita fell down steep registering 0.46% of annual growth during the above referred period causing a high rate of unemployment. The precariousness of employment was associated with meager economic growth between 1982 and 2008, which could generate only 354,306 jobs annually on an average in the formal sector of the economy. However, the unemployment persisted in the economy at an annual increasing pace until the end of the economic recession in 2011.

Soon after the devaluation of currency in Mexico 1994, a short-term macroeconomic policy succeeded in maintaining inflation at levels less than a single digit (the inflation rose to 52% as hyperinflation during mid-1990s), at the expense of maintaining the peso-dollar exchange rate appreciated, with poor results in terms of driving exports and employment. The critical examination economic model of Mexico exhibits the structural incapacity to generate economic growth mainly in the industrial manufacturing sector causing inability to generate employment and raise productivity. This is also explained by the trade and industrial policies applied during 1981–1999 period which was based exclusively on market efficiency criteria and on cost-benefit calculations to minimize the financial market distortions. The trade and industrial policies implemented by several governments till 2012 have been passive as they aimed at removing barriers that prevent the resources assigned to the so-called "free market" economy. Counting on the positive side of industrial policies introduced during the period 1981–2012, it is observed that the governments tended to make the state regulations flexible, curb state and private monopolies, and gradually minimize tariffs (also eliminate cross-border tariffs in some sectors delineated under NAFTA) to encourage global competition. However, the neoliberal ideologists in Mexico have not laid their foundation of trade and economic growth on industrial reforms to drive globalization of factors of production on a real-time basis and stay competitive in the global marketplace. All adopted a passive trade and industrial policy that simply left the development of manufacturing industry in the hands of market forces to ride a "free play." The market forces in the context of globalization and regional economic integration controlled the industrial scenario in Mexico and determined the entry and exit of companies. Accordingly, the country will be incapable of implementing active trade and industrial policies that promote economic development. The slow economic growth that the Mexican economy has been facing for the last 24 years (1981–2015) is the result of insufficient growth in the manufacturing industry as a priority sector.

The post-economic recession period in the country is being managed by the recently elected government, which took over the economic challenges since 2013. The National Development Plan 2013–2018, unveiled in June 2013, explicitly considers the industrial policy as a tool for development. This new economic development plan envisages active policies that tend to promote the industrial production index and augment exports avoiding unnecessary distortions in competitive markets. The new plan emphasizes non-subsidized industrial growth and minimizes interventions by the state in production or investment to draw a true portrait of the country on industrialization and sustain the market competitiveness. It advocates the economic and industrial efforts to be laid on correcting market failures, re-orienting production to key sectors and markets, deregulating economic restrictions in the sectors of international market development, and coordinating actions between the private and the public sector players. This economic development plan stresses the urgent need to create stronger forward and backward linkages between exports and the rest of productive activities to boost Mexico's economic growth and internal markets (Bird-Moreno 2013). The main objective of the new industrial policy is to achieve efficient operation of the markets and promote competition, given that this is believed to be the best route to enable private initiative to make decisions concerning investment, production, and employment. As a result of the structural reforms to exploit NAFTA satisfactorily, the focus has been laid on improving privatization in industrial sectors, intellectual property rights, and human and physical infrastructure. The new industrial policy proposes essentially to resolve the points of distortions in the market, monopolies, oligopolies, incomplete markets, and asymmetric information.

However, these liberal economic principles are based on a series of programs promoting industry, both horizontal and vertical in character, seeking to strengthen foreign direct investment (FDI), industrial production, and market competitiveness. There are four distinct policies laid toward attracting FDI as discussed below:

1. The policy combines intellectual and physical property rights protection, and financial and fiscal incentives to promote transnational companies[1] in new strategic sectors. The diverse industrial growth brings manifold economic development as witnessed in the Mexican economy over the twenty-first century in the automotive and the emerging aerospace industry. More than 260 aerospace companies now operate in Mexico, exporting some $4.3 billion in aircraft and parts last year. The Mexican government has set a target of $12 billion in such exports by 2020.
2. Another factor in the policy envisages the support for locating multinational companies in the electronic, software, and computing industry. The requirements and regulations for importing are still evolving under NAFTA. It is the responsibility of the importer to define what certificates are required and from whom to obtain them. The Mexican government strictly enforces all customs regulations, particularly when it comes to potentially under-valued Asian-origin goods. The liberalization combined with NAFTA trade movement has led to lower prices and more rapid diffusion of business in computer and software industry throughout the economy. However, such economies of scale penetration of foreign

firms have paralyzed the domestic computer firms as they became non-competitive in the market. Both countries saw an increase in computer production, but Mexico's production was contract-based mainly for export to the USA (e.g., Dedrick et al. 2001).

3. Another policy perspective is raised toward the highly concentrated activities of large-scale and network economies, such as electricity, telecommunications, and oil and natural gas. In the case of Mexico, most of these sectors are state-controlled except telecommunications. In these sectors, government support basically consists of developing flexible regulatory frameworks that promote and strengthen competition between agencies.
4. Finally, the territorial policy has been designed to measure the so-called clusters, particularly of small- and medium-sized companies and activities in which a large number of small firms operate to develop the leadership under the guidance of large transnational companies. Such perspective in the industrial policy is to encourage the small and medium enterprises of Mexico to gain market competitiveness and grow global through potential exports and exploring the contract manufacturing opportunities.

Despite dynamics of new industrial policy, two challenges appear to drive the manufacturing sector in Mexico internationally competitive. The first challenge is to improve the capability and competency to form an endogenous nucleus of technological momentum in the manufacturing sector to drive the industrialization movement in the country in all sectors, and the second challenge is to construct enterprise taxonomy from small and medium level to national and transnational. These reforms represented a turn toward a market economy and passive trade and industrial policy whose only objective was to remove the distortions to the market that have seriously damaged the country's potential for growth. To drive growth in the Mexican economy, not only is an active, strategic trade, and industrial policy required but also this policy must exist within the frame of a broader economic policy that promotes economic development in Mexico. In order to develop an internationally competitive and active industrial policy, the government should reduce the income inequality, provide financial subsidies to the small and medium enterprises, and encourage exports to overcome the huge differences between regions and sectors inside the country, and consequently eradicate industrial differentiation. The challenge that lies in building a new economic development model is to drive the industrial sector strategically with key manufacturing responsibilities. A new economic model for economic development is required that enables the country to repair the damage of the current model and envisage active trade and industrial policy as a lever for economic development.

The Loose Ends of Industrial Policy

The industrial policy comprises the strategies for the growth of the secondary sector of the economy by improving the design of manufacturing industries as well as the services and primary activities. Thus, the industrial policy of the country is also analogous to the production development policy. The public policy makers need to integrate the industrial policy from the perspectives of innovations, technology, design, and market competitiveness to be achieved by the country and attain the proposed objective (Peres and Primi 2009). In developing countries, the industrial policies are complex as they are multi-focused arguing for protections to native and infant industries, on the one hand, and catering to the various trade agreements, on the other hand. The various industrial policy instruments can be grouped into the following categories:

- Science, technology, and innovation policies: The objective of these policies is to increase national capacities to use, absorb, modify, and generate scientific and technological knowledge, and to stimulate innovation activities in the organizations that make up innovation systems. The industrial policy support for this category of industries should include contestable funds, tax elasticity, and admissible subsidies to drive R&D on innovation and technology for manufacturing. Good industrial policies should provide incentives, skills, information and technical support, resources, and technological policies.
- Trade policies: These policies are decisive for establishing the level of international competition and international market access faced by domestic firms. Instruments include multilateral and bilateral free trade agreements, the liberalization of FDI inflows, and export promotion schemes delineating the special economic zones, export-oriented units, and maquiladoras-contract manufacturing units.
- Policies to promote industries sector: It has been observed that in the industrial policy reforms approach, Mexico has not laid enough

> insights on developing the incentives for the various sectors of industries within the prevailing taxonomy. This group could include policies with specific intervention goals in strategic sectors (such as agribusiness, consumer products, consumer durables, computer industry) or industries or size of the firms. The most widely used instruments to promote the industrial sector include concessional loans, tax incentives, government subsidies to selected sectors, and public procurement. The industrial policy should also include instruments to promote productive articulation in industrial clusters Perez and Alvarado (2014).

Industrial reforms in Mexico need to foster a business-friendly environment in major industrial sectors including agribusiness, consumer goods, industrial machinery, and automobile and transport industries by creating economic incentives to drive international market competitiveness. A wide variety of instruments are used in these policies: tax and financial incentives, the development of efficient regulations, a competitive real exchange rate, and regulatory adjustment (Peres 2006). The reforms on industrial policy should also delineate the measures set for antitrust regulations and competition policies, along with laws that aim to underpin the proper functioning of the market and thus ensure efficient resource allocation. The antitrust and market competition laws should cover all instruments that affect the functioning and structure of markets and competition, including a number of trade-policy tools such as host country practices, countervailing measures, and safeguards (ECLAC 2012). The trend of economic growth, industrial production, and international trade of Mexico in the shifting industrial policy regime is exhibited in Table 2.1.

The data exhibited in the above table reveal that the economic growth in Mexico is inconsistent and has discretely established the diminishing rate of economic growth since the economic recession. This situation has been evidently caused due to the low investments, industrial production, and deficit balance of trade occurred in the country. Upon analyzing the trade and economy growth during 2010–2014, it may be stated that the low industrial production has driven the decline in the economic growth and pushed the trade balance to the negative bracket.

Structural change in the industrial policy still needs to be enforced strictly in Mexico toward higher productivity activities categorizing the companies in the special economic zones as export-oriented units, and

Table 2.1 Economic growth, industrial production, and international trade of Mexico (2010–2014)

Indicators	*Measure*	*2010*	*2011*	*2012*	*2013*	*2014*
Economic growth	Annual variation in	5.1	4.0	4.0	1.4	2.1
Investment	percent	1.3	7.8	4.8	−1.6	2.1
Industrial production		4.6	3.4	2.9	−0.6	1.8
International trade						
Trade balance	Billion US	−3.0	−1.4	0.0	−1.2	−2.4
Exports	dollars	298 (29.9)	349 (17.1)	371 (6.1)	380 (2.5)	398 (4.6)
Imports		301 (28.6)	351 (16.4)	371 (5.7)	381 (2.8)	400 (4.9)

Figures in parentheses indicate annual variation in percent. *Sources* Mexican National Institute of Statistics (INEGI) and author calculations

to drive intensive innovation and technological knowledge in manufacturing and marketing. Of the two approaches based on structural change, the transformation of target productive activities that are more closely related to comparative advantages needs to stem from the existing structure of factor of productions (Lin 2012). The government should play a key role in implementing the industrial policy to promote a production development strategy by deriving comparative advantages on factors of production in the sector and focusing on the following areas:

- Providing information on new industries on factors of production
- Coordinate investments in related industries and improve infrastructure
- Offer subsidies on selected industrial sectors to increase their market competitiveness
- Attract new industries through business incubation
- Promote opportunities for FDI.

The economic growth of Mexico showed a decline soon after the recovery from the economic recession began in 2013, largely because of the change of the political regime. A slowdown in both the manufacturing and construction sectors as well as weak economic activity in the USA caused GDP growth to moderate in the early 2013. However, Mexico's Central Bank revised the growth forecasts and now expects the economy to grow between 2.0 and 3.0% in 2015. The growth projections for 2016, by the Central Bank of Mexico, have shown a marginal increase in economic growth between 2.5 and 3.5%. However, to achieve this target, it is necessary for the government to implement the new economic development plan along with a rigorous industrial policy to attract investments and improve the balance of trade situation.

US Industrial Policy

Industrial policy is often embedded in the concept of a "developmental state." As a principal key determinant within a developmental state, the industrial policy generally focuses on encouraging R&D, driving innovations and technology emerging from R&D investments for commercial use. Historically, industrial policy in the USA has been developed in close relation with the military sphere and has been aimed at stimulating competition and innovation, in addition to promoting education and human capital formation (Buigues and Sekkat 2009). The state supports for R&D through grants and budgetary allocations of state patronage institutes contribute to the innovation and technology breakthroughs giving impetus to raise productivity and market competitiveness by attracting businesses to adopt these innovations for international growth. Industrial policy as a tool includes R&D subsidies for the government, university, or private business research centers. It also has the provisions of preferential tax treatment, credit opportunities, and direct subsidies for the specific sectors of the economy and regions. Some types of business regulations such as auto fuel-efficiency standards, or financial regulations aimed at channeling credit to preferred sectors, or industrial activities at subsidized rates could also be seen as industrial policy interventions within the state jurisdictions of the country. However, in the recent economic crisis of market downturn (2007–2011), the federal government provided a very large bailout package for the automotive industry as this segment was badly affected due to the consumer credit defaults and declining consumption trends in the USA. The trend of industrial production and capacity utilization of industrial plants and infrastructure in the USA during and post-economic recession period is exhibited in Table 2.2.

The data exhibited in the above table reveal that the industrial production increased by 5.2% in 2014 as compared to the previous year. The capacity utilization rate for manufacturing moved up by 4.0% by

Table 2.2 Industrial production and capacity utilization in the USA (2007–2013)

Function	*Measure*	*2007*	*2008*	*2009*	*2010*	*2011*	*2012*	*2013*	*2014*
Industrial production	Percent change	2.7	−4.7	−13.6	6.1	3.4	4.1	2.6	5.2
Capacity utilization	Percent utilization	78.7	74.6	65.6	71.1	73.9	75.5	76.1	80.1

Source Federal reserve statistical release, December 15, 2014

the end of 2014 against the previous year. Such growth trend indicates the positive dimension of industrial production and utilization of plant capacities and industrial infrastructures in the country. On analyzing further data from the source mentioned in the above table, it is observed that factory output is estimated to be above its late-2007 pre-recession peak in both October and November in 2014. In November, the indexes for both durables and nondurables increased more than 1%, and the output of every major industry group increased or remained unchanged. Among durable goods industries, the output of motor vehicles and parts jumped 5.1% as a result of an increase of 900,000 units at an annual rate in total motor vehicle assemblies. Miscellaneous manufacturing, wood products, and machinery each recorded gains exceeding 1%. Among nondurable goods industries, output advances of more than 2% were registered by petroleum and coal products and by apparel and leather. The indexes for food, beverage, and tobacco products and for plastics and rubber products both increased by 1.4%.

As the globalization is seeding technologies through many emerging markets predominantly India and China in leading industrial technologies such as advanced batteries, high-speed rail, hybrid automobiles, solar modules, offshore wind turbines, and machine tools, the USA finds itself competing against or even catching up with foreign companies and engineers. Historically, the country has been the undisputed leader of next-generation technology, from semiconductors to IT to space. The composition of global demand has changed dramatically over the past few decades. For the first time in recent history, more than 50% of the global middle class lives outside North America. Meanwhile, many next-generation engineered products are in high demand not by the US or European customers but by those in Asia, Latin America, and the Middle East. The customization of innovation and technology has driven the manifold growth of small enterprises that handle industrial innovation and technology for new products as seed companies and transfer the commercial right to potential companies for diffusing the breakthroughs. The rapid expansion of small, inventive companies that grow up to become large ones innovating at scale is one of the hallmarks of US leadership. The country should continue to encourage this model, and more executives of large companies should embrace it (Manyika et al. 2011).

Recognizing the importance of manufacturing industry in the country's growth and in the creation of jobs, the second release of industrial policy was issued in 2013 to promote investments in the manufacturing industry, clean energy, infrastructure, and education. In the employment sphere, the plan aims for education and training to provide US citizens the skills needed for global competition through public–private partnerships. In the case of manufacturing industry, the goal is to revitalize it through the following three broad objectives (OSTP 2012):

- Partnering with businesses and communities to invest in manufacturing new innovations products
- Ending tax breaks to ship jobs overseas and making the USA more competitive
- Bringing jobs back attracting investment to the USA

The revival of manufacturing in the USA will entail innovations that raise competitiveness, expand job opportunities, and advance the construction of a clean energy economy. To pull this off successfully, a clustering of large-scale public policy initiatives is required that could, as a combination, fairly be described as industrial policies. The military-based industrial policy has indeed been a major force shaping the development trajectory of US capitalism for at least a century.

Industrial bailout policies in the USA add unique support to the manufacturing sector. In 2008 and 2009, General Motors (GM) and Chrysler received $65 billion in loans from the federal government. The loans were provided by the government to stabilize the financial condition of the companies. These bailouts had an important precedent in the 1979 government bailout of Chrysler. In this prior case, the federal government provided $1.5 billion worth of loan guarantees as well as "voluntary" quotas on foreign cars being imported into US markets. One can make a reasonable case for both bailouts on the grounds that, in

1979 as well as in 2009, the collapse of GM and Chrysler would have caused massive unemployment and more general economic hardship, especially in the Midwest. But when the tools of industrial policy are cobbled together amid a crisis, we cannot expect the results to be stellar, beyond preventing the firms from shutting down outright. The 2009 GM bailout, for example, imposed devastating concessions on autoworkers, including the elimination of 21,000 union jobs, while the United Auto Workers itself had to accept GM stock of uncertain value to replace $10 billion in guaranteed health care funds.

Over the past four decades, states and municipalities in the USA have competed among themselves, sometimes intensively, to attract businesses to locate with them. The main advantage in this competition has been various types of tax incentives. Foreign auto companies have been among the most favored recipients of such support since 2006 that include Kia Motors, Honda, Toyota, and Volkswagen. These efforts have achieved some success in their primary aim of attracting businesses to their locations. But they have done so almost entirely on a zero-sum basis by reducing job creation in neighboring states and localities that have not offered the same incentives.

Export Trends in Mexico

Trade liberalization as an impact of NAFTA has been associated with the dynamic moves of Mexico into global markets and its rising importance in non-oil exports. Mexico has ranked among the top ten countries in terms of increasing its share in the world (non-oil) market since 1985 (Brid-Moreno et al. 2005). This positive performance is particularly evident in the evolution of its manufactured exports. Mexico ranked fifth among countries with the largest increases in their share of world manufactures exports during 1994–2001, and then, it was pushed to second place behind China. The export drive in the manufacturing sector in the country started during the late 1980s, before NAFTA came into force. The boom was partly rooted in the trade liberalization processes that began at that time, but also in the sectoral development programs initiated during the previous phase of state-led industrialization. NAFTA opened an unprecedented window of opportunity to export to the USA, the largest world market. In 1994, total exports represented 16% of Mexico's real GDP. By the year 2000, this figure had more than doubled, reaching 35.1%. Although subsequently it declined somewhat, in 2003, it still stood at 34.9%. The export drive was based on the dynamism of manufactured exports, which meant a shift for Mexico, whose main exports had traditionally been primary commodities—shrimp, coffee, cotton, and tomatoes.

Since the mid-1980s, the external sector has undoubtedly been the most dynamic component of demand for Mexican manufacturing. In 1988, exports were equivalent to 49.7% of the total value added by the manufacturing industry. In 1994, it climbed to 71.9%, and by 2003, it even exceeded by 61% due to various value additions. NAFTA contributed positively toward the export performance of the country as it forced firms to seek external markets to recover from the economic crisis of Mexico in 1994 and overcome the severe depreciation of the domestic currency to the US dollar in the following year, which caused foreign exchange crisis in the country.

This export boom in Mexico began in 2001, and it stood among the most successful competitors in many industrial and consumer goods export segments of the US market. The maquiladoras, which are the contract manufacturing enterprises, constituted a vital force behind this export drive in Mexico. In the early 1990s, they provided more than half of total exports of manufactured goods and over 40% of the total exports. Other important contributors to the export boom included foreign manufacturing firms in automobile parts, pharmaceuticals and consumer goods segments, and new ventures engaged in floating FDI. The contributions of FDI have been largely in the manufacturing sector, mining and metal products, industrial chemicals, food, beverages, and tobacco. One of the major contributions of NAFTA toward making the FDI more attractive in Mexico is that this agreement eliminated significantly the investment barriers, ensured basic protections for investors, and provided a mechanism for the settlement of disputes between investors and a partner country. This trilateral agreement provided non-discriminatory treatment for foreign investment in certain sectors and envisaged explicit country-specific liberalization commitments. Exemptions from NAFTA investment provisions include the energy sector in Mexico in which the Mexican government reserved the right to prohibit foreign investment. It also included exceptions related to national security and to Canada's cultural industries (Villarreal and Fergusson 2015).

FDI came in at a record US$35.2 billion (2.8% of GDP) during 2013. However, it should be noted that US$13.2 billion of this came from a single transaction toward the purchase of Cervecería Modelo by AB InBev (Belgium–Brazil) during the second quarter of this year. At the same time, direct investment by Mexican firms abroad fell to US$10 billion, less than half of the 2012 figure and the lowest since 2009. Portfolio inflows maintained their momentum, despite greater global volatility than in the previous years (2010–2012), which accounted for US$50.4 billion remitted in the country during 2013, the second highest amount on record of US$81.3 billion received in 2012. During the above reference year, there was a US$13 billion increase in foreign reserves, resulting in an end-year stock of US$168.6 billion in 2013. Overall, Mexico's international trade profile appears solid during the post-economic recession period, which makes the country trade competitive in the international market and with sustainable purchasing power parity. Its current account deficit, despite widening, remains far lower in both relative and absolute terms than many other emerging economies, including Brazil, and is easily covered by capital inflows. However, the weak levels of FDI remain a sore spot, which should be taken care of by the structural reforms over the near future (KPMG 2014).

The export drive was not uniformly distributed across all its manufacturing industries; it was highly concentrated in only a few. Motor engines and auto parts, automobiles, and computers and other electronic equipment accounted for more than half of the total exports. Parallel to the export boom in manufactures, the Mexican economy has experienced a massive penetration of imports, mainly manufactured goods, since the 1980s. It was expected that after decades of protectionism, trade liberalization would provoke an intense, but temporary, flood of imports. The swift growth rate of Mexican imports since the second half of the 1980s was induced not only by the elimination of non-tariff barriers to foreign trade but also by the expansion of domestic demand amid a persistent appreciation of the real exchange rate. Facilitated access to external funds resumed at that time and likewise played a role. After decades of tightly restricted access to foreign products, Mexican consumers began to eagerly satisfy their demand for a wide variety of goods and brands from abroad. However, to some extent, such import demand also mirrors the strong relations between exporting firms and foreign suppliers. The case of maquiladoras, which make up the most successful export sector to date, is typical because they rely on imported inputs and materials and have weak relations with local suppliers. Another factor that boosted import penetration to the domestic market, and that should not be ignored, is the breakdown of some internal linkages in domestic productive structure, as local producers have been put out of business by foreign competition.

The updated scenario of international trade of Mexico with the USA indicates that exports to Mexico in 2013 were \$226.2 billion, which were up by 4.7% (\$10.2 billion) from 2012 and market an overall increase of 132% from 2003. An increase of 444% is recorded since 1993, the pre-NAFTA period. The US exports to Mexico accounted for 14.3% of overall US exports in 2013. On another side of the international trade, the US goods imports from Mexico totaled \$280.5 billion in 2013, driving an increase of 1.0% (\$2.9 billion) from 2012, and accounted for an overall rise of 103% from 2003. The imports from Mexico to the USA have been augmented by 603% since the pre-NAFTA period (1993), establishing the fact the NAFTA significantly stimulated the international trade dynamics for Mexico as a partner country (USTR 2015). Sustaining high long-term economic growth should be a top priority on the national agenda. The rate of economic growth would have to be even higher to significantly improve the living standards of the people in rural geo-demographic settings. The evolution of employment in Mexico after NAFTA has clearly fallen short of the expectations, although it has been restructured in favor of international trade-related activities, but the overall employment growth is still underachieved.

Financial Integration and International Trade

As an emerging market economy, Mexico has taken advantage of globalization to implement structural policies and modernize regulation in order to strengthen its financial system. The country should meticulously drive the financial integration in view of the benefits of international integration for the money, bond, and foreign exchange markets for improving the international trade conditions of the country. The international financial competition has broadened the range of intermediaries and investors leading to more transparent pricing, higher liquidity, and lower transaction costs in the domestic markets. It has also enlarged the scope of investment alternatives to attract more specialized and sophisticated business partners. This has generated a cycle of increased integration, modernization, competition, and need to achieve higher efficiency. Mexico's monetary policy framework is gradually getting closer to that of its counterparts, and this is not only the case for the Banco de Mexico's instruments but also for its communication. The Central Bank of Mexico publishes statements summarizing the meetings of its Monetary Policy Committee (MPC). Its governing body is proactive in delivering speeches focused on monetary policy issues and the outlook for the Mexican economy. The use of interbank rates to analyze the ability of the central bank to communicate its messages to the financial markets relies on the ground that the interbank money market is highly liquid (Garcia-Herrero et al. 2015).

NAFTA has also given its member countries opportunity to develop policies toward a high level of financial integration within the financial instruments as well as to develop requisites to manage international financial integration for flawless money and banking movements in the region. The governments of the USA and Canada have provided, within limits, the atmosphere which has allowed this state of integration to exist. This state of integration may not be optimal in the sense of regional differences or in the sense of overall efficiency of money. However, given the national and regional priorities, it may be argued that North America is an optimum currency area, with the provisions of regional and cultural differences. The government in Mexico implemented the financial integration policies on stabilization program aimed at inducing a rapid macroeconomic adjustment, mainly by enlarging domestic savings and eliminating, for good, fiscal dominance by curtailing expenditures and broadening tax revenues. Exchange controls began to be gradually dismantled, and compulsory direct financing from commercial banks began to be replaced by liquidity requirements. The new requirements took the form of marketable debt instruments which provided banks with an incentive to foster the development of the government debt market. Increased financial integration has been particularly evident in the foreign exchange market. Increased integration is also evident in the fixed income market, mainly in the government bond segment. Intermediation in the primary and secondary markets continues to be carried out predominantly by traditional, large deposit-taking institutions. However, subsidiaries of foreign institutions, which have focused more on securities trading, have gained importance in the economy over the period of globalization.

According to a recent analysis by the Bank of Mexico, the increase in foreign participation also corresponds to a period of greater competition among commercial banks when measured in terms of overall income, lending activity in the mortgage market, and consumer credit. Greater competition and financial innovation, together with macroeconomic stability and improvements in regulatory and supervisory frameworks, have allowed for a gradual restoration of credit by commercial banks and other intermediaries. These conditions have increased the effectiveness of the credit transmission channel of monetary policy. In the foreign exchange market, increased competition has led to an extension of active trading hours to other time zones and a significant reduction in bid–ask spreads. As participation in the foreign exchange market has extended to time zones outside the USA, the hours in which the peso is traded more actively have shifted accordingly. Financial integration has contributed to the development of deeper and more liquid capital markets. The central bank has therefore been able to execute monetary policy without having undesirable effects on the functioning of markets. In conducting its operations, the Bank of Mexico has tried to rely mostly on marketable instruments, further promoting market development. Financial integration, mainly reflected in the increased competition in domestic markets, has contributed to a more developed and sounder local financial system. Exposure to global capital markets has increased competition as well as the number of intermediaries and investors, leading to more transparent pricing and lower transaction costs (Sidaoui 2008).

However, there is a high degree of heterogeneity in domestic financial markets across countries, and these differences remain largely unaltered despite financial globalization and financial development. There were large differences even among advanced economies, with the USA ranked first. Since the recent financial downturn, there has been a significant reevaluation of the effects of financial market integration. Financial integration tends to increase investor leverage and risk-taking, over and above the opportunities that it affords for portfolio diversification and inter-temporal borrowing and lending. In order to manage the dichotomy of financial opening and increased risk-taking, it is required to increase the value of existing asset holdings by increasing the collateral value of investors' portfolios to enhance the borrowing capacity and financial integration process. Also, it is necessary to reduce the overall consumption risk so that financial integration reduces precautionary saving and leads to an increase in investor's desire to borrow (Devereux and Yu 2014).

The governments of developing countries and leading emerging markets also need to explore the possibility of raising private capital for industrial development as it is an enormous source of global wealth that has not historically played as significant a role in development as its scale would suggest. The private capital sector is contemporary to industrial growth and is constantly active toward seeking investment opportunities. However, it only commits to those prospects that fall within the scope of predetermined risk and reward. Due to a variety of factors, many opportunities in developing countries such as Mexico are often perceived as of high risk or uncertain for the majority of investors. Institutions that offer to guarantee portions of loans made for such investments help investors rebalance their assessments of risk and reward and subsequently unlock considerable capital into developing countries. For example, in the past decade, the World Bank has approved 28 guarantees worth a total of $1.4 billion. These guarantees have stimulated more than $5 of private capital for every dollar spent by the Bank (World Bank 2010).

Another scope of attracting domestic and international investments is sovereign-wealth funds, which are typical of stretched investment nature for reasonably longer periods and are often more flexible in their investment rules than other types of investors. The concept of sovereign-wealth funds is not new as some countries have recently been forming innovative enterprises to develop coalitions for bringing together such diverse players. For instance, Chinese funds, Middle Eastern funds, multinational corporations, and local industrial development funds from the emerging markets and developing-country governments might be sell explained serving with this concept (Bensoussan et al. 2013).

Research and Development Spending

Expenditures for R&D include recurring and capital expenditures, both public and private on creative work undertaken systematically to increase knowledge including knowledge of humanity, culture, and society, and the use of knowledge for new applications. R&D covers basic research, applied research, and experimental development aspects in an international socioeconomic growth sector. The share of expenditure to the GDP of Mexico and the USA toward R&D to promote industrialization and serving the mankind is exhibited in Table 2.3.

It may be observed from the above table that the USA has the highest spending concentration on R&D. However, Mexico needs to improve its share of expenditure toward R&D to provide innovation and technology to push the industrialization and market competitiveness of the

Table 2.3 Expenditure on research and development in NATFA region (percent of GDP)

Country	*2010*	*2011*	*2012*	*2013*	*2014*[P]
Mexico	0.46	0.43	0.50	0.50	0.50
USA	2.74	2.76	2.79	2.80	2.80

P Provisional data
Source World Bank, Battelle-R&D Magazine, International Monetary Fund, CIA Fact Book

country. The geographic concentration of R&D is more apparent when looking at specific countries. The USA is by far the largest R&D performer ($429 billion in 2011), accounting for just under 30% of the global total, but down from 37% in 2001. Overall, the global R&D performance remains highly concentrated in three geographic regions including North America, Asia, and Europe while North America (the USA, Canada, and Mexico) accounted for 32% ($462 billion) of worldwide R&D performance in 2011. The ranking of the top ten countries as measured by R&D spending remained unchanged during 2014, with the USA reprising its role as the dominant force in global research across numerous industries. The projected investments on R&D in the USA during 2014 have shown declining trend in defense and aerospace R&D but tended to increase in energy-related research, increase in life science R&D, and toward establishing strong growth in information technology. Except for a decline in the 1970s at the point where industry surpassed government as the dominant research sponsor, the US total commitment to R&D has ranged between 2.5 and 3% of GDP for decades.

The intensity investment toward the R&D has been correlated with macroeconomic growth, which has laid the foundation of US technological innovation. This evidence of impact and economic return may account for much of the stability in the share of GDP. In addition, there may be a stabilizing portfolio effect in the complementary roles of public and private research, as well as the diversity of societal objectives and commercial markets they encompass. The reliable trend in research intensity continued in 2013 (2.8%), although multiple contemporary factors influence the prediction of 2014 activity. Though many individual firms and some industries increased their investment, industry investment in R&D was in slow pace during 2013 due to the slow global economy but continued to rationalization of R&D activities in selected industries.

There has been a dramatic change in the extent of globalization involved in research, as well as shifts in the way funds are spent. With the initiative of China on aggressive R&D programs, Southeast Asia has become the world's largest region for research investments, a trend expected to continue through at least the end of the decade. Collaborations with technology firms and research organizations in the USA and Europe are also increasing as Asia seeks to leverage global scientific knowledge and capabilities. However, major spending on infrastructure investments for R&D continues to be the center of budgetary attentions. R&D capabilities also follow markets for technology-enabled products. Automobiles are a good example since the major manufacturers have R&D operations around the world. In the commercial sector, innovation capabilities tend to follow the wealth created by manufacturing and catalyzed by accelerating product development cycles and sometimes by regulation.

Governments around the world, and particularly in Asia, recognize the importance of investing in the building blocks of innovation-based economies. The US government tends to seed innovation with investment in basic research and some tax and policy incentives, but the free market decides which technology is deployed at large scale. China, on the other hand, has fixed a macroeconomic goal of spending 2.2% of GDP on research by 2015, toward becoming an innovation-based economy by 2020. Such a command approach can sometimes accelerate the translation from research to development. R&D is a long-term investment in the future, serving as the cornerstone for innovation-driven growth. R&D investments are the foundation for generating new knowledge through basic research and ultimately for generating products and services through applied research and commercialization (Grueber and Studt 2013).

Advanced manufacturing is emerging as a potential driver of future economic growth to optimize the manufacturing potential and ensure continual improvement in innovation and technology management processes, to stay abreast in international markets, and to introduce timely new products. It is this paradigm shifting toward advanced manufacturing to spin off entirely new industries and lead to production methods that are most likely to stay in the USA because they are hard to imitate. Global competition in advanced manufacturing is growing at a rapid pace as innovation and technology life cycles are accelerated, which open the opportunities for new industries to emerge in the global marketplace. The industrial life cycle starts with the basic concept for a technology and grows with the focus on differentiation and commercialization. For many technologies, scientific knowledge created through basic research provides key insights that enable the basic concept, which is often validated through applied research. The development efforts at mature stage drive the technology toward developing a prototype of a commercial product and finally commercialization, scale-up activities, and develop the commercially viable product. At this stage, companies typically recapture the costs of technology investment through profits in the scale-up phase (OSTP 2012).

Disruptive Tendencies in Markets

A disruptive innovation initially grows in a niche market and gradually penetrates in the existing market cultivating its demand among the consumers. Over a period of time, the new product or idea completely redefines the industry. A disruptive innovation helps in developing a new market and value network, but drives to disrupt the long-standing market demand and value network displacing an earlier technology. Disruptive innovation may be described as the process that improves a product or service in a different way against the normal market drivers, typically first by developing a new consumer segment in a new market or by defecting the consumers from the existing market. Most of the disruptive innovations are radical as they skip some stages of the process of the existing products and technologies to gain competitive advantages in the market quickly. In contrast to disruptive innovation, a sustaining innovation does not create new markets or value networks but only evolves the existing ones with better value, allowing the firms within to compete against each other's sustaining improvements. In view of the globalization and marketing practices of the emerging companies, it has been observed that market disruption has become a growth function for technology and its application.

Clayton M. Christensen has revolutionized the concept of disruptive innovation, which is referred as technology mudslide hypothesis (Christensen and Overdorf 2000). This is a simple notion expressing that an established firm fails because it is unable to cope up with the changing technological advances with the competing firms. In this hypothesis, attributes of a firm can be explained with the analogy of creepers—one which finds its own path to climb and the other that survives as a parasite to climb. Products emerging out of the disruptive technology are like parasites, which are built on the products available in the market with popular technologies. Disruptive innovation products largely focus on low cost and utilitarian values of the consumers. Good firms are usually aware of the emerging innovations underneath the market, but their business environment does not allow them to intersect the disruptive innovations as they are risky to pursue due to low profit, and may drain resources of the firm. Generally, a firm's existing value networks place insufficient value on the disruptive innovation to allow its pursuit by another firm. Start-up firms live with different value networks until disruptive innovation is able to invade their value networks, grow parallel in the market and create a me-too entry, and strengthen its chances of co-survival in the existing market.

Disruptive innovation may be a product or a service designed for a new set of customers by defecting them from the existing stream of buying. Generally, disruptive innovations are technologically straightforward, convincing to consumers, and generate value for money. Some disruptive innovations offer more for less to customers through a different package of attributes that have higher significance to the consumers in the bottom-of-the-pyramid market segment than to those of the mainstream market. Christensen argues that disruptive innovations can damage successful brands and well-managed products of reputed companies that are responsive to their customers and have invested resources in conducting excellent R&D to support innovation. These companies tend to bypass markets that are most susceptible to disruptive innovations as there appears the risk of low profit and scope of business growth. Thus, disruptive technology provides products and services with a focus on the customer and drives strategically counterproductive impact on the existing products in a market. However, in a positive sense, the disruptive innovation may be considered as the constructive integration of attributes to the existing technology. Disruptive innovations generate radical insights that could help in improving the economic benefits to consumers and provide better opportunities for the firms to grow in the mass market.

As companies tend to innovate faster, customers' needs evolve over the period and set demand for the products with new technologies in the market. However, most organizations develop complicated, high-technology, and expensive products for customers. High-technology, high-value products help companies to succeed in the premium market segment by maintaining high price–high profit ratio. Such strategy encourages disruptive innovations at the bottom of the market and allows consumers at the bottom of a market to access the products. Major attributes of the disruptive innovations include:

- Low-price profile
- High perceived use value
- Low gross margins
- Small target markets
- Simple products and services
- Attractive solutions

The bottom-of-the-pyramid market offers lower gross margins and is non-competitive to other firms to develop strategies to move upward in the market and create space at the bottom of the market for new disruptive competitors to emerge.

Disruptive market behavior and streamlined differentiations in products and services by the companies exist simultaneously in the competitive marketplace. As companies introduce differentiated products in the markets, disruptive products grow underneath the mainstream retailing in the mass market as well as in the bottom-of-the-pyramid market segment. The prominence of disruption of products and services in the market causes serious threats to the mainstream marketing strategies of the companies and might also cause failure of business in specific markets or consumer segments. One of the most consistent patterns in business is the failure of leading companies in combating with the unnoticed disruptions emerging in the market whenever new technologies or product differentiations are introduced. The reason at the grassroots why companies succumb to disruptive products is the defection of their customers to the low-end disruption. However, to stay sustainable within the industries and competitive marketplace, companies must be able to spot disruptive technologies and protect their market and consumer segments that are serving mainstream customers (Bower and Christensen 1995).

Most companies position differentiated and new competitive products in high-end markets by promoting high-cost technology, high price, and developing high brand equity for gaining sustainable competitive advantage. However, as the new products are positioned in the high-end markets, there exists the threat of new entrants. Sometimes, the companies choose to launch the differentiated products in a market niche catering to the consumer needs in a limited territory. Companies gain the first mover advantage in low-end markets by positioning the differentiated and new competitive products through low-price offers and creating high perceived use value for the products among consumers. However, new products takeoff in the low-end markets slowly but fetch wider outreach among consumers. Companies need to play safe in this market segment as disruptive innovations might grow here and cause damage to any new differentiated products brought to this market segment. Hence, most companies introduce low-cost differentiations in the low-end markets.

The low-end disruptive innovation products are targeted to customers who are satisfied even with the partial performance of the product but derive high emotional satisfaction, while new market disruption aims at the new consumer segment to cater both high product performance as well as emotional satisfaction. Low-end disruption in the market takes place when the demand for the product exists but products are unavailable. Consumers have the latent desire to experience the high-end products but often these products are not affordable. Consequently, at some point, the performance of the disruptive products overshoots the needs of certain customer segments, and at this point, a disruptive technology may enter the market and provide a product with high perceived use value, gaining a reasonable market share. In low-end disruption, the disruptive product is focused initially on serving the least profitable customer, who is happy with the partial performance of the product. Such customers will be willing to pay a lower price than others and have higher satisfaction on having the product over its performance. Once the disruptive products gain a sustainable market share, it seeks to improve its profit margins over the established brands, and in order to achieve higher profit margins, the disruptive products enter the differentiated price segment where the customer is willing to pay a little more for higher quality. Hence, the disruptor firms set the innovation process for the products to meet the desired quality and establish as a black market product. Over time, the disruptive products will move to up-market and focus on penetrating into attractive consumer segments. This business situation makes the disruptive products spur out of the niche. The new market disruption occurs when a product fits a new or emerging market segment that is not being served by the existing incumbents in the industry (Rajagopal 2015).

Sustaining innovation pioneered by established companies ensures its competitive status in a market by enhancing and improving the existing products' performance in an expected way that customers value

(Christensen and Overdorf 2000). However, disruptive innovation usually originates from newcomers and upsets the market status by fundamentally altering the way customers think about product performance because it exceeds their expectations in an unexpected way. In comparing both innovation types, it can be seen that sustaining innovations are the type of technological outcomes that can be outperformed by large and established competitors within a short period of time, while disruptive innovations cannot be imitated or outdone by established companies due to the number of difficulties faced by them (Kim and Mauborgne 2005). With disruptive innovation, the vital concern is to make such a leap that the relevant offering provides a better product/service than anything that existed beforehand. It is almost impossible for established companies to cope with the change as they are focusing on their sustained innovation that helps to maximize profits and keep making their products more desirable. However, established companies can be disruptive by attracting low end of customers as in the case of the portable digital music player. Many companies are in search of an innovative strategy to move on to a market where there is no competition yet. In view of that, many academics and managers are trying to find a systematic framework for a strategic innovative business model. The disruptive technology largely serves to the low-end or new niche market customers, and upon establishing a strong market foothold, it enters the market competition and engages in continuous R&D to improve the performance of products and services. The R&D strategy comprising simplification of usage of technology and application of new products drives the disruptive innovations (Yu and Hang 2010).

Notes

1. Transnational companies are engaged in diversified business portfolios in the region but hold common ownership. Such companies serve diverse markets and support national economic growth as well as stay competitive in the international markets.

References

Andersen, P. H. (2006). Regional clusters in a global world: Production relocation, innovation, and industrial decline. *California Management Review, 49*(1), 101–122.

Bensoussan, E., Ruparell, R., & Taliento, L. (2013, August). *Innovative development financing*. New York: McKinsey Insights, McKinsey.

Bower, J. L., & Christensen, C. M. (1995). Disruptive technology: Catching the wave. *Harvard Business Review, 73*(1), 43–53.

Brid-Moreno, J. C. (2013). Industrial policy: A missing link in Mexico's quest for export-led growth. *Latin American Policy, 4*(2), 216–237.

Brid-Moreno, J. C., Vladivia, J. C. R., & Santamaria, J. (2005). *Mexico: Economic growth exports and industrial performance after NAFTA*. Mexico: Economic Development Unit, CEPAL.

Buigues, P. A., & Sekkat, K. (2009). *Industrial policy in Europe, Japan and the USA: Amounts, mechanisms and effectiveness*. Basingstoke, UK: Palgrave Macmillan.

Christensen, C. M., & Overdorf, M. (2000). Meeting the challenge of disruptive change. *Harvard Business Review, 78*(2), 66–76.

Dedrick, J., Kraemer, K. L., Palacios, J. J., Tigre, P. B., & Junqueira-Botelho, A. J. (2001). Economic liberalization and the computer industry: Comparing outcomes in Brazil and Mexico. *World Development, 29*(7), 1199–1214.

Devereux, M. B., & Yu, C. (2014). *International financial integration and crisis contagion*. Federal Reserve Bank of Dallas (Globalization and Monetary Policy Institute Working Paper No. 197).

Garcia- Herrero, A. G., Girardin, E., & Marmolejo, A. L. (2015). *Mexico's monetary policy communication and money markets* (Working Paper 15/15, BBVA Research). Retrieved on July 7, 2015 from https://www.bbvaresearch.com/wp-content/uploads/2015/05/WP15-15_MexMP.pdf.

Grueber, M. & Studt, T. (2013). 2014 Global R&D funding forecast, *R&D Magazine*, December 1–35. Retrieved on July 07, 2015 from http://www.battelle.org/docs/tpp/2014_global_rd_funding_forecast.pdf.

Kim, W. C., & Mauborgne, R. (2005). *Blue ocean strategy: How to create uncontested market space and make the competition irrelevant*. Boston, MA: Harvard Business School Press.

KPMG. (2014). *Investments in Mexico*. Report, KPMG Cardenas Dosal, S.C., Mexico City, Mexico.

Lin, J. Y. (2012). *New structural economics, a framework for rethinking development and policy*. Washington, DC: World Bank.

Manyika, J., Pacthod, D., & Park, M. (2011, May 1). Translating innovation into US growth: An advanced-industries perspective. *McKinsey Quarterly*, McKinsey and Co.

OSTP—Office of Science and Technology Policy. (2012). *A national strategic plan for advanced manufacturing*. Washington, DC: Executive Office of the President of the USA, National Science and Technology Council.

Perez, R. P., & Alvarado, J. (2014). The revival of industrial policy. In R. P. Perez (Ed.), *Strengthening value chains as an industrial policy instrument*.

Methodology and experience of ECLAC in Central America (pp. 31–70). Chile: Economic Commission for Latin America and the Caribbean (ECLAC), Santiago.

Peres, W. (2006). *El (lento) Retorno de las políticas industriales en América Latina y el Caribe*. Serie Desarrollo Productivo, (Spanish) no. 166, ECLAC, Santiago. In UNCTAD, Trade and Development Report. Geneva, Switzerland.

Peres, W., & Primi, A. (2009). *Theory and practice of industrial policy: Evidence from the Latin American experience*. Desarrollo Productivo series, No. 187 (LC/L.3013-P), Santiago, Chile, Economic Commission for Latin America and the Caribbean (ECLAC), United Nations.

Rajagopal. (2015). *Butterfly effect in competitive markets: Driving small change for larger differences*. Basingstoke, UK: Palgrave Macmillan.

Sidaui, J. (2008). The impact of international financial integration on Mexican financial markets. In *Financial globalization and emerging market capital flows* (BIS Papers # 44, 341–361). Basel, Switzerland: Bank for International Settlements.

Villarreal, M. A. & Fergusson, I. F. (2015). *North-American Free Trade Agreement, Congressional Research Service* (CRS Report # R42965), Washington, D.C.

World Bank. (2010). *Innovative finance for development solutions: Initiatives of the World Bank group*. USA: World Bank.

Yu, D., & Hang, C. C. (2010). A reflective review of disruptive innovation theory. *International Journal of Management Review, 12*(4), 435–452.

CHAPTER 3

Market Integration in NAFTA Region

The North American Free Trade Agreement (NAFTA) has given an advantage to the USA and Mexico to gain a competitive advantage in manufacturing by offering infrastructure and services required to turn the industrial production cost effective. It has been estimated by the World Trade Organization (WTO) that about 50% of global trade flows emerge through the preferential trade agreements between the countries. This trend indicates the growing importance of the regional agreements over the preferential or bilateral trade agreements between the countries as they are comprehensive and offer wider benefits. This chapter discusses the fundamentals of integration process in the North American trade and economy and delineates how the market integration has been driven by exports, imports, and manufacturing investment. The chapter analyzes the impact of market integration on the economy responding the pertinent questions that remain unresolved, whether the market integration through regional trade agreements delivers the desired benefits to the developing nations as compared to the one with the develop trade and economy conditions.

Besides other issues like financial, environmental sustainability, and cross-border migration, the NAFTA largely focuses on tariff elimination in vital primary and manufacturing sectors to keep the trade flows dynamic among the partner countries. Accordingly, the market integration could be driven by exports, imports, and manufacturing investment made by the member countries which, taken together, have been responsible for 90% of regional imports during 2002–2012. The cross-border

Rajagopal and V. Zlatev, *Business Dynamics in North America*,
DOI 10.1007/978-3-319-57606-0_3

tariffs for automobile parts exports, textiles, and agricultural produce have been eliminated among the member countries in a phased manner. It has been observed that in fact half of world trade does not pay tariffs, while in the most favored nations (MFN), tariff is zero, and the most protected products are excluded from many "preferential" agreements pulling down the trade contribution through the preferential trade agreements to as low as 16% in comparison to regional trade agreements. In this estimate, the European Union is regarded as a single country for the all preferential agreements (Medvedev 2006).

Market Integration Effects

NAFTA may also be considered as an intra-regional agreement signed between countries from a single region unlike inter-regional trade agreements wherein members belong to different groups or regions. This agreement has been built over some bilateral agreements that were in force since the 1980s among the USA, Canada, and Mexico. Some propose the establishment of customs unions and others seek the establishment of free trade areas. In line with the specification of trade agreements, there are some shallow agreements that only seek the elimination of tariffs or the reciprocal granting of tariff preferences instead of including commitments like investments, intellectual property, the resolution of disputes, and regulatory measures for international trade like NAFTA (Robert Lawrence 2006). Most countries of South America have signed as many as 65 trade agreements, of which 54 have been negotiated with other developing countries, within and outside of the region, and 11 with developed countries until 2010 (WTO 2011). However, 15 of the existing trade agreements have been negotiated with Asian countries that have come into force in the first decade of the twenty-first century and that reveal their successes in achieving growth in trade and economy through regional trade. After the recovery of the USA from the recent economic recession (2007–2010), the commercial integration among the developing countries with emerging markets has become a matter of primary importance alongside the financial integration by regulating the investment measures and foreign exchange rate regimes. Although the mechanisms for trade and financial integration and international cooperation among the emerging markets like Mexico have proliferated, such dynamics is largely governed by the political ideologies and interventions, the status of the domestic economy, and international diplomacy.

The trade agreements have driven the Latin American countries with enormous opportunities to explore international markets and develop market competitiveness. Besides, the trade development measures to attract foreign direct investment and lower or eliminate the tariff barriers have also reflected global trends in reference to the typology of these agreements. While the majority of trade agreements are bilateral, some include the free trade agreements, which have set a very comprehensive scope for trade and economic development. Notably, some free trade agreements signed by Peru, Colombia, and Chile with the USA and the European Union have helped in gearing up the trade and economy of these countries. However, the bilateral agreements signed with Asian countries, especially by Chile and Peru, pose a limited scope with regard to regulatory commitments but are very ambitious with regard to their levels of opening trade and eliminating tariffs. These agreements also have a strong potential, given the economic dynamism of this region. Other agreements are *plurilateral* involving a large number of countries on extended geo-economic parameters like the Trans-Pacific Strategic Economic Partnership Agreement, negotiated by Chile, New Zealand, Brunei Darussalam, and Singapore, which is now being broadened to include the USA within the framework of the negotiations for the Trans-Pacific Partnership Agreement (TPP).

Many agreements are emerging as intra-regional within the Latin American geographic region, however, since the mid-twentieth century, numerous inter-regional agreements including cross-continent free trade and bilateral agreement with trans-Pacific and trans-Atlantic countries have also taken place with Mexico, Chile, Peru, Brazil, and other South American countries. In general, in the agreements among countries of the region, the focus has been largely on tariff liberalization and regulatory matters. By contrast, with the countries outside of the region, the agreements of the South American countries are more ambitious and include significant regulatory commitments, especially the agreements signed with the USA or the European Union.

Over the trend of trade liberalization as experienced in the Latin American countries in the early decade (2001–2010) of the twenty-first century, NAFTA has created a single market with the USA and Canada that has helped to propel Mexico into the top ranks of manufacturing exporters. The economic reforms policies of Mexico that are set for implementation in 2015 have received global attention, and in recent months, global auto and food manufacturing giants have expressed possibilities of multi-billion dollar investments within new facilities and industrial infrastructure. However, with the implementation of economic reforms policies concerning regulations on investments, property rights, repatriation of profit and transfer of funds, and fiscal policies toward corporate taxation, Mexico stands out as an attractive destination with ample opportunities for international business and trade. Mexico has several setbacks ranging from the high rate of inflation, low-skilled workforce, and internal security to gain strong international competitiveness which has caused relatively slow GDP growth. However, the country exhibits a stable monetary and fiscal position and prospects to cater its rising demand as the US economic turns dynamic after 2012 overcoming the effects of the recent economic recession (2007–2010). For the past two decades (1991–2010), the annual GDP growth in Mexico has averaged about 2.7%, which is apparently low by the standards of emerging economy and not enough to enhance living standards substantially across the various socioeconomic segments. The main factor causing the slow growth rate is the chronically weak productivity in the manufacturing and services sectors since the pre-NAFTA period, and it is necessary for the country to find ways to spur higher productivity to reach the targeted growth of 3.5% as anticipated after the economic reforms. The plans for enhancing the investment in the manufacturing and services sectors and improving the exports not only to the NAFTA member countries but also to other preferential trade agreement led countries would help the country to achieve the desired growth rate.

Modern, highly productive, and globally competitive Mexico has flourished under NAFTA and other rounds of market liberalization. Today, Mexican multinationals such as FEMSA, Grupo Alfa, Grupo Bimbo, Grupo Lala, Mabe, and Walmex have become leaders in some of the most competitive markets in the world. But policy changes have barely touched the other Mexico, where traditional enterprises operate in the same old ways and are experiencing falling labor productivity. While the largest modern companies have been ratcheting up productivity by 5.8% annually, productivity at traditional Mexican enterprises—tiny stores, bakeries, and low-skill manufacturers—has been declining by 6.5%. Worse, employment is growing faster in the traditional economy, in effect shifting labor from high-productivity to low-productivity work—the opposite of what any economy wants. Upon overall observation on NAFTA and its impact on the economy of Mexico as the growing country among the other two member countries, one of the pertinent questions that remain unresolved is whether the market integration in the treaty has delivered the desired benefits to Mexico as a developing nation. Mexico lags far behind its emerging-market peers in outstanding bank loans. We estimate that Mexico's annual credit gap—the difference between what companies would be expected to borrow and what is actually loaned—is $60 billion a year. Three-quarters of that gap is underlending to small- and medium-size enterprises, which in other economies create new products and services and deliver the most employment growth. The private sector has a critical role to play in bridging the two Mexicos. Even in auto manufacturing, where top global competitors are maximizing plant productivity, 80% of companies are small, traditional shops, with fewer than ten employees. These subcontractors provide low-cost labor to global parts makers and assemblers and have one-tenth the productivity of producers in the top 10%. Some global companies are already working with their small suppliers, providing technical know-how and even access to capital for new equipment and technology. Mexico needs more of this kind of development (Rubio and Remes 2014).

The important factors that stoke rapid growth in emerging economies exist in Mexico: a young and growing labor force, abundant natural resources, and access to export markets (in Mexico's case a strategic location next to the USA and membership in NAFTA provide uniquely privileged access). In addition, Mexico has opened up its economy to trade and foreign investment installed extensive reforms. Since 2000, it has also been able to boast sustained macroeconomic and fiscal stability. Yet year after year, rapid growth remains elusive. GDP expanded by just 1.1% in 2013 and probably came in between 2 and 2.5% in 2014. That's less than the 3% plus global average and far below the 5% plus the rate of fast-growing developing economies. Government economists and foreign investors are once more calling for GDP growth rates of 3–4% this year, and some project even higher rates after that. But can Mexico do it this time? There are reasons for optimism. The USA is enjoying a robust recovery, raising demand for cars and other goods that flow from Mexican factories. The US auto sales topped 16 m units in 2014 and could break 17 m in 2015, and more than 10% of these cars are Mexican imports. At the same time, rising wages in China and a search for simpler supply chains make Mexico more attractive.

Since the NAFTA was signed, large Mexican producers and locally owned operations of multinationals have invested in modern plants. In Mexico, the plants of the world's leading autos and auto parts makers are as productive as many US plants and, we estimate, that productivity across all large modern enterprises has risen by 5.8% a year since 1999. In stark contrast, in traditional enterprises, productivity is falling by 6.5% a year. A decade ago, Mexican small businesses were, on average, 28% as productive as the large companies; now, they are less than 10% as productive. In between are mid-sized companies a mix of traditional and modern establishments whose productivity growth has been close to flat, at about 1.0% a year. Businesses remain small and informal because they have incentives to remain so and lack access to the capital that would enable them to operate formally and grow. Policies that were intended to help small businesses survive now provide perverse incentives to stay small. This ranges from tax exemptions and electricity subsidies to zoning rules that keep modern operators out, insulating mom and pop businesses from modern competitors that would force them to become more productive. Even if companies want to operate in the formal economy, they face barriers and prohibitive costs. The cost of registering a company (in terms of annual income) is seven times the US cost. Required social security contributions average around 28% of salaries, and labor laws make it costly to dismiss workers, discouraging formal hiring. Weighing these costs against the unlikely possibility of being caught and prosecuted for operating informally, companies choose to stay informal and enjoy higher margins than their formal peers (Bolio and Remes 2015).

Attributes of NAFTA

The North American market is one of the richest in the world. Companies based in Canada have preferred access to a market of 461 million people, with a combined GDP of over US$17 trillion. At the time that NAFTA was implemented, the US–Canada FTA was already in effect, and US tariffs on most Mexican goods were low. NAFTA opened up the US market to increased Mexican imports and the Mexican market to the USA and Canada, creating one of the largest single markets in the world. Some of the key NAFTA provisions included tariff and non-tariff trade liberalization, rules of origin, services trade, foreign investment, intellectual property rights (IPR) protection, government procurement, and dispute resolution. Labor and environmental provisions were included in separate NAFTA side agreements. The 1994 NAFTA, together with its 1989 predecessor, the Canada–US Free Trade Agreement, has eliminated most barriers to trade within Canada, the

USA, and Mexico, easing the cross-border flow of goods, services, capital, and technology. NAFTA formed the world's largest free trade area and has resulted in economic growth and rising standards of living for all three partner countries. NAFTA has opened up vast new business opportunities, not only for companies located within one of the three partner countries but also for foreign firms interested in the huge North American market. As a result, international investors now can access the entire North American market from a Canadian location. The salient features of NAFTA include:

- Tariff elimination on trade between Canada, the USA, and Mexico;
- Provision of a standard of "national treatment" for foreign investors in other signatory countries;
- Ensured secure market access;
- Improved dispute settlement mechanism;
- Increased access to government procurement opportunities, for companies located in member countries;
- Improved cross-border movement of business people and professionals among the signatory countries; and
- Stronger protection of IPR.

Given that the US–Canada FTA was already in place, most of the market opening measures resulted in the removal of US tariffs and quotas applied to imports from Mexico, and Mexican trade barriers applied to imports from the USA and Canada. At the time that NAFTA went into effect, about 40% of US imports from Mexico entered duty-free and the remainder faced duties of up to 35%, with a trade-weighted average rate of about 7%. Mexico's trade-weighted tariff on US agricultural products averaged about 11%. Also affecting US–Mexico trade were both countries' phytosanitary rules, Mexican import licensing requirements, and US marketing orders. The marketing orders were designed to set national guidelines for product quality, market promotion, and supply levels. The most significant Mexican products that were affected by US marketing orders included tomatoes, onions, avocados, grapefruit, oranges, olives, and table grapes.

The market opening provisions of the agreement gradually eliminated all tariffs and most non-tariff barriers on goods produced and traded within North America over a period of 15 years after it entered into force. Some tariffs were eliminated immediately, while others were phased out in various schedules of 5–15 years. The US import-sensitive sectors, such as glassware, footwear, and ceramic tile received longer phase-out schedules. NAFTA provided the option of accelerating tariff reductions if the involved countries agreed.[1] The agreement included safeguard provisions in which the importing country could increase tariffs, or impose quotas in some cases, on imports during a transition period if domestic producers faced serious injury as a result of increased imports from another NAFTA country. It terminated all existing drawback programs by January 1, 2001. A duty drawback is a refund or waiver in whole or in part of customs duties assessed or collected upon importation of an article or materials which are subsequently exported.

Some of the more significant changes took place in the textiles, apparel, automotive, and agricultural industries. Elimination of trade barriers in these key industries is as summarized below:

Textiles and Apparel Industries: NAFTA phased out all duties on textile and apparel goods within North America meeting specific NAFTA rules of origin over a 10-year period. NAFTA rules of origin for textiles and apparel define when imported textile or apparel goods qualify for preferential treatments. For most products, the rule of origin is "yarn forward," which means that goods must be produced from yarn made in a NAFTA country to benefit from preferential treatment. Prior to NAFTA, 65% of US apparel imports from Mexico entered duty-free and quota-free, and the remaining 35% faced an average tariff rate of 17.9%. Mexico's average tariff on US textile and apparel products was 16%, with duties as high as 20% on some products (Business Roundtable 2004).

Automotive Industry: NAFTA phased out Mexico's restrictive auto decree. It phased out all US tariffs imports from Mexico and Mexican tariffs on US and Canadian products as long as they met the rules of origin requirements of 62.5% North American content for autos, light trucks, engines, and transmissions and 60% for other vehicles and automotive parts. Some tariffs were eliminated immediately, while others were phased out in periods of 5–10 years. Prior to NAFTA, the USA assessed the following tariffs on imports from Mexico: 2.5% on automobiles, 25% on light-duty trucks, and a trade-weighted average of 3.1% for automotive parts. Mexican tariffs on US and Canadian automotive products were as follows: 20% on automobiles and light trucks, and 10–20% on auto parts (Business Roundtable 2004).

Agriculture: NAFTA set out separate bilateral undertakings on cross-border trade in agriculture, one between Canada and Mexico, and the other between Mexico and the USA. As a general matter, US–Canada FTA provisions continued to apply on trade with Canada. Regarding US–Mexico agriculture trade, NAFTA eliminated most non-tariff barriers in agricultural trade, either through their conversion to tariff-rate quotas (TRQs) or ordinary tariffs. Tariffs were phased out over a period of 15 years with sensitive products such as sugar and corn receiving the longest phase-out periods. TRQs allowed NAFTA partners to export specified quantities of a product to other NAFTA countries at a relatively low tariff, but subjected all imports of the product above a predetermined threshold to a higher tariff. Approximately, one-half of US–Mexico agricultural trade became duty-free when the agreement went into effect. Prior to NAFTA, most tariffs, in agricultural trade between the USA and Mexico, were fairly low on an average though some US exports to Mexico faced tariffs as high as 12%. However, approximately, one-fourth of US agricultural exports to Mexico (by value) were subjected to restrictive import licensing requirements (Business Roundtable 2004).

Foreign Investment: NAFTA removed significant investment barriers, ensured basic protections for NAFTA investors, and provided a mechanism for the settlement of disputes between investors and a NAFTA country. NAFTA provided for "non-discriminatory treatment" for foreign investment by NAFTA parties in certain sectors of other NAFTA countries. The agreement included explicit country-specific liberalization commitments and exceptions to national treatment. Exemptions from NAFTA investment provisions include the energy sector in Mexico in which the Mexican government reserved the right to prohibit foreign investment.

Intellectual Property Rights: NAFTA built upon the then-ongoing Uruguay Round negotiations that would create the Trade-Related Aspects of Intellectual Property Rights (TRIPS) agreement in the WTO and on various existing international intellectual property treaties. The agreement set out specific enforceable commitments by NAFTA parties regarding the protection of copyrights, patents, trademarks, and trade secrets, among other provisions.

Dispute Settlement Procedures: NAFTA's provisions for preventing and settling disputes were built upon provisions in the US–Canada FTA. NAFTA created a system of arbitration for resolving disputes that included initial consultations, taking the issue to the NAFTA Trade Commission, or going through arbitral panel proceedings. NAFTA included separate dispute settlement provisions for addressing disputes over antidumping and countervailing duty determinations.

Government Procurement: NAFTA opened up a significant portion of federal government procurement in each country on a non-discriminatory basis to suppliers from other NAFTA countries for goods and services. It contains some limitations for procurement by state-owned enterprises (Villarreal and Fergusson 2015).

Besides the three principal sectors discussed above, NAFTA provisions for services companies established a set of basic rules and obligations in services trade among partner countries. The agreement expanded on initiatives in the US–Canada FTA and the Uruguay Round of multilateral trade negotiations to create internationally agreed disciplines on government regulation of trade in services. The agreement granted services providers certain rights concerning non-discriminatory treatment, cross-border sales and entry, investment, and access to information. However, there were certain exclusions and reservations by each country. These included maritime shipping (USA), film and publishing (Canada), and oil and gas drilling (Mexico). Although NAFTA liberalized certain service sectors in Mexico, particularly financial services, which profoundly altered its banking sector, other sectors were barely affected. In telecommunications services, NAFTA partners agreed to exclude provision of, but not the use of, basic telecommunications services. NAFTA granted a "bill of rights" for the providers and users of telecommunications services, including access to public telecommunications services; connection to private lines that reflect economic costs and available on a flat-rate pricing basis; and the right to choose, purchase, or lease terminal equipment best suited to their needs. However, NAFTA did not require parties to authorize a person of another NAFTA country to provide or operate telecommunications transport networks or services. NAFTA did not bar a party from maintaining a monopoly provider of public networks or services, such as Telmex, Mexico's dominant telecommunications company (Villarreal and Fergusson 2015).

Economic Integration and Growth

Two basic observations arise from international data on economic development. The first is the persistent divergence of income per capita across countries over a sufficiently long period of time. This well-known tendency is striking, as developing economies typically exhibit unexploited business opportunities that would otherwise allow them to grow faster than industrial nations, thereby catching up with the leaders. We know that, as a general trend, absolute convergence has not occurred. Economists refer to the first as total factor productivity (TFP), estimated on the basis of measures of output and inputs, as well as certain production function assumptions. The second observation is that a large part of economic growth can be attributed to the efficiency with which production inputs are applied, in addition to the intensity of their use. The success of a few countries, who have managed to multiply their income levels quite rapidly, has largely resulted from booming TFP. Furthermore, productivity differences at the firm level within an industry are a puzzle that prevails even in advanced countries. Firm survival is frequently linked to higher levels of efficiency. These observations make the study of productivity a central object of inquiry. On the other hand, the fact that TFP is estimated as a residual implies that it summarizes our ignorance regarding what makes one economy or firm more efficient than others (Sánchez 2015).

During the last three decades, Mexico has been undergoing a process of expanding economic integration with the USA. Deeper relations between the two countries have been built on their geographic proximity, especially as a result of the opening up of the Mexican economy, which began in 1983 with a phase of unilateral reduction of tariffs and other barriers to trade. Ever greater openness has been achieved through the NAFTA since 1994, which included Canada, the USA, and Mexico. Despite the important role that Canada plays in intra-regional transactions, the following discussion focuses on the growing economic links between the USA and Mexico. Enhanced economic integration between these two countries is multifold. The most dramatic reflection of this relation is the consistently high growth of their bilateral trade in goods and services, which surpasses that of their respective GDPs. Specifically, highly dynamic Mexican exports to the USA have implied markedly more Mexican imports from north of the border. Additionally, bidirectional tourism has been increasing, and workers' remittances from the USA are an important source of inflows in Mexico's balance of payments. At the same time, foreign direct investment between the two countries and from other nations has been growing in view of advantages from business opportunities arising from their greater commercial interaction. From 1980 to 2010, Mexican exports to the USA rose from 5.0% of GDP to 23.1%, while Mexican imports from the USA increased from

5.7% of GDP to 14.0%. During the same period, FDI from the USA to Mexico grew by more than 1.8 times in constant dollars, while workers' remittances, most of which come from the USA, increased 32 times (Sánchez 2011).

To gain some insight into Mexico's productivity problem, it is useful to examine sectorial productivity performance. Due to a lack of reliable data on capital by sector, the developing countries need to focus on labor productivity. For this exercise, GDP has been in four sectors: agriculture, the manufacturing industry, the nonmanufacturing industry, and services. For the period under consideration, on average, total labor productivity dropped 0.3% per year, with rises in the first two segments of the economy and falls in the latter two. Without an attempt to provide a formal explanation of the contrasting sectorial development, the following conjectures are relatively safe.[2] The fastest-growing sector in terms of productivity was agriculture, with an average annual rate of 1.2%, mainly reflecting a sharp reduction in the labor force dedicated to this activity. Average productivity growth in manufacturing was 0.2% per year, surprisingly low given the undeniable efficiency levels of some sub-sectors such as automobiles and electronics exposed to competition in international markets. Nonmanufacturing exhibited the sharpest contraction in productivity, at negative 1.7%. This dismal result is driven mainly by utilities in the hands of state monopolies, and construction, of which a large fraction is self-construction suffering from low-scale and lagging technology.

Policy makers are expected to use all the information on hand, including the best estimates of theoretical models, to foment a favorable setting for productivity. Sometimes, this may simply mean incrementally removing obstacles, thereby allowing private participants to strengthen the existing institutions that facilitate economic activity (Easterly 2008). Additionally, implementation of measures to fuel efficiency must not be considered in isolation. The absence or presence of other policies or institutions that could be necessary should be taken into account. A leading example is that of privatization, in which the lack of an appropriate regulatory framework or governance rules in some countries has produced unintended consequences, including the stripping of privatized company assets (Hoff and Stiglitz 2005). Many factors impinge on a country's productivity dynamics, making it necessary for any explanation to consider the issue in a multifaceted way. The pursuit of higher productivity growth is challenging. Policy makers should avoid looking for a non-existent panacea, while at the same time recognizing the need for continuous progress. In Mexico, the bar is also high. Productivity performance has been underwhelming, but a recent program of structural change could yield benefits along the path to greater modernization, if essential building blocks such as the rule of law are reinforced and the reforms are implemented adequately and deeply. Mexico has undertaken a program of structural reforms of various areas of the economy. The aim is to tackle some of the evident problems of low efficiency briefly described, by allowing or increasing competition as well as facilitating investment and market operations. Results from these measures depend on the depth of their actual implementation and, in any case, should be viewed as steps along a road that needs to be paved with further changes.

Productivity and Growth in the USA

There is large untapped potential to increase productivity and growth in the USA, MGI finds. Businesses can achieve three-quarters of the necessary productivity growth acceleration in the current regulatory and business environment. Companies can achieve one-quarter of the acceleration by more widely adopting best practice. Even in such sectors as retail, where US businesses have a strong productivity record, there is scope to do more (e.g., by taking lean practices from the stockroom to the storefront). Aerospace companies may be leading global exporters but they have yet to adopt lean practices in the systematic way seen among best-in-class automotive players. The public sector and regulated sectors such as health care, which have not faced as strong competitive pressure, offer another large opportunity. Health care players have just begun to adopt lean. Hospitals have room to improve how nurses spend their time at some hospitals; nurses spend less than 40% of their time with patients and to improve their discharge and admissions processes. Implementing emerging business and technology innovations can achieve a further half of the necessary acceleration. Opportunities lie in enhanced supply chain integration, greater responsiveness to evolving customer preferences and behavior, and innovating in what and how goods and services are provided to customers.

Manufacturing industrial production in Mexico fell at a 1.0% annual rate in the first quarter of 2015, which has been faster than the 0.7% pace of decline in the overall economy. Production activity fell sharply as the adverse weather conditions disrupted construction, transportation, trade, and commercial activity, making the severe winter of 2015 a repeat performance of 2014. The sudden rise in the value of the dollar affects trade competitiveness. The US economy is growing faster than most advanced economies, and our central bank has ended quantitative easing and is talking about raising interest rates while other nations' central banks are beginning quantitative easing. More spending was prominent toward imports as the export growth slows, weakening domestic production growth. The rapid declines in oil and natural gas prices were turned beneficial to energy users but caused a similarly rapid decline in investment in energy drilling, exploration, and the material supply chain. A large inventory buildup this winter drove the inventory to sales ratio to unwanted highs, contrasting with last year's lean inventories. An inventory drawdown should subtract 1.1% points from growth in the second quarter of 2015 versus adding 1.4% points in the second quarter of 2014. Consumers have been cautious and risk averse, and they used much of their windfall oil savings to pay down debt, muting the positive impact on the economy.

The USA finds itself competing against or even catching up with foreign companies and engineers in leading industrial technologies such as advanced batteries, high-speed rail, hybrid automobiles, solar modules, offshore wind turbines, and machine tools. Historically, the country has been the undisputed leader of next-generation technology, from semiconductors to IT to space. It pretty much owned these sectors. But today, even in an industry such as space, the USA finds itself relying on Japan, Russia, and Western Europe to launch its satellites. The composition of global demand has changed dramatically over the past few decades. For the first time in recent history, more than 50% of the global middle class lives outside North America. Meanwhile, many next-generation engineered products are in high demand not by the US or European customers but by those in Asia, Latin America, and the Middle East (Manyika et al. 2011).

After experiencing a steady loss in its relative importance in the last three decades, including through recession episodes, the US manufacturing output has rebounded strongly from the Great Recession of 2007–2010. The Great Recession was, in fact, the first US recession since the early 1980s to be followed by a significant recovery in the share of manufacturing value added in total GDP of the USA. At the same time, there have been significant differences between the performances of the durables versus non-durables sectors. The nearly 20% increase in the US manufacturing output following the recession (between 2009 and 2013) has been almost entirely driven by the higher production of durable goods. Although this rebound is in part the natural consequence of a stronger cyclical decline for durables than for non-durables, the difference in performance has been remarkable. Whereas durable goods production surpassed its pre-recession level in 2011 (Q3), a quarter before overall real GDP of non-durable goods production remained about 10% lower than its pre-recession level (and 5% above its trough) as of 2013 (Q3). Compared with the recoveries after the 1990 and 2001 US recessions, the increase in durable goods production has been markedly stronger during the ongoing recovery, whereas the rebound in non-durable goods has been weaker than that observed after the 1990 and 2001 recessions.

The strength of the durable sector has in turn been concentrated in just a few sub-sectors. Three sub-sectors are responsible for the observed rebound in durables: computer and electronics, motor vehicles, and machinery. While it is possible to argue that the increase in vehicles and machinery is mostly cyclical, computer and electronics have exhibited a robust positive trend during the past decade (Houseman et al. 2011), including through the Great Recession. In contrast, most sub-sectors within non-durable goods have continued to decline or have shown a slow rebound after the Great Recession, including chemicals, plastics, and rubbers. The exception has been petroleum products, which has recovered to pre-crisis levels. After a steady decline in much of the last three decades, the US share in global manufacturing output has largely stabilized around 20% since the Great Recession. Interestingly, after a strong increase during most of the previous decade, China's share in global manufacturing has also stabilized, around the same level. The decline in the US manufacturing production during the Great Recession was comparable to the declines observed in other G-7 countries but the recovery paths have been different. The rebound has been relatively strong in the USA and Germany, but has been muted in France and Italy.

Although the dynamics of employment in the US manufacturing sector is not the focus of this paper, its differences from the dynamics of the output are worth noting. In contrast to manufacturing output, which has broadly remained on an upward trend despite experiencing declines during recessions, manufacturing jobs have been on a declining trend, with a large further drop in the Great Recession. In particular, manufacturing employment declined by about 19% between the start of the 2001 recession and end of 2007; it declined another 15% during the Great Recession and has only increased by about 2% since the recovery started in mid-2009. Post-recession employment growth has been strongest in durable goods manufacturing (in particular, in computers and electronics, and machinery), while employment in the non-durable goods sector has remained stagnant.

Market Dynamics

Scenario planning is a disciplined method for imagining possible futures that companies have applied to a great range of issues. Royal Dutch/Shell has used scenarios since the early 1970s as part of a process for generating and evaluating its strategic options. Shell has been consistently better in its oil forecasts than other major oil companies, and first, it saw the overcapacity in the tanker business and Europe's petrochemicals. In the early 1980s, Anglo-American Corporation of South Africa convened an international group of experts to explore South Africa's future through scenarios, which provided a catalyst for profound political reform. Even the Dutch Central Planning Bureau, a leading government agency traditionally wedded to econometrics and time series analyses, issued wide-ranging, 25-year global scenarios (Schoemaker and van de Heijden 1992).

The USA also ranks highest in flow of people, reflecting its openness to immigration and its ability to attract a steady flow of international talent. Its supportive business environment, well-developed financial markets, leadership in innovation, and strong legal and political institutions create a sturdy foundation for US participation in global flows. The country has also made a concerted effort to reduce the costs of and barriers to international trade with 20 bilateral free trade agreements with nations around the world. Until 2012, when it was surpassed by China, the USA was the largest participant in flows of goods trade for many decades. As the world's largest consumer market, it remains the world's biggest importer of goods. Unlike other advanced economies, the USA is a major importer of R&D-intensive goods such as cars and computers and runs a trade deficit in R&D-intensive goods. The R&D-intensive manufactured goods also account for more than half of the US goods exports, with machinery, electrical and high-tech goods, and medical goods alone worth nearly one-third of the total exports. The USA continues to rely on imports to cover its energy needs; petroleum, natural gas, and nuclear fuel imports accounted for nearly one-fifth of total imports in 2012, although the current boom in shale gas and tight-oil production could reduce the US energy import requirements. The USA has been a net exporter of services for more than three decades. With leading positions in business, technology, and finance, it has a particularly strong record on exports of knowledge-intensive services. Exports of professional services and financial services account for one-third of all US service exports. The US-generated entertainment, media, and online content are eagerly consumed by people all over the world and help support the country's services trade surplus. Payments of royalties and license fees for copyrighted content account for more than 20% of all service exports, compared with an average of 8% for other developed economies.

The EU is the most integrated trading bloc. Almost 60% of its total goods trade was intra-regional in 2012 compared with 52% in 1990. Trade between the USA, Canada, and Mexico was 41% of all trade in these economies in 1994, when NAFTA came into effect, and peaked at 45% in 2000. However, that share fell back to 39% in 2012 as NAFTA's constituent countries began to trade more actively with China, which increased its share of total NAFTA trade from 5 to 13% as it captured a share of NAFTA low-cost production from Mexico. Trade between the Association of Southeast Asian Nations (ASEAN) group of countries remains far lower than trade within the EU and NAFTA at just 22% of their value of total trade in 2012, modestly higher than the 16% share in 1990. However, over the past decade, there has been little progress in boosting intra-regional trade. Relatively small economies that rank high on their participation in flows tend to be waypoints. They do not originate or receive large flows for domestic consumption but, rather, channel and redistribute flows from many sources to many destinations, building leading positions as hubs. We profile Singapore, which is highly connected across all flows but the most prominent in goods trade. Other examples include the Netherlands, which is a major hub only for data and communication flows; Belgium, a significant waypoint for flows of goods and services; and Luxembourg, notable for financial and services flows (Manyika et al. 2014).

Like manufactured goods, global commodities flows are being shaped by several trends. First, the increasing participation of emerging economies is reshaping global commodities flows as both producers and consumers. Second, digitization is enabling new efficiencies in operations, which are necessary to help navigate the world that is likely to be characterized by continuing high and volatile resource prices.[3] Finally, we expect to continue to see increased volatility in commodities flows because of surging demand, supply constraints, and a higher correlation between commodity prices that stems from a more tightly interconnected world. Emerging economies are becoming larger participants in the global commodities markets, with rising levels of production, consumption, and investment. These economies have significantly raised their share of both import and export commodity flows over the past decade. The emerging world's share of the global value of metals, minerals, and oil and gas exports increased from 49% in 2002 to 62% in 2012. These countries now produce more than two-thirds of oil and gas exports more than half of which come from the Middle East and nearly 60% of mining exports half of which originate in Latin America. The future outlook for this continuing shift of global goods flows to and from emerging markets will, however, be shaped to a large degree by national policies. The policy continues to have a marked impact on manufacturing flows with many governments focused on expanding or reinvigorating their manufacturing sectors as a strategy to grow exports, attract investment, and create jobs.

Manufacturing is a highly significant sector for flows of trade and FDI. In trade flows, it is responsible for two-thirds of global trade in goods and is growing fast: Exports of manufactured goods have risen by 11% a year in nominal value over the past decade to 2012. Global trade in manufactured goods rebounded strongly after 2009 and had exceeded pre-recession levels by 2011 to reach $11 trillion, although growth stagnated between 2011 and 2012. In FDI flows, manufacturing industries have grown by 3% per year over the past decade, compared with 10% in the case of overall FDI between 2002 and 2012. However, manufacturing has increased its share of total goods greenfield FDI, from 52% in 2002 to 67% in 2011.

As manufacturers invest in local assembly facilities in emerging economies, the nature of trade is also changing, with intermediate manufactured goods, which includes parts, components, and commodities, making up a greater share of cross-border flows of goods. Eventually, as large global manufacturers achieve scale in emerging markets, they may pull many of their suppliers to enter these regional markets, too, which could slow the growth of trade in intermediate goods. However, there are other factors too that may reshape manufacturing flows in the future. For instance, rising labor costs in China may continue to shift more labor-intensive manufacturing to countries such as Mexico, Vietnam, and Bangladesh, which could see a resulting increase in exports. Over the next 10 years (2015–2024), the shift in manufacturing production and investment toward emerging markets is likely to continue, judging by investment flows to emerging economies that increased from 17% of global FDI flows in 1990 to 58% in 2012. Since the recession, emerging economies have also accounted for a growing share of global FDI inflows, from 43% in 2008 to 58% in 2012. The automotive industry provides an interesting demonstration of this dynamic. Major manufacturers including Renault, Volkswagen, GM, Ford, Toyota, and Honda are all increasing their production capacity in emerging economies.

By 2025, half of global consumption growth is projected to come from emerging markets, with much of that growth in manufactured goods. This shift is already well under way. Most demand for cars, for example, comes from emerging markets. China displaced the USA as the largest car market in the world in 2009 and has produced more vehicles every year since. Indeed, the recent global recession has accelerated this change in the profile of global consumption, which, in turn, has helped to support the recovery. As consumption grows, emerging economies' imports of final goods have been rising rapidly, from $151 billion in 2002 to $702 billion in 2011, i.e., 19% a year. China's growing appetite for imports makes it a leading consumer for a wide range of products from advanced economies, such as North American aircraft (for which China is the largest export market) and European automobiles (for which China is the second largest export market).

The USA remains a magnet for those seeking economic opportunity and the chance to study at some of the world's best academic institutions. From 2000 to 2011, the USA attracted more than one-quarter of the world's flow of college-level international students on average. In 2013, some 800,000 international students were attending the US colleges and universities. In 2010, the total of foreign-born migrants in the USA reached 40.3 million, twice the number in 1980 and more than one-fifth of the world's total migrants. The foreign-born migrants contribute significantly to the US innovation ecosystem; they lead one-quarter of the science and technology companies established between 1995 and 2005 and have founded more than 50% of start-ups in Silicon Valley. Today, 14% of the US population is made up of immigrants, compared with a global average of around 3%. The US high-tech companies have created many of the major Internet-based platforms, from search engines to social media that are powering worldwide flows of data and communication. In 2011, the USA accounted for the greatest share of international telephone call minutes worldwide, equaling the total of the next three countries combined. Despite its strength in connectedness across major flows, the US benchmarks low on flow intensity even in comparison with other large economies. China, for example, is almost twice as flow-intensive, at 62%, as the USA, at 35%. With a flow intensity of 110%, Germany's reading is more than three times that of the USA. This may indicate the significant further potential for the USA to expand its participation in flows.

Innovation and Technology Transfer

Innovation capital has been a crucial contributor to economic prosperity in developed economies. It drives productivity improvements and, in turn, overall economic growth. Analysis of the relationship between innovation capital and economic development indicates that innovation directly contributed to 53% of labor productivity growth in the period analyzed. These productivity improvements enable us to do more with less; in other words, to create a greater quantity and value of goods and services per hour of labor in an economy. This could include the replacement of manual tasks by automated software or improved "leaner" organizational processes leading to decreased waste during a manufacturing process.

Growth from more knowledge comes in two ways: direct and indirect. The direct impact is from firms who invest in knowledge and then appropriate the gains from that investment: perhaps via a patent, or a copyright or trade secret. The contributions in exhibit 4 measure only this direct component. But there is another indirect effect whereby knowledge raises output. This arises from firms who do not themselves invest in knowledge, but instead use the knowledge created by others. Many universities, for example, make new knowledge public for all firms to use. Sometimes, institutional design supports free transfer of knowledge, for example, open source software. Or consider Apple's App Store: It creates value for its inventor and also for a number of external developers who found that it offered a new route to market to make apps both possible and profitable. In short, innovation investments yield returns not only to those making the investment but also to other parts of the economy. The size and mix of innovation capital relative to GDP vary considerably by country, to some extent reflecting their economic structure. Small- and medium-sized businesses (SMBs) are playing a growing role in the rise of the market for cloud services. By 2015, their share in the market is expected to reach USD 28 billion—with an expected profit pool of USD 3.5 billion—representing 40–50% of the total cloud market opportunity.

The Trade-Related Intellectual Property rights (TRIPS) agreement established minimum international standards. Chapter 17 of the NAFTA addresses the intellectual property obligations.[4] While the TRIPS provisions are incorporated into NAFTA by reference, NAFTA also contains provisions that go beyond TRIPS, and hence, NAFTA is regarded as TRIPS-plus. In terms of national laws, Mexico had the greatest burden of adjustment. The USA had the least since the global standards negotiated during the Uruguay Round reflected US laws and practices the most. In 1997, Mexico put into effect a new copyright system, customs law allowing the seizure of pirated goods, protection for plant varieties, and semiconductor chips. In Mexico, protection for computer software and databases is provided for under copyright law, that is, as artistic expressions. Mexico also created an agency—the Mexican Institute for Industrial Property (IMPI)—to implement IPR laws. In the USA, the copyright laws were revised to recognize the moral rights of authors. Previously, the US laws recognized the economic rights of authors, but did not formally protect against mischaracterization and alteration of an author's work. Furthermore, the US laws used to require the secrecy of a patent application until it was granted. Critics of this provision pointed out that secrecy creates uncertainty for contemporary innovators who do not know if some other innovator has developed a particular technology. Under the amended Act, the US laws now require the patent application to be published 18 months after filing, so long as the inventor files abroad. If the inventor only applies for a patent application in the US market, the underlying technology is kept secret until it is granted. But on Mexican innovation performance, Lederman and Maloney (2003) conclude that NAFTA is not enough. They assess the national innovation system in Mexico—consisting of the private sector, public sector, and academia—to be inefficient. The key problem appears to be the lack of coordination among universities, private businesses, and government agencies, and the lack of networking activities to stimulate knowledge spillovers. Even Mexican firms, such as the pharmaceutical company Avimex which has a high (15%) R&D to sales ratio, have had to look for joint venture partners in foreign countries, like the USA, due to the lack of networking opportunities locally.

NAFTA is also positively associated with US licensing payments. This means that the ability of Canada and Mexico to market (license) their technologies in the USA has been enhanced by NAFTA. Inward FDI is also enhanced by NAFTA, especially FDI into Mexico. However, NAFTA appears to have had an insignificant effect on the outward FDI of all NAFTA countries. Other factors were more important in their ability and incentive to invest capital abroad. Alternatively, other regions and markets were just as important as (or more important than) the NAFTA market. The associated intellectual property reforms are also important factors determining technology trade. Stronger patent protection in the Canada and Mexico attracted FDI and licensing from abroad, but not in the USA since the latter already represents a large market and has a very strong system of intellectual property protection. Stronger patent protection, by stimulating local innovation, also contributed to the ability of NAFTA members to engage in FDI abroad as well as transfer technologies abroad via licensing. There was, however, some evidence that stronger patent rights in Mexico enabled foreign firms to exercise greater market power in Mexico. Stronger patent rights, for example, are associated with a reduction of FDI into Mexico, holding other factors constant. The USA also appears to have exercised greater market power abroad where patent protection is stronger. Holding other factors constant, the US outward FDI also decreased in response to tighter intellectual property protection abroad (Park 2011).

Franchising

Franchising is found to be a most popular mode of entry for the consumer goods companies in Mexico as it is yet underexplored. However, it has been widely used as a rapid method of expansion within major developed markets in North America and Western Europe, most notably by fast food chains, consumer service businesses such as hotel or car rental, and business services. A key indicator that franchising carries this constraint is the fact that marketing budgets at local levels are usually restricted to short-term promotions rather than market development. This is consistent with the concept that franchising is a rapid replication strategy. For example, consider the expansion of US-based Weight Watchers into Mexico. Weight Watchers is a highly successful dieting business that franchises its programs to operators of local clubs and groups of people motivated to lose weight and maintain their new lighter shape. It is an expansion into Mexico, which was the result of an opportunistic network initiative by a member of the US executives' network. It encountered some cultural differences compared with the USA or Canada. In some parts of the country, the attitude still prevailed that being overweight was not bad because it indicated sufficient affluence to eat well (Arnold 2013).

Franchises are developing very fast in Mexico. In 2005, the experience in our country confirms that franchises constitute a very useful option for acquiring capital in a short time as well as security. The first franchises in Mexico were established in the early 1980s and most of them were American. After a few years, Mexican businesses realized that franchises were a solid way to grow, and national franchises started to increase. Franchises have not been in Mexico for a long time; hence, laws and regulations are still at an early stage, but everyday there is an advance. Although the Industrial Property Law regulates franchises, the Mexican Congress just modified legislation to give more legality and security to franchises. This modification benefits both franchisees and franchisors. This regulation is a big step because it is creating a franchise culture supported by laws. Statistics show that in 2009, there were 70% of the franchises constituted of Mexican origin, 24% from the USA, 4% from Spain, and Canada and Brazil had 1% of the market among other countries. Firms from other Latin American countries are finding Mexico as their best option to expand internationally and are focused on exploring secondary markets such as Veracruz, Quintana Roo, Puebla, and Estado de Mexico.

The franchise sector in Mexico grew 9% in 2013, continuing to be one of the most important sectors in the country's economic growth. Conservative estimates indicate that this sector will grow between 11 and 13% in 2014. Franchises in Mexico are regulated by Article 142 of the Industrial Property Law and Article 65 of its Regulations. Franchise agreements must be registered before the Mexican Institute of Industrial Property in order to be effective against third parties. Foreign franchisors not having a permanent establishment for tax purposes in Mexico but obtaining an income from a source located within the Mexican territory are normally taxed on income (federal tax), and the tax is paid in Mexico by the foreign franchisor through retention or withholding (10%) made by the corresponding franchisee. There are no barriers to franchisers of any products or services in Mexico.

The franchise sector in Mexico is regulated by Article 142 of the Industrial Property Law and Article 65 of its Regulations. On January 26, 2006, an amendment to the Mexican Franchise Regulations (Article 142) was published in the Mexican Official Gazette, stating a new definition of franchise, mandating requirements for franchise agreements, and providing new standards for pre-sale franchise disclosure. The amendment mainly protects franchisees that report abuses from franchisers, either at the execution of the agreement or when terminating it, which was affecting the growth of the franchise sector. The Mexican Association of Franchises (AMF) lobbied for the change, demanding more legal security for the franchise sector in Mexico. There are no restrictions applicable on remittance of royalties and fees, apart from normal reporting requirements. Royalties and fees face withholding taxes at the following rates: 15% on payments for technical assistance; the use of models; plans; formulas; know-how; copyright; artistic, literary and scientific works; and the rights to use theatrical and television films and radio recordings; and 40% for the use of patents, trade names, trademarks, and publicity. In the case of payments made to residents of a tax haven jurisdiction, the 40% rate applies. Fees from construction activities are subject to a tax withholding of 30% if the projects do not give rise to a permanent establishment. Mexico has yet to place any limits on how much subsidiaries can be deducted for payment of royalties and fees to parent companies, as long as those payments do not exceed the amounts to be paid to a third party (USCS 2009).

Direct Marketing

With the establishment of large international firms in Mexico and their emphasis in adopting similar marketing strategies to those of their international home base in addition to more and better educated consumers with higher quality expectations, the marketing services industry has evolved into a more segmented and specialized sector offering the US companies a complete array of possibilities from which to choose. Today, the choices firms have for promoting their products range from marketing campaigns through one-to-one contact at point-of-sale displays to mass exposure through billboards or Internet campaigns. Companies in Mexico invested about $11.7 billion in marketing services to promote their products and services in 2012, with electronic media and in point of sale promotion (POP) as the most important vehicles of promotion. The breakdown of marketing tools in Mexico includes publicity (printed and electronic media) 73%, direct marketing 19%, market research 4%, public relations 3%, and design 1%. In order to satisfy clients' demands, direct marketing has evolved combining different methods of promotion, including Internet promotional campaigns. The most important promotional tools chosen by companies were direct mail and telemarketing.

Intellectual Property Rights

IPR in Mexico are protected by a combination of national laws and international conventions and agreements. Mexico is a member of the WTO and the World Intellectual Property Organization (WIPO). It has signed the Paris Convention for the Protection of Industrial Property, the Patent Co-operation Treaty (PCT), and the Union for the Protection of New Plant Varieties (UPOV). Mexican law protects IPR, and recent changes have stiffened penalties for violations; nevertheless, enforcement remains weak, and pirated goods are commonly found throughout Mexico. Piracy in the country primarily affects the entertainment, pharmaceuticals, software, publishing, and clothing industries. To improve enforcement, Mexico created an IPR enforcement unit in 2003 that combines federal prosecutors and police forces. Public awareness campaigns have also been published in newspapers and shown on television and at cinemas to discourage consumers from purchasing pirated goods. Despite attempts to improve enforcement of the law, consumer demand for pirated goods remains strong, and the sale of pirated goods represents a large source of informal employment in Mexico.

The Law for the Promotion and Protection of Industrial Property came into force in June 1991 and was revised and renamed the Industrial Property Law (Ley de Propiedad Industrial) in 1994. The 1991 law lengthened the initial term for trademarks to 10 years (from 5) and increased the patent term to 20 years (from 14). For the first time in Mexico, legislation extended eligibility for product patents to pharmaceuticals, chemicals, biotechnology products, metal alloys, and agrochemicals. Inventions not patentable include biological processes for producing and reproducing plants and animals, biological and genetic material as found in a natural state, animal breeds, and human tissue and plant varieties. Trademarks are protected for 10 years, but those not used for 3 consecutive years may be canceled. In order to recognize the priority of a mark, reciprocity need no longer exist with the country of origin of the application. The law requires universal novelty of industrial designs/utility models (only local or national novelty was required before). Commercial and industrial applications that retain information on an individual or entity are considered trade secrets. Mexico's Federal Copyright Law (Ley Federal de Derechos de Autor) was implemented in March 1997, replacing the 1963 Federal Copyright Law. The copyright law grants the author both moral and patrimonial rights (moral rights make the author the first and only perpetual owner of the rights of his or her works; patrimonial rights allow the owner to "exploit the work exclusively or authorize others to exploit the work"). The 1997 law expanded the definition of copyrightable materials and brought Mexico into compliance with its obligations under the NAFTA. Although the legislation decriminalized copyright violations, it increased financial penalties.[5]

The National Copyright Institute (Instituto Nacional de Derechos de Autor—INDA), an independent agency of the Ministry of Education, is responsible for the administrative enforcement of the copyright law. The institute is permitted to conduct investigations, request appropriate inspections, perpetuate temporary termination of copyright violations, and impose penalties. The Mexican Institute of Industrial Property (Instituto Mexicano de Propiedad Industrial—IMPI) oversees broad IPR enforcement and intervenes in copyright infringements that involve commerce. The law protects all original works that can be "disclosed or reproduced by any means" from the moment they are tangible, regardless of whether they have been registered. In May 2004, Congress altered the Federal Law against Organized Crime (Ley Federal Contra el Crimen Organizado) to categorize copyright violation and trademark counterfeiting as punishable crimes. Persons charged with piracy now face 20–40 years in jail, along with monetary fines. Criminal penalties apply only to repeat offenders who traffic in pirated goods. In December 2006, IMPI created a unit, known as the Alianza para la Prosperidad y Seguridad de America del Norte, to investigate the points of entry that register the most contraband goods. The unit works with Canada and the USA to share information and best practices in combating piracy. Nonetheless, the piracy remains widespread.

Notes

1. Congressional Quarterly Almanac 1993, pp. 171–175, 180–181.
2. Own calculations of average annual changes based on data from INEGI and the Groningen Growth and Development Centre 10-Sector Database, July 2014.
3. Resource Revolution: Tracking global commodity markets, McKinsey Global Institute and the McKinsey Sustainability & Resource Productivity Practice, September 2013.

4. Article 1701 of NAFTA references previous international IP conventions while article 1702 states that member countries may provide higher levels of protection.
5. The Economist Intelligence Unit (2010), Intellectual Property Rights Environment in Mexico, The Economist.

References

Arnold, D. (2013). *The mirage of global markets: How globalizing companies can succeed as markets localize*. New Jersey: FT Press.

Bolio, E., & Remes, J. (2015, March 11). Mexico, destined to always underachieve? *Financial Times*.

Roundtable, Business. (2004). *NAFTA: A Decade of growth* (pp. 33–46). Washington, DC, February: The Trade Partnership Group.

Easterly, W. (2008). Institutions: Top down or bottom up. *American Economic Review, 98*(2), 95–99.

Hoff, K., & Stiglitz, J. E. (2005, November). *The creation of the rule of law and the legitimacy of property rights: The political and economic consequences of a corrupt privatization* (Working Paper No. 11772). NBER.

Houseman, S., Kurtz, C., Lengermann, K. P., & Mandel, B. (2011). Offshoring bias in U.S. manufacturing. *Journal of Economic Perspectives, 25*(2), 111–132.

Lawrence, R. Z. (2006). *Regionalism, multilateralism and deeper integration, Washington*. DC: Brooking Institution.

Lederman, D., & Maloney, W. (2003). (2003), NAFTA is not enough. In D. Lederman, W. Maloney, & L. Serven (Eds.), *Lessons from NAFTA for Latin America and the Caribbean countries* (pp. 171–215). Washington, DC: World Bank.

Manyika, J., Bughin, J., Lund, S., Nottebohm, O., Poulter, D., Jauch, S., et al. (2014). *Global flows in a digital age: How trade, finance, people, and data connect the world economy*. McKinsey and Co: McKinsey Global Institute.

Manyika, J., Pacthod, D., & Park, M. (2011, May 1). Translating innovation into US growth: An advanced-industries perspective. *McKinsey Quarterly*, McKinsey and Co.

Medvedev, D. (2006). *Preferential trade agreements and their role in world trade* (World Bank Policy Research Working Paper# 4038). Washington, DC: World Bank.

Park, W. G. (2011). Technology trade and NAFTA. In A. Tavidze (Ed.), *Progress in economics research* (Vol. 25). New York: Nova Publishers.

Rubio, L., & Remes, J. (2014, April 1). The two Mexicos. *McKinsey Quarterly*, McKinsey and Co.

Sánchez, M. (2011). *Mexico's economic integration and outlook*. Bank for International Settlements, Basel, Switzerland: BIS central bankers' speeches.

Sánchez, M. (2015). *Productivity, growth, and the law*. Bank for International Settlements, Basel, Switzerland: BIS central bankers' speeches.

Schoemaker, P. J. H., & van de Heijden, C. A. J. M. (1992). Integrating scenarios into strategic planning at Royal Dutch/Shell. *Planning Review, 20*(3), 41–46.

USCS. (2009). *Franchise services sector in Mexico, United States Commercial Service, Us Department Of Commerce*. Retrieved July 28, 2015, from http://www.franchise.org/sites/default/files/ek-pdfs/html_page/Mexico_Franchising-in-Secondary-Markets_April-2009_3.pdf.

Villarreal, M. A., & Fergusson, I. F. (2015). *The North- American Free Trade Agreement, CRS report # 7–5700*. Washington, DC: Congressional Research Service.

WTO, World Trade Report. (2011). The WTO and preferential trade agreements: From co-existence to coherence.

CHAPTER 4

Structural Growth in Trade

This chapter focuses on the growth of trade and economy in the USA and Mexico as compared to the world trade relative to income growth since 2001. The spatial and temporal analysis has been done in reference to manufacturing, services, and corporate social responsibility of large companies. This chapter critically examines the global trade slowdown and analyzes its structural and cyclical nature among the North American countries. The available evidence suggests that the explanation may lie in the slowing pace of international vertical specialization rather than increasing protection or the changing composition of trade and GDP. This chapter discusses the structural growth in business in reference to product portfolio, market share, international trade, investment, and contribution of corporate business to GDP in the manufacturing sector. The chapter holds discussions on the impact of corporation social responsibilities on the structural growth of international trade within cross-cultural and socio-political relations.

There has been unprecedented turmoil in the world economy due to the recession in the USA during 2007–2011. The recovery of the economy has been slower than expected, and as a result, it affected the worldwide trade. The international trade scenario in mid-2020 has appeared to be in a fragile state, with growth likely to decline below the performance of 2014 and 2015. The average performance of trade and economy in developed countries since the 2008–2009 economic and financial crisis is set to continue, with the added threat of the loss of momentum in developing countries over the past few years. However, the growth of

Rajagopal and V. Zlatev, *Business Dynamics in North America*,
DOI 10.1007/978-3-319-57606-0_4

manufacturing and services sector in the international destinations has stabilized the external environment and reduced the impact of shocks of economic recession in the North American region by economic prosperity and stability in the medium run. The changing political scenarios with diverse political ideologies in the developed and emerging countries are also contributing uncertainties in the international trade. Despite some favorable diplomacy on international trade among the developed countries like the USA and Canada in the North American region, the widespread effect from unforeseen shocks, bashing regional and global growth even more sharply, cannot be ruled out.

Upon recovering from the historic low of the Great Recession during 2007–2011, world trade had shown an increase of less than 3.0% during 2012–2012 as compared to the pre-economic recession average growth of 7.1% over the two decades from 1987 to 2007. This slowdown in the performance of international trade has raised widespread concerns in the American continent as most Latin American and Caribbean countries have a higher dependency on trade and economy among the Canadian and American trade patterns. One of the many pertinent questions that emerge is whether the slower growth in trade simply reflects the sluggishness of gross domestic product (GDP) of the country, or whether a deeper structural shift in the international trade patterns needs to be carried out. The global trade slowdown has appeared as the strongest phenomenon in the decade of 2020 and prompts trade analysts to investigate into the long period of subtle trade in the developing countries and critically examine the structural changes that are required in the trade—GDP relationship. Some studies explain that a long-term elasticity of trade with respect to income was 1.3 between 1970 and 1985, which rose to 2.2 in the period 1986–2000, but reverted to 1.3 in the 2000s. This is a unique phenomenon seen at the end of the twentieth century, which confirms the existence of significant structural breaks in the trade–income relationship in the 1990s relative to the preceding and subsequent periods. The decline in the trade elasticity in 2000 was set in before the global financial crisis, which affected in the post-crisis global economic environment. A study revealed that an increase of 1% in income was associated to 150 and 70% increase in trade during the period 2001–2007 and 2008–2013, respectively. These results indicate that the growth in the trade–income relationship driving global trade is slow not only because GDP growth is sluggish but also because the trade relationships with international partners have changed. However, the cyclical effects in trade and economy have dominated during the economic crisis as trade tended to collapse from 2008 until 2010. The dynamics of current global trade has shown a decline in the trade growth with a long-term impact on the international economy (Constantinescu et al. 2015).

The factors affecting international trade include protectionism, and considerable structural changes in trade and aggregate demand through international vertical specialization are needed, as has been evidenced in the USA and China. Though the long-run trade elasticity increased during the decade of 1990s as production split internationally due to high production sharing practices among manufacturing industries, such as automobiles, and converged into automated global supply chains, it decreased in the 2000s as this process of production sharing decelerated due to political and economic diplomacy in the North America and Europe. Other factors may have contributed to the lower responsiveness of trade due to tariff and non-tariff restrictions. However, the current fluctuations in trade performance demand that countries need to boost aggregate demand, concentrate on trade-intensive components, and amplify the liberal trade policies and investments in the international markets (Bems et al. 2013).

The global trade scenario in the post-economic recession reveals that the growth in the USA tended to slow down in mid-2020 and built through the quick cleansing of its investment policies in manufacturing, services, and international trade segments. There is an urgent need for a more aggressive use of monetary policy in support of manufacturing and trade liberalization following comparative trade and location advantages. The manufacturing sector in the USA has been affected adversely during the post-recession period, and many industries have relocated their manufacturing and service facilities. However, during 2015–2016, unemployment has dropped steadily to the level registered before the crisis hit, and real earnings have begun to pick up that has indirectly supported the trade and economy of the country at large. However, in view of the weak underlying employment rate, and high levels of debt and exporters struggling with fluctuating exchange rate syndrome in the trade partnering countries, there are no guarantees that the economy will enjoy a robust period of growth anytime soon (Trade Development Report 2016).

The dynamic trade models are built by analyzing the international trade uncertainties. Such models indicate that the trade of goods and services can generate positive effects on economic growth in reference to knowledge of the domestic markets, where goods can be understood as new ideas, designs, or managerial processes that lead to increased productivity, while international trade may produce incentives for local markets. International markets and trading practices generally act as diffusion sources for innovation and technology to attract potential buyers. Hence, the potential for economic benefits is largely associated with innovation, brand recognition, patent registrations, and improvements over the competing firm's products that make the companies competitive in the international marketplace. Carrying out trading operations in international destinations drives producers to react to a changing business environment and engages in the innovation process. These innovations are carried out in setting new business models, or following necessary adjustments toward improving operational efficiency in packaging, inventory, logistics, and transportation methods due to local market requirements and infrastructure. Innovative adjustments are also made in reference to product attributes, use value, and life cycle to induce consumers with new experiences. In order to stay market competitive, companies in the international marketplace also stay proactive toward improving the production process, minimizing defects level by adapting to lean manufacturing methods, and complying with foreign regulations. International trade is a continuous process governed by political and economic policies, philosophies, and perspectives. Every destination generates knowledge through research or experience. However, when countries trade goods and services that embody original ideas, knowledge is indirectly transferred to the trading partner who learns by induction. Accordingly, international trade facilitates convergence of new technologies across countries. The amount of technological diffusion depends on how much a country trades and who its trade partners are, which is largely a politico-economic symbiosis (Kali et al. 2007).

As the economic situation in the USA has stabilized over the recession period, developing countries have greatly increased their share in global exports of manufactures. The global share of export for developing countries grew from around 10% in 1980 to nearly 45% by 2014. The global value chains that have extended the reach of international production networks in some key tradable sectors of the global economy have supported the international trade to grow over the stagnated share of many countries since 2000. These developments combined with the trade liberalization have facilitated international trade, and both global value chains and liberal trade policies have been widely viewed as a promising indicator of the potential for globalization. The international trade in the twenty-first century, thus, played a significant role toward supporting industrialization and accelerating the economic development of countries in particular, and regions in general. One of the principal reasons for the growth of export-led industrialization is the success of the promising strategy embedded in globalization policies in the emerging markets. The total export orientation has been a success of the first-tier East Asian economies, while the expansion of exports of manufactures was supported by industrial policy and macroeconomic management resulting in the fastest and most sustained record of catch-up development in the modern era. Among many Asian countries, India, China, South Korea, Taiwan, and Singapore have set the strong examples of export-led industrialization. Over the years, variants of this approach have spread to other countries and regions, though they have not been able to fully emulate the advantage of being first-movers in the region. In 2014, Asia alone accounted for nearly 90% of developing-country exports of manufactures to the world, and for 94% of South–South trade in manufactures. Nevertheless, a number of developing countries outside the Asia region engage in significant trade in manufactures, with many more pursuing such trade in the hope of realizing the promise of export-led industrialization (Trade Development Report 2016).

It has been observed that tariffs tend to be inflationary and free trade is deflationary. However, many arguments express that protectionism has generally created inflation in developing economies, though the experience of the developed countries including the USA was very different on this aspect. Tariffs in most of the developed countries were never associated with rising prices, and trade liberalization with declining prices (Batra 2001). High tariffs were always followed by a steep decline in the cost of living. Despite the greater complexities associated with open economy macroeconomics, the policy conclusions for a closed economy remain remarkably unaffected. While Keynesians and heterodox economists believe that government should actively intervene, conservatives remain skeptical about the desirability of such interventions (Stiglitz et al. 2006). Mainstream economic theory suggests that economic welfare is maximized when distortions are minimized. Accordingly, a removal of distortions of both macroeconomic and microeconomic nature would have beneficial effects on economic activity and the rate of growth (Igor 2000). The growth and development in a country or region may result to be slower in a normal process than in a stirred process of reforms. It has been observed that move toward liberalization stimulated privatization in Latin American countries. However, most cases of privatization failure can be linked to poor contract design, opaque processes with heavy state involvement, lack of re-regulation, and a poor corporate governance framework (Lopez and Chong 2003). The tariff and quantitative restrictions often impede the process of trade liberalization. The higher the average level of dispersion of tariffs and para-tariffs in terms of customs duties and taxes, the more the distortion of international trade. The measure applied to evaluate the level of tariffs and para-tariffs is the weighted average rate of tariff and para-tariff charges, which is used to weigh their respective shares in regional or global imports (Pritchett and Sethi 1994).

The trade and economic policies of the USA are considered as a global benchmark for development in the international trade. More specifically, the economies of Central America, Mexico, and the Caribbean are closely linked to the economic and trade policies of the USA through strong dependency on manufacturing and production networks, remittances, and tourism. For most of these economies, growth in 2016 has been slightly slower than in 2015, partly as a consequence of growth deceleration in the USA. The domestic currency in Mexico losing nearly 25% against the dollar during 2015 had pulled down the international trade performance during the first half of 2016. However, the government policies on reducing tax structure on exports could provide some stimulus to growth by boosting manufacturing exports. However, the emphasis on fiscal consolidation might continue to diminish public investment performance. Though many Central American and Caribbean countries enjoyed improved terms of trade in the region as a whole, the drop in the value of exports (−15%) was the result of falling prices. In real terms, export volumes increased 2.9% (Trade Development Report 2016).

Manufacturing Performance

Manufacturing industries in North America as well as those spread globally face a plethora of challenges as they keep navigating in a changing international trade and economy platforms. Global economic and political disorder, and new technology demands, driving continuing innovation are some of the most unstable variables that always keep the manufacturing industries unwarranted. Increasing cost of manpower across the geo-demographic segments has become challenging for the companies as the skilled labor costs are growing, and taxes and regulations are strangling progress. Despite the location advantages over the manufacturing costs in terms of labor, infrastructure, inventory, and logistics costs, the North American region still falls in the preferred manufacturing global regions. Manufacturers are implementing new technologies to expand aggressively in the lead markets, investing in machines and human capital to augment production capacity, optimizing manufacturing operations, and upgrading manufacturing facilities at local and international destinations. However, comparative wages, managerial and technical know-how, and production-level skills are not enough for many manufacturers to match with the export requirements and demand in the global markets. There are many challenges involved in closing the skills gap, but by encouraging manufacturing consortiums, services communities, and market research operations, the government can make great strides in recovering the manufacturing and export gaps that rose during the economic recession.

Acquiring skilled workforce in the USA and Canada to improve the productivity levels has always been a challenge and a source of competitive advantage for the manufacturers across the changing demographics, competition from emerging markets, gaining first-mover advantages, and technology advances. However, the challenge of cultural and language differences remains an obstacle for many US and Canadian companies in the region in considering establishing production and export facilities in Mexico. Failure to understand these differences may overrule the location advantages in Mexico. The average compensation per employee in US manufacturing was $37.71 per hour in 2015 as compared to US$5.91 per hour in Mexico during the same reference period (Levinson 2017). The location advantage in references to taxes, cross-border tariffs, infrastructure, and wages has been higher in Mexico as compared to the USA and Canada. Due to the strength of the dollar since the second half of 2014, most other countries have seen average compensation per hour expressed in US dollar decline. However, over a longer period, labor costs in most European countries have also increased relative to those in the USA.

International trade, which was growing manifold since the mid-1980s, has been connected to the globalization and production sharing of manufacturing through cross-border production networks like ***maquiladora***[1] in Mexico and other low-cost production facilities. Those companies leading in the international markets outsource selected activities to specific locations and manage the assembly, branding and marketing of the final product, and play the central role. Vertical specialization and economies of scale have enabled large companies to increase profits in the manufacturing of standardized goods by exploiting the location advantages with desirable combinations of relatively high labor productivity, low wage and infrastructure costs, and favorable tax conditions. Such international manufacturing facilities have structurally adjusted industrial growth in the global macroeconomic context in which low manufacturing facility chains like maquiladora have emerged. However, increases in their global share of manufacturing exports did not show similar increases in wage shares of national income relative to the global average. During the favorable international trade and economy conditions, the shares of global manufacturing exports rose faster than relative shares of wage income.

As stated in the pre-text, the business and manufacturing sector of Latin America and Mexico depend largely on the US economy, which accounts for 82% of the region's economic output being the largest trading partner for both Mexico and Canada, and accounting for almost 80% of exports of NAFTA countries. The manufacturing sector in the USA has not grown as fast as the rest of the economy and, as a result, its share of total output has increased from 2% in 1970 to 12% in 2015, though the total value of US manufacturing production reached a record of more than $2.0 trillion by the end of 2014. The North American Free Trade Agreement (NAFTA) gave location advantages in manufacturing in Mexico after it was implemented in 1994. Consequently, the output increased to 18.7% of Mexican GDP in 2000, though it had fallen to 16.2% by 2014. Canadian manufacturing also benefited from NAFTA, helping exports, such as energy, motor vehicles and parts, industrial machinery, aircraft, telecommunications equipment, and electronics, grow. However, since 2000, the share of economic activity represented by the sector has fallen from 14.8% to the current 10.6% (Levinson 2017).

The location advantage has also been proved beneficial for Canadian companies to use the production facilities in Mexico. Bombardier, a leading multi-disciplinary Canadian company, has participated in many Mexican industrial sectors for over three decades. However, its most important investments are in the aerospace field, toward developing an aircraft cluster in Querétaro—an industrial state in the country. The Canadian company entered the Mexican market in 1981, exploring the first contract to build train wagons for the metropolitan subway transport system. In 1992, Bombardier acquired the National Train Wagon Builder (Concarril) contract and set bases in Ciudad Sahagún, Hidalgo, where it builds wagons for Monterrey's subway and Guadalajara's electric train. The aerospace division of the company established a manufacturing center in Querétaro, where 200 million dollars were invested in 2005. In two decades, the company has invested more than 500 million dollars.

Trends in structural transformation of international trade in different regions and economies since 1970 indicate that these have been closely related to patterns of capital accumulation, income, production, and learning linkages. Most emerging markets tended to diversify their manufacturing and marketing operations toward higher value-added sectors like automobiles, energy products, consumer electronics, and financial services in order to augment both income and employment. However, most countries required the economic restructuring to develop effective backward and forward linkages for exploiting the diversified activities. The need for diversification in manufacturing and services sectors can largely be explained as the call of the hour in the global markets for business sustainability and market competitiveness. Accordingly, most emerging markets such as Brazil, Russia, India, China, South Africa, Mexico, Chile, Vietnam, and Indonesia have initiated divergent patterns of structural transformation over the past few decades.

The international trade and economy scenario in developed regions like the USA and Europe have been varying over the transitory trade regime from the mid-twentieth century to twenty-first century. The share of global manufacturing of the USA, following the end of the economic recession, has declined from 28% in 2002 to 16.5% in 2011. During the post-recession period, the share of the USA has risen to 18.6% until 2015, the largest share since 2009. These estimates are based on the value of each country's manufacturing in US dollars. However, part of the decline in the US share was due to a 23% decline in the value of the dollar between 2002 and 2011, and part of the rise since 2011 is attributable to a stronger value of the US dollar. Manufacturers in many countries have been allocating higher financial resources toward research and development relative to their value-added manufacturing and marketing process. It has been found that the manufacturers in the USA spend approximately 11% of value-added resources on research and development. A large proportion of research and development of the manufacturers in the USA takes place in high-technology sectors, such as pharmaceutical, electronics, and aircraft manufacturing, whereas in most other countries, the largest share of research and development is utilized in the medium-technology sectors such as automotive and machinery manufacturing (Levinson 2017).

Exploring new markets for diversified manufacturing of emerging countries can play an important role in stabilizing market share and reducing economic effects associated with long-standing economic and international trade arrangements. Trade can thus outgrow with improvement in domestic and international markets. In addition, international agreements can be an important external anchor and catalyst for institutional change by breaking through domestic impediments to reforms. Lessons can be learnt from Chile and Mexico, which provide important role models for the Latin America and Caribbean regional trade. It is evident that over the years, institutional strengthening and trade policy reforms in both countries have allowed them to establish a successful inflation-targeting framework, lower public debt, open the trading regime, and build a strong regulatory and oversight framework for the banking system. The effects of such associated factors have boosted the international trade and economy scenarios of Chile and Mexico. However, in order to achieve significant results of trade openness measures in Mexico, further institutional reforms will be necessary with a focus on reducing macroeconomic instability, improving the investment climate and institutional framework, scope for prolific corporate venturing, and putting in place business education and innovation system capable of fostering technological advancement and productivity growth. In addition, regional trade integration will have to be supplemented with multilateral actions on other trade sectors to maximize the gains from trade liberalization and reduce the possible operational costs.

Access to international markets has also been improved by growing trade blocks at the regional level. Such accessibility to the markets is further reinforced by reducing the trade barriers through far-reaching business communication strategies, product and market development programs, and customer relations. This situation has given a boost in determining the market opportunities as narrowing the trade barriers helped in deregulating certain sectors of trade such as financial services. However, there may be some exceptions to this common pattern. The global marketplace equipped with the application of global communications has become the focus of the global business arena that makes the world markets remain open and involve in the fair competitive practices.

The globalization moves have opened up high comparative advantages in many manufactured goods through partnership deals to explore business in the emerging economies. They generally display an increasing specialization trend and high consumer values. Leading alliances between the major multinational enterprises may be seen in reference to production, finance, and technology and supply chain along with other complementary activities (Rajagopal 2007).

The major setback due to the economic recession during 2007–2011 in the USA has been the decline in the manufacturing sector. Total production in the manufacturing sector fell over 20%, marking the largest drop in more than 60 years. While it took 5 years (2012–2016) for the manufacturing sector to recover, the US economy started to grow sustainably adding more jobs than early decade of 2010. Such renaissance of economy enhanced expectations for continuing growth in manufacturing and services industry, and stronger market competitiveness in the global markets. However, manufacturing had a weaker start than anticipated in early 2015, and the overall economic growth was restricted by a variety of challenges including weather conditions, slower GDP growth globally, the drop in global oil prices, and a strong dollar, making exports more expensive and imports more affordable. As of June 2015, manufacturing production was 0.2% below the November 2014 level. General Electric (GE) Company would be reducing the size of its financial business and focus on industrial growth by looking at the possibility of strategic investment in manufacturing. Under the plan, GE expects that by 2018, more than 90% of its earnings will be generated by its high-return industrial growth. The company is investing in the type of innovations that will drive cutting-edge manufacturing and economic growth (Cushman and Wakefield 2015).

The global manufacturing scenario is changing continuously in reference to the shifts in political and economic policies. Accordingly, the regional industrial performances are also affected in most regions in the world. In the USA, the Midwest remained a vital part of the manufacturing industry, though the Southeast and Mid-south regions also gained a significant share of manufacturing investment. In Canada, non-energy products from Central Canada, British Columbia, and other oil-consuming provinces that are manufactured as exported have shown promising growth, while oil price recovery played an important role in determining the extend of investment in the manufacturing sector during 2015. However, a significant recovery in the manufacturing industry in the region continued at a modest but steady rate during 2016. The growing volume of consumer spending in the USA has shown a positive trend in manufacturing, and it has been observed that such economic recovery would be benefiting to both Canada and Mexico trade environment. However, the manufacturing industry in North America would stand in a better position in the longer run to compete globally for investment and augmenting employment.

Product Portfolios

Despite the international diplomacy and regional trade integration across various trade zones of North America, Latin America and Caribbean, Europe, Africa, Commonwealth Countries, and Asia, the recent global economic thinking on policy reforms needs region-specific attention to structural transformation and industrial development. The economic fundamentals advocate that macroeconomic stability and well-functioning markets should be the key considerations to improve the international trade situation. It is argued by several economists and international trade experts that such macroeconomic enlightenment can be achieved through structural transformation initiating automation process in manufacturing and trade-related services. In an open economy, international trade is largely based on the comparative advantage matrix that directs resources to optimize the manufacturing and services sector contributions to the GDP. The contemporary political and economic ideologies on trade policy in most countries have been striking a balance to foster growth to the domestic as well as international trade. Observing the international competition and economic governance trends, most countries encourage diversification in manufacturing and services sectors in tune to the growth of technology. Such diversification is regarded as productive and plays as a key to economic development. Developing countries produce a relatively narrow range of goods, while developed countries are engaged in a broad range of economic activities covering the fundamental insights of trade theory (Rodrick 2007). The principle of comparative advantage states that the gains from trade arise from specialization, and this maxim has surfaced the location advantage that prompted the manufacturing industries to move to low-cost locations to gain price competitiveness. Such production decisions segregated the manufacturing and services industries to selected geo-demographic segments in the region. Accordingly, since the beginning of the twenty-first century, manufacturing industries in the USA have been relocated to Mexico to seek cost advantage in production by way of labor costs, infrastructure benefits on cost, and logistics.

The manufacturing sector, which is contributing 12.32% to GDP of the USA,[2] is rapidly rising by enhancing productivity to its greatest strength. It is emerging as a major contributor to the growth of the US economy during the post-economic recession period of 2007–2011. Higher productivity offers multiple benefits including stronger and sustainable market competitiveness in manufacturing, higher real wages, and a rising standard of living. During the economic recession period of 2007–2011, the decline in industrial productivity has caused a gradual decline in employment in manufacturing. The manufacturing sector has shown strong performance in the past 25 years despite difficult periods of adjustment through the 1970s and 1980s. The manufacturing sector remained strong despite shocks to the world economy, including those in some of the strongest US export markets during the Asian financial crisis of 1997. According to United Nations estimates, China displaced the USA as the largest manufacturing nation in 2010. The value added in manufacturing in China has reached US$3 trillion as compared to US$2.2 trillion for the USA. These estimates are calculated in US dollars, and the reported manufacturing value added of many countries, including China, Germany, and Japan, declined in 2015 due to the strengthening of the dollar. Japan, which ranked third in manufacturing value-added segment at US$810 billion in 2015, declined by 29% between 2012 and 2015, a period in which its currency declined 40% against the dollar (Levinson 2017).

Industry competitiveness depends largely on the ability of the company to develop alliances with other companies and converge with the innovation, technology, and demand. Products that are labor intensive, high volume, and non-complex are more likely to be supported by the offshore workstations from the low-wage countries such as India and China to provide business to the USA and Canada in the North American region. As stated in the pre-text, Mexico has the competitive advantage in many labor categories for the North American region, which explains why the production of many automobile parts suppliers migrated south of the border of the USA. Advanced technology products, complex products, and products restricted by national security tend to be developed and produced in the advanced countries, but there is no guarantee that this generalization will last as developing countries increase their capabilities and cost differentials converge. Small companies that have been more vulnerable to the effects of global competition than the large multinational companies are commonly short of resources to move production, research and development, and other market operations to gain a better competitive advantage. Traditionally, the ability to closely integrate product development and production has allowed companies to explore advances in product design and production efficiency, thus pushing the envelope in terms of innovation and productivity. If the production portion of the value chain loses its luster in North America, it remains to be seen whether manufacturers in the region can hold on to their lead in global innovation and continue to march up the value chain to higher value-added, and more profitable, products and services (Giffie 2008).

Globalization is characterized by a variety of contradictions prominently pertaining to the risks of trade openness and prompting inflationary economic conditions in the developing economies. However, the process of globalization has increased the access to the markets as the remote markets have been reduced following the political and economic changes worldwide. Market access has also been improved by growing trade blocks at the regional level. Such accessibility to the markets is further reinforced by reducing the trade barriers through far-reaching business communication strategies, product and market development programs, and customer relations. Such situation has given a boost in determining the market opportunities by narrowing the trade barriers helped in deregulating certain sectors of trade such as financial services (Rajagopal 2007). It has been observed that international trade has consistently grown faster than GDP and has been an important driver of world growth. The openness in trade has revealed benefit in augmenting overseas investment and reduced barriers that discourage greater participation by firms in international markets (Alexander and Warwick 2007). A longitudinal research study reveals that trade openness eliminates most of the explanatory power of investment, generates a significant positive impact on growth per capita, and allows economic growth to precede investment, rather than the reverse. Therefore, in open economies, trade openness could replace investment, and investment may not be a determinant of growth as is traditionally assumed. Governments in relatively open economies should give priority to liberalizing their trade rather than initiating policies that induce savings and investments (Mehanna 2006). The most significant factors to openness are population of a country and distance to potential trade partners. Countries with larger populations trade less, as do countries that are relatively more remote. Furthermore, after controlling for trade policy, there is little evidence of a positive correlation between openness and economic development (Guttmann and Richards 2006).

Implementing NAFTA has benefitted the manufacturing sector in the USA and Canada over the years. Canadian manufacturing also benefited from NAFTA, helping exports such as energy, motor vehicles and parts, industrial machinery, aircraft, telecommunications equipment, and electronics grow. However, the share of economic activity represented by the sector has fallen from 14.8% in 2000 to the 10.6% in 2014. The consumer demand in the USA has collapsed following the recession of 2007–2011, which has caused industrial output to decline in both Canada and the USA. However, the extent of the plunge in consumer demand was relatively less severe in Mexico during the above referred period.

The nature of technology and the knowledge acquisition for manufacturing change at different stages of industrial development. Trade openness in the free trade regimes has also affected the economic growth and profit of individual firms in developing countries. It is found that the less efficient firm loses market shares in its home market at the beginning of trade liberalization. Only for a more advanced level of liberalization, it does take advantage of a larger access to foreign demand. Trade liberalization may, therefore, harm its profits too strongly, forcing it to leave the market. Although its incentives decrease with trade liberalization, the high-technology firm may be willing to take it over for low organizational and technological costs of firms' integration (Bertrand and Zitouna 2006). A study analyzing the contribution of openness of trade in a given market structure reveals that around 30–50% for small European economies and 20–30% for larger European countries are put in by the foreign firms. On the contrary, market structure is less affected by openness in the USA and Japan (Mirza 2006). However, continuous trade reforms and the increasing influence of the World Trade Organization, and policy formulation for developing-country markets require continual examination of the link between profitability and trade for more developing countries than have been analyzed so far (Shahnawaz 2005). Trade openness triggers competition, and to maintain or achieve competitiveness and profitability, a manufacturing firm or enterprise must respond to a range of challenges, including rapid improvements in technology, declining employment and output, globalization of markets, and environmental requirements. In addition, substantial changes in government policy have

Table 4.1 Total industrial production index in North America (base 2010 = 100)

Period	*USA*	*Canada*	*Mexico*
2000	101.6584	111.7473	90.8164
2001	98.48787	107.2482	89.54731
2002	98.79596	108.9398	89.58778
2003	99.9966	109.0422	90.78603
2004	102.6337	110.8367	94.34508
2005	105.9883	112.9998	96.78593
2006	108.3514	112.3435	101.0072
2007	111.0694	111.4276	102.4102
2008	107.1241	107.736	101.7956
2009	94.80094	95.41282	95.62671
2010	99.99996	100	99.9965
2011	102.9298	104.8612	103.4547
2012	105.8025	104.8705	106.3292
2013	107.8261	106.4261	105.8877
2014	110.9772	110.8528	108.714
2015	111.3201	110.0191	109.7881

Source OECD Data https://data.oecd.org/industry/industrial-production.htm (Retrieved on February 20, 2017, and presented in Table 4.1 after calculating the quarterly averages for each year)

had important impacts in many countries, as have the increasing levels of global trade (Hyland et al. 2007).

The industrial productivity in the North American region since 2000 has been varying over the years. However, NAFTA has provided an advantage in augmenting industrial manufacturing and market competitiveness. The industrial productivity index on the base price of 2010 has been exhibited in Table 4.1. However, all the three countries—Mexico, Canada, and the USA—have experienced an increasing trend in growth during the post-economic recession period.

Productivity levels can vary considerably within any economy depending on the principal and auxiliary economic activities, the size of the trade, and the extent of employment availability with the economy. It is observed that labor productivity tends to be high in the labor-oriented industries such as mining, agriculture, and natural resources-based manufacturing. The bulk of mining production is undertaken by large and capital-intensive firms that form the industrial conglomerate in developing countries like Mexico and Latin American countries. Typically, the productivity level of manufacturing tends to be well above the national average, although it varies as microenterprises and informal jobs displaying relatively lower productivity coexist with large firms that use high technology and skilled labor, and therefore have higher productivity. The lowest output per worker is generally in agriculture, especially in Latin American countries where most producers are small peasants who use less mechanized technologies. Contrary to manufacturing, the productivity of services depends on the type of activity. Among many services activities, finance, insurance, real estate, business services, transport, storage, and communications have relatively high levels of productivity (though initially, this may simply reflect price movements), while community, social and personal services, and government services tend to have much lower output per worker. Productivity in trade, restaurants, and hotels is quite varied but tends to be rather low in most developing countries like Mexico, where a large segment of informal commerce exists (Trade Development Report 2016).

The lowering of trade barriers made globalization of markets and production a theoretical possibility, and technological change has made it a tangible reality. Since the mid-twentieth century, global market has seen major advances in communications, information processing, and transportation technology including, most recently, the explosive emergence of the information technology. The technology drivers play a significant role in global business. The global expansion of the multinational companies has been highly stimulated by the technological advancements in the designing, manufacturing, and marketing of consumer and industrial products. The services were also improved by many technological breakthroughs. The Internet revolution has triggered the e-commerce as an open access channel, as a strong driving force for the global business in the consumer and industry segments. Improved transport and communication now make it possible for firms to be in continuous contact with producers anywhere in the world. This makes it easier for companies to split production of a single good over any distance. Storage and preservation techniques have revolutionized the food industry, for example, so that the idea of seasonal vegetables is no longer relevant today as anything can be exported all year round anywhere. The new global marketplace accelerates competition, thereby reducing the lead time for companies with new products, services, or technologies to reach and service their target market. To survive and grow in this type of economic environment, a business will need strategic markets where it can expand its sales and be competitive. Businesses, both large and small, are turning to niche markets where competition is reduced. Economic globalization is a new worldwide economic order, in which a majority of nations prescribe to the free enterprise system. The triad market refers to the USA and Canada, Japan, and Western European countries. The triad powers essentially function in the countries of their spatial spread, and other regions have become less important for survival and considered as marginal or less opportunistic. In the triad market, time and distance play a major role in helping the executives to make quick and appropriate strategic decision.

Revenue Optimization Management

As strategic assumptions lead the policy decisions in a country, the political and economic capabilities and promised profiteering goals need to be redefined to sustain and integrate competencies of manufacturing, and trading in an economy. Accordingly, organizational capabilities need to be developed by the companies within industries segments to serve as the core thread of market competiveness. The financial indicators related to the international marketing consist of corporate bond yield, factor income, the value of a local currency with reference to US dollars, and money supply. Besides, the extent of foreign direct investment (FDI) in a country also reveals its financial strength. A foreign investment is classified as a direct investment if the foreign investor holds at least 10% of the ordinary shares or voting rights in an enterprise and exerts some influence over its management. The higher yields of the corporate bonds indicate the soundness of the financial conditions in a country. Corporate bond interest rates and associated yield spreads are the core topics in financial economics. The factors that affect the level of changes in these variables are important to many financial analysts. An examination of these variables and the relationships between them, as well as possible linkages between yield spreads and stock market behavior, is the focus of major financial analysis. In particular, changes in yield spreads between high and medium quality corporate bonds and Treasury bonds are examined, as are the changes in the spread between the differing quality corporate bonds. Variations in the interest rates are given in financial market history and are taken for the financial analysis as the guideposts. Changes in macroeconomic factors such as inflation and the business cycle cause these fluctuations. Investor perception of risk, of course, affects both interest rates and stock market valuations. Interest rates tend to move together due to common influences, such as inflation. Although this is true, the differences between corporate and government bond interest rates, and between corporate bonds rates on different quality bonds, are not constant. Other vital financial indicators include the exchange rate, stock trends, and long-term interest rates. The sensitivity of longer-term interest rates to expectations about future short rates is also operative in a short term.

Recent changes in the business landscape have triggered the need to create an optimized organization. Globalization seems to dominate the competitive horizon. The concept is not new, but the intensity of the challenge to get on with it is. Globalization entails new markets, new products, new mind-sets, new competencies, and new ways of thinking about business. In times to come, many organizations may have to evolve new models for attaining global agility, effectiveness, and competitiveness. Additionally, organizations may also have to devise means to consolidate their dispersed capabilities to provide unparalleled value to the customers at reasonable cost. Organizations seldom have time to adapt themselves to the rapidly changing business landscape. Ways of working are becoming obsolete with each passing day. Innovation and self-discovery have become new catalysts for growth.

Sustainable development is a prime global concern. It has been emphasized that the business sector will only be more effective if it incorporates into its policies social and environmental responsibilities. Poverty and environmental damages affect the business sector and, thus, need to be resolved and prevented to create a good and prosperous business environment. It is also noticed that global competitiveness is the key element to survive in business, and it is a task that the business sector along with governments has to confront. The economic reforms in a country are complex and multi-dimensional processes that involve the development and implementation of many public policies at intermediate levels during the reforms. The economic reforms thus will not have a constant speed and will often be subject to modifications in the policies that bring changes in the performance and structure of economic activities. The economic reforms can be assessed by examining their corresponding policy measures and implications. However, entire economic progress may not be interpreted as an outcome of the reforms. The growth and development in a country or a region may result to be slower in a normal process than a stirred process of reforms.

Besides the macroeconomic factors in the destination country, international diplomacy and behavior of financial markets also cause the volatility of the exchange rates. Inflation rises in a country due to price escalations, hike in interest rates, and higher circulation of money in the society. Countries with a consistently low inflation rate exhibit a rising currency value as its purchasing power is high relative to other currencies. During the mid-twentieth century, Japan, Germany, and Switzerland had observed low rate of inflation while the USA and Canada could bring down the inflation during the 90s. The controlled inflation helped these countries to stabilize the foreign exchange rate for a longer period.

Interest rates, inflation, and exchange rates are highly correlated. There are two types of interest rates that prevail in the economy—interest rate for lending and for investments. In general, when the lending interest rates are lowered, more people are able to borrow more money. Consequently, consumers have more money to spend, resulting in the growth of the economy as well as an increase in inflation. By manipulating interest rates, central banks attempt to influence both inflation and exchange rates. Higher interest rates on investments attract foreign capital and cause the exchange rate to rise. Besides the interest rates, the social expenditure in the six least return areas including government expenditure on public health, education, housing, public infrastructure, social security, and military also inflate the economy of the country disrupting the stability of foreign currency exchange rate. The disequilibrium in the balance of payment, which is the sum of total income and expenditure in a country leading to either surplus or deficit in the economy, significantly affects the volatility of foreign currency exchange rates. Developing countries with high international debt, high social expenditure, low exports, high imports, and low foreign investment often suffer from the instability of foreign exchange rates. Low exports scenario in a country often contributes to economic as it increases the expenditure on imports and reduces the overall income of the country. International diplomacy promoting international trade by means of regional trade agreements or by revaluating the lead currency values (appreciation or depreciation) has a global impact on the foreign currency exchange rates. The extent of bad debts due to willful or circumstantial defaults in repayments causes liquidity crunch in financial institutions. This, in turn, lowers the investor confidence resulting in decline in investments, rise in the inflation of a country, and fluctuations in the foreign currency exchange rates. Companies intending to establish their production and business operations in the destination countries should evaluate the causes and effects associated with the foreign currency exchange rates and act accordingly.

Variability in the foreign exchange rate significantly affects the trade and economy of a country. The foreign and domestic market structures are woven around the exchange rates, which largely govern the corporate decisions on export, import, and investments. The exchange rates trends in destination countries also determine a company's operating efficiency and sustainability in the market. However, managers over the past have developed strategies to manage foreign exchange exposure in new ways by considering the manufacturing units flexible to adjust the financial commitments according to the movements of the exchange rates. A company can also shift sources of raw materials, subassemblies, and components to other destinations adopting the production sharing strategies that ensure the stability of exchange rates. Above all, globalization has leveraged most multinational companies to assume alternate strategies, if exchange rate changes affect operating performance to pull down the competitive advantages at the destination market (Lessard and Lightstone 1986). The forward market currency options and currency futures facilitate international trade and investment by allowing firms to hedge, or reduce the foreign exchange risks inherent in international transactions. The forward price of a foreign currency often differs from its spot price. If the forward price (using a direct quote) is less than the spot price, the currency is selling at a forward discount, and in case the forward price is higher than the spot price, the currency is selling at a forward premium. The forward price represents the aggregate prediction of the spot price of the exchange rate in the future in the marketplace (Antle and Ensor 1982). Thus, the forward price helps international businesspeople forecast future changes in exchange rates. These variations can affect the price of imported components as well as the competitiveness and profitability of the exports of a company. If a currency is selling at a forward discount, the foreign exchange market believes the currency will depreciate over time. Firms may want to reduce their holdings of assets or increase their liabilities denominated in such a currency. The currencies of countries suffering balance of payment (BoP) deficits or high inflation rates often sell at a forward discount. On the contrary, if a currency is selling at a forward premium, the foreign exchange market assumes that the currency will appreciate over time. Firms may want to increase their holdings of assets and reduce their liabilities denominated in such a currency. The currencies of countries enjoying BoP surpluses generated of trade or low inflation rates often sell at a forward premium. Thus, the difference between the spot and forward prices of a country's currency often signals the expectations of a market regarding macroeconomic policies and prospects of the country.

Import–Export Scenario

The world merchandise trade remained sluggish at 2.7% in 2015 as measured by the average of exports and imports. This figure was revised downward from a preliminary estimate of 2.8% released in April 2016 based on available data at the time. Slow global trade growth was accompanied by a modest increase in world GDP, which grew 2.4% in real terms at market exchange rates in the same period. Several factors contributed to the lackluster performance, including an economic slowdown in China, recessions in other large developing economies including Brazil, falling prices for oil and other primary commodities, strong fluctuations in exchange rates, and financial volatility driven by divergent monetary policies in developed countries. Faster economic growth and rising import demand in developed countries partly made up for weaker demand elsewhere, leaving trade growth and output growth nearly unchanged compared with the previous year (2.8 and 2.5%, respectively, in 2014). The year 2015 marked the fourth consecutive year with trade volume growth below 3%, and the 4th year in a row with world trade growing at nearly the same rate as world GDP. Growth rates for trade and GDP in 2015 remained below their respective averages since 1990 of 5 and 2.7%. The slow pace of trade growth relative to GDP growth over the past 4 years stands in contrast to the period from 1990 to 2008, during which world merchandise trade volume grew 2.1 times as fast as world GDP on average. The recent uninterrupted spell of slow trade growth is unusual but not unprecedented, and its importance should not be exaggerated. Overall, world trade growth was weaker between 1980 and 1985, when 5 out of 6 years saw trade growth below 3%, including 2 years of outright contraction (World Trade Organization 2016).

The US Census Bureau and the US Bureau of Economic Analysis, through the Department of Commerce, announced that the goods and services deficit was $44.3 billion in December 2016. Exports during the referred period were $190.7 billion while the imports marked $235.0 billion. For 2016, the goods and services deficit increased $1.9 billion, or 0.4%, from 2015, and the exports decreased $51.7 billion or 2.3%. Imports decreased $49.9 billion or 1.8%.[3] Referring to the annual performance in export and import in the USA, it has been observed that for 2016, the goods and services deficit was $502.3 billion, increased to $1.9 billion from $500.4 billion in 2015. Exports were $2209.4 billion in 2016, down $51.7 billion from 2015. Imports were $2711.7 billion in 2016, down $49.9 billion from 2015. The increase in the goods and services deficit in 2016 reflected a decrease in the goods deficit of $12.5 billion or 1.6% to $750.1 billion and a decrease in the services surplus of $14.4 billion or 5.5% to $247.8 billion. Table 4.2 exhibits the triennium ending (2014–2016) performance of US exports and imports in goods and services with the balance of trade situation.[4]

In order to promote manufacturing and increase international trade performance, foreign trade zones (FTZs) serve as designated geographical areas within the USA to facilitate international trade by encouraging the duty- or quota-free entry of imports. The FTZs provide in habiting companies free trade environment and a liberal regulatory regime with an infrastructure appropriate for carrying out trade and industrial operations. Enterprises operating within these zones benefit from a variety of incentives such as duty drawbacks on inputs or capital goods used in the production for exports. They are usually located in or near customs port of entry and legally considered outside the customs territory of the USA. The FTZs in the USA are located within 60 miles from customs supervising office, whereas sub-zones have no limit and can be located at the zone user's private facility (Seyoum 2017). However, some pockets of excellence have grown simultaneous in sub-sectors, such as information technology-related services of India, and in enclaves of manufacturing dynamism in Mexico including *maquiladora*. These manufacturing and services sub-sectors attracted a heavy FDI in the North American market (World Trade Organization 2016).

NAFTA has played a significant role in the recovery of employment growth during the 2010 decade and helped the companies to stay competitive in the international market along with a surge of production by *maquiladoras* that supported cost-effective manufacturing in labor-oriented industry sector. However, an acceleration in FDI, labor productivity, and market competitiveness helped the companies of the USA and Canada to grow significantly in the 2000s. However, the economic recession that struck the North America during 2007–2011 raised several concerns about consumer credit, consumer spending, low corporate profits, and sustained industrial growth. Consequently, the sluggish

Table 4.2 International trade performance of the USA during 2014–2016 (in million dollars)

Period	*Balance*			*Export*			*Import*		
	Total	*Goods*	*Services*	*Total*	*Goods*	*Services*	*Total*	*Goods*	*Services*
2014	−490,176	−752,169	261,993	2,376,577	1,633,320	743,257	2,866,754	2,385,489	481,264
2015	−500,361	−762,565	262,203	2,261,163	1,510,303	750,860	2,761,525	2,272,868	488,657
2016	−502,252	−750,074	247,822	2,209,418	1,459,843	749,575	2,711,671	2,209,917	501,753

Source US Census Bureau and US Bureau of Economic Analysis NEWS US Department of Commerce, Washington, DC 20230, February 7, 2017

growth of manufacturing sector and low productivity were observed during the above referred period. Indeed, the overall economy showed no increase in productivity during this period. Rapid trade and financial liberalization has emerged as a quick-fix strategy to stabilize the economy and made the market an important *maquila* exporter with only limited domestic production linkages. On the Mexican economic front, the overvalued exchange rate and the changing role of the public sector have been the additional factors contributing to the slow growth performance of Mexico's economy. The period following the NAFTA agreement, characterized by trade and financial liberalization, led to a strong increase in manufacturing exports, from only 10% of total exports in 1981 to more than 80% in the early 2000s, decreasing only slightly thereafter. However, as exports increased, imports kept pace, resulting in an increase in the imports-to-GDP ratio from 12.9% in 1981 to 31% in 2010. With domestically produced intermediate goods accounting for only 25% of the total value added, few backward and forward production linkages could be established (Palma 2005). The declining investment rate of the 1980s was reversed during the 1990s, but the investment-to-GDP ratio has been stagnant at 20–21% since then. Thus, despite preferential access to the largest and most dynamic market in the industrial world and large inflows of foreign investment, the Mexican economy has been unable to establish the linkages needed to stimulate a dynamic process of industrialization and economic growth. This is largely due to a delinking of the exporting sectors from the domestic economy (Cruz 2015; Palma 2005; Trade Development Report 2016).

Manufacturing dynamism in Mexico has moved up due to heavy FDI presence and has benefited from preferential access to the North American market. Mexico has been relatively resilient to the decline in exports compared with other developing economies, recording a fall of 3 and 4% during 2014–2015, respectively. China, however, experienced a large decline of 14% in imports. Mexico's decline in imports was not as drastic, falling by 2% during 2015. Mexico has been improved its performance on international trade as the world share of exports of the country has increased by 575% in 2015 over 1980 resulting in the big leap from 0.4% to 2.7%. It has shown a phenomenal growth in export value over the pre-NAFTA period. Exports from Mexico have shown an annual percentage change of 7% during 2010–2015. Table 4.3 exhibits growth in international trade among NAFTA countries—the USA, Canada, and Mexico—during the period 2010–2015 (Trade Development Report 2016).

Table 4.3 Growth in international trade among NAFTA countries: World share in exports and imports (annual percentage change)

Period	*Exports*			*Imports*		
	USA	*Canada*	*Mexico*	*USA*	*Canada*	*Mexico*
2014	3.1	5.6	6.6	4.7	2.8	6.9
2015	−0.9	4.4	4.0	6.5	0.7	13.3
2010–2015	3.2	4.3	5.6	3.7	2.5	7.4

Source World Trade Organization (2016), World Trade Statistics-2016, p. 90

Exports of Mexico jumped during December 2016 by 6.6% to USD 33,232.0 million as oil sales climbed 49.9% and non-oil sales rose 4.9%. By sector, sales increased for agricultural products (+11.9%), mining (+2.1%), and manufacturing (+4.6%). Within non-oil exports, those to the US rose 3.5% and to the rest of the world went up 11.6%. Imports advanced 4.2% to USD 33,204.0 million as non-oil purchases increased 1.9% while oil products jumped 28.9%. Among sectors, imports rose for intermediate goods (6.8%) while fell for consumer goods (−5.2%) and capital goods (−0.8%) for the above referred period. Mexico recorded a trade surplus of USD 28 million in December of 2016 compared to a trade gap of USD 715 million a year ago. Exports rose 6.6% to USD 33,232 million as oil sales jumped 49.9% and non-oil shipments increased 4.9%. Among categories, exports rose for agricultural products (+11.9%), mining (+2.1%), and manufacturing (+4.6%). Within non-oil exports, those to the USA increased 3.5% and to the rest of the world, sales went up 11.6%. Imports rose 4.1% to USD 33,204 million, as non-oil purchases went up 1.9% and oil jumped 28.9%. Among categories, imports rose for intermediate goods (+6.8%) while fell for consumer goods (−5.2%) and capital goods (−0.8%). Considering full 2016 year, the trade gap narrowed 10.1% year-on-year to USD 13,135 million as exports shrank 1.9% and imports declined 2.1%. The balance of trade in Mexico averaged −281.41 USD million from 1980 until 2016, reaching an all-time high of 1710.25 USD million in March of 2013 and a record low of −3292.30 USD million in October of 2008.[5]

International Investment

FDI has been an integral part of the economic relationship between the USA and Mexico since NAFTA implementation. The USA is the largest source of FDI in Mexico. The stock of US FDI increased from

\$17.0 billion in 1994 to \$92.8 billion in 2015. While Mexican FDI in the USA is much lower than US investment in Mexico, it has also increased since NAFTA, totalling \$16.6 billion in 2015. The liberalization of Mexico's restrictions on foreign investment in the late 1980s and the early 1990s played an important role in attracting US investment to Mexico. Up until the mid-1980s, Mexico had a very protective policy that restricted foreign investment and controlled the exchange rate to encourage domestic growth, affecting the entire industrial sector. A sharp shift in policy in the late 1980s that included market opening measures and economic reforms helped bring in a steady increase in FDI flows into Mexico. These reforms were locked in through NAFTA provisions on foreign investment and resulted in increased investor confidence. Under NAFTA, Mexico gave US and Canadian investors' non-discriminatory treatment of their investments as well as investor protection. NAFTA may have encouraged US FDI in Mexico by increasing investor confidence, but much of the growth may have occurred anyway because Mexico likely would have continued to liberalize its foreign investment laws with or without the agreement (Villareal 2016).

Government investment policies such as FDI and joint venture programs (JV) with the benefits of tax flexibility, low interest rates, and flexible policies of repatriation of funds including profits attract foreign companies toward such destinations. Developing countries encourage FDIs in selected sectors and allow foreign companies to participate through JVs in manufacturing and business operations in the consumer sector. FDI and JV opportunities are offered by both the developed and developing countries, and as the globalization is rapidly growing, there appear bidirectional movements of companies in carrying investments in both types of destinations. The outward FDI of China is steadily increasing and is targeting the USA as a beneficial destination for investments in potential manufacturing sectors like consumer electronics, automobile parts, consumer durables, and mass consumer products. However, Chinese FDI in the USA faces challenges in cultural, marketing, and technological aspects besides the fitness of politico-business ideologies (He and Lyles 2008). Technology and managerial know-how elements are also important determinants of comparative advantage for the companies to choose the right overseas destination for manufacturing and business operations. Destination markets that have low cost for accessing technology like information and communication technologies for use of Internet and mobile communications and offer low charges for online banking and insurance services, and encourage seamless office operations, appear to be the right choice for multinational companies for doing business. In some countries, governments restrict the import of technology in the generic areas such as food, textile, etc., if any threat is foreseen toward the disruption of the local economy.

Most companies, while exploring the opportunities for manufacturing products in the destination markets, look for optimizing the investment on manufacturing infrastructure by way of incurring expenditure on construction of own plant and installing machineries. Companies prospecting to manufacture in destination countries search for the production infrastructure of local companies that are engaged in manufacturing similar or identical products and analyze their plant utilization capacity. Accordingly, the foreign firms negotiate with the local companies to share their manufacturing infrastructure to make use of their unused plan capacity. The *government drivers* for globalization include diplomatic trade relations, customs unions, or common markets. The government drivers add favorable trade policies, foreign investment regulations, bilateral or regional trade treaties, and common market regulations. The introduction of global norms and standards like ISO certifications by governments may be one of the effective measures to promote globalization through uniform quality perspectives. In the past, the government barriers to foreign market entry protected the domestic markets and made the global marketing an uphill task. WTO has been instrumental in promoting government drivers for improving trade in the developing countries.

Notes

1. A maquiladora in Mexico is a production facility or company that operates under preferential tariff programs established and administered by the USA and Mexico. Maquiladoras serve as assembly facilities, manufacturing units using raw materials, and use production equipment that are allowed to enter Mexico as duty-free. Product manufactured in the maquiladoras can be exported to the USA at preferential tariffs.
2. World Bank (2016), World Development Indicators (Table 4.2), World Bank Headquarters, Washington, DC.
3. US Census Bureau and US Bureau of Economic Analysis data for December 2016 on US international trade in goods and services at https://www.bea.gov/newsreleases/international/trade/2017/trad1216.htm retrieved on February 21, 2017.

4. US Census Bureau and US Bureau of Economic Analysis NEWS US Department of Commerce, Washington, DC 20230, February 7, 2017 at file:///D:/Academic%20documents/Books/Palgrave%20Book%206/Material/US%20Export%20and%20Imports%202014-2016.pdf retrieved on February 21, 2017.
5. Trading Economics (2017), Mexico Balance of Trade at http://www.tradingeconomics.com/mexico/balance-of-trade retrieved on February 21, 2017.

References

Alexander, C., & Warwick, K. (2007). Governments, exports and growth: Responding to the challenges and opportunities of globalization. *The world economy, 30*(1), 177–194.

Antle, B., & Ensor, R. (1982), *Management of Foreign Exchange Risk*, London: Euromoney Publications.

Batra, R. (2001). Are tariffs inflationary. *Review of International Economics, 9*(3), 373–382.

Bems, R., Robert, C. J., & Yi, K. M. (2013). The great trade collapse. *Annual Review of Economics, 5*(1), 375–400.

Bertrand, O., & Zitouna, H. (2006). Trade liberalization and industrial restructuring: The role of cross-border mergers and acquisitions. *Journal of Economics & Management Strategy, 15*(2), 479–515.

Constantinescu, C., Mattoo, A., & Ruta, M. (2015). *The global trade slowdown: Cyclical or structural?* IMF Working Paper, Strategy WP-15-6, Policy and Review Department, International Monetary Fund, Washington, DC.

Cruz, M. (2015). Premature de-industrialization: Theory, evidence and policy recommendations in the Mexican case. *Cambridge Journal of Economics, 39*(1), 113–137.

Cushman and Wakefield (2015). *Manufacturing in North America*, A Cushman and Wakefield Special Report, August, Chicago, IL.

Giffie, C. (2008). *Made in America.* New York: Deloitte Research, Deloitte Headquarters.

Guttmann, S., & Richards, A. (2006). Trade openness: An Australian experience. *Australian Economic Papers, 45*(3), 188–203.

He, W., & Lyles, M. (2008). China's outward foreign direct investment. *Business Horizons, 51*(6), 485–491.

Hyland, P. W., Mellor, R., & Sloan, T. (2007). Performance measurement and continuous improvement: Are they linked to manufacturing strategy? *International Journal of Technology Management, 37*(3–4), 237–246.

Igor, P. (2000). *Growth and reforms in Latin America and the caribbean in the 1990s.* United Nations Economic Commission for Latin America and the Caribbean (ECLAC), Working Paper, Economic Division.

Kali, R., Méndez, F., & Reyes, J. (2007). Trade structure and economic growth. *The Journal of International Trade & Economic Development, 16*(2), 245–269.

Lessard, D. R. & Lightstone, J. B. (1986). Volatile Exchange Rates Can Put Operations at Risk, *Harvard Business Review, 64* (4), 107–114.

Levinson, M. (2017). *U.S. Manufacturing in International Perspective*, Congressional Research Service, CRS Report 7–5700, Washington, DC.

Lopez, S. F., & Chong, A. (2003). *The Truth about Privatization in Latin America*. Yale ICF Working Study No. 03–29, October.

Mehanna, R. A. (2006). Open first, then invest. *Journal of Transnational Management, 11*(2), 53–76.

Mirza, D. (2006). How much does trade contribute to market structure? *Economica, 73*(289), 59–74.

Palma, J. G. (2005) Four sources of "de-industrialization" and a new concept of the "Dutch Disease", In J. A. Ocampo (Ed.), *Beyond reforms: Structural dynamics and macroeconomic vulnerability* (71 – 117). Palo Alto, CA: Stanford University Press, and Washington, DC: World Bank and ECLAC.

Pritchett, L., & Sethi, G. (1994). Tariff Rates. *Tariff revenue and tariff reforms—Some new facts, World Bank economic review, 8*(1), 1–16.

Rajagopal. (2007) Trade openness and inflation in Latin American countries. *Economic Studies of International Development, 7*(1), 75–96.

Rodrick, D. (2007). Industrial development: Some stylized facts and policy directions. In United Nations (Ed.), *Industrial development for the Twenty-first century: Sustainable development perspectives*. New York: Department of Economic and Social Affairs, United Nations.

Seyoum, B. (2017). US foreign trade zones and import intensity examining determinants of import intensity in US foreign trade zones. *European Business Review, 29*(1), 103–122.

Shahnawaz, S. (2005). Profitability and trade in developing countries. *International Trade Journal, 19*(3), 269–284.

Stiglitz, J.E., Ocampo, J.A., Spiegel S., French-davis, R., & Nayyar, D. (2006). *Stability with Growth: Macroeconomics, liberalization and development*. New York: Oxford University Press.

Trade Development Report (2016) Structural transformation for inclusive and sustained growth, *Trade Development Report*, UNCTAD, New York.

Villareal, M. A. (2016). *U.S.-Mexico Economic Relations: Trends, Issues, and Implications*. Congressional Research Service, Paper 7–5700, Washington, DC.

World Trade Organization. (2016). *World Trade Statistics-2016*. Geneva: WTO Headquarters.

PART II

Operationalizing Business in Destination Markets

CHAPTER 5

Venture Collaborations and Management

Growth in international trade is not linear, but often discrete and unpredictable. Companies engaged in cross-border trade in North American region need both the strategic directions and ability to shift their approach to drive on a sustainable growth path in the long term. It has been observed that companies are leaning towards venture collaborations in the international markets to gain global–local push in business and enhance their performance in the competitive marketplace. The discussions in this chapter outlines the shifts of corporate mind-set need to make the business strategies effective and the patterns of common venture collaborations. This chapter discusses corporate and human resources management followed by the companies in doing business in North America. How trade moves with corporate alliances, partnerships, acquisitions, mergers, and joint ventures in most companies as a part of the core international business strategy have been critically examined in this chapter.

Globalization in the business environment has caused a series of changes in the process of recruitment, global staffing, organizational management, and rewards. The changes are affected by globalization highlighting the difference between standardized and localized human resource processes. Sales firms need to respond fast to staffing demand, changing organizational structure, and economic indicators to stay ahead in competition (Sparrow 2007). Firms make continuous efforts to attract the talents of competing companies to make sustainable business growth. Open competition for the talents of competitive firms had

Rajagopal and V. Zlatev, *Business Dynamics in North America*,
DOI 10.1007/978-3-319-57606-0_5

been rare before the globalization, but is now an accepted fact. Fast-moving organizations continuously require new talent because when a good employee walks away, the business takes a hit. The recruitment strategies need to be set around the socioeconomic benefits of employee, career paths, and training efforts. However, a market-driven approach allows employees to stay long with the firm and develop loyalty so that the firm can use highly talented people for competitive growth in the long term. Compensation is only one of many useful retention mechanisms. Firms can also redesign jobs to reduce employee turnover. Firms can promote loyalty of salespeople to particular client accounts or work teams. Generally, sales firms do not count on talent and hire people who are not in high demand, and place key players in locations where they are not constantly tempted by job offers. Such approaches result in high turnover of salespeople affecting the business of the firm. Firms can outsource, strengthen recruitment, standardize jobs, cross-train employees, and organize work around short-term projects to derive advantage of talented human resources (Cappelli 2001).

Human Resources Management

Human resources management (HRM) has led to many changes consequent upon the changing patterns international HRM practices due to globalization effect. Apparently, the shifts in the HRM practices indicate the degree of convergence with key variables of talent, capability, competence, and performance in driving the organizational competitiveness in the global marketplace. However, critically examining the contemporary HRM trend reveals a different picture with many differences due to a variety of limiting factors, ranging from economic stages of development to business strategies, national culture, and fixed enterprise mind-sets (Rowly and Benson 2002). Hence, firms should plan for recruiting best salespeople considering the following organizational requirements:

- Identifying requirement
- Pooling staff needs
- Classifying job specific criteria for recruiting
- Specialist, Generalist, Auxiliary sales force
- Defining job perspectives
- Delineating probationary criteria
- Scheduling announcement

In driving high-value talent in a company, managers need to market the workplace environment, and create job offerings and employment relationships that provide mutual value for firms and their employees. Firms can use 9Ps comprising product, price, place, promotion, people, performance, psychodynamics, posture and proliferation to create compelling job offerings that attract high-value employees. Many firms use relationship-marketing concepts to build long-lasting employment relationships that create mutual value for the firm and its employees. Firms should also generate high-value employment relationships, which include greater employee commitment and satisfaction and lead to greater employee advocacy of the firm and lower levels of employee turnover (Schweitzer and Lyons 2008).

Recruiting managers forms a major part of overall resourcing strategies of sales oriented firms, which seek to identify and secure the salespeople needed for the organization to stand competitive and achieve its goals at different temporal spans. Recruitment activities are responsive to the increasingly competitive market where human resource managers make efforts to secure suitably qualified and capable recruits at all levels. To be effective these initiatives need to include how and when to source the best recruits internally or externally. Common factors associated with the success of either human resources strategies may be as stated below:

- Well-defined organizational structures with sound job design,
- Robust task and person specification and versatile selection processes,
- Reward, employment relations, and human resource policies,
- Commitment for strong employer branding, and
- Employee engagement strategies.

Job designs and recruitment process should be based on performance control, accountability, influence, and support determinants. It is necessary for a firm to have efficient salespeople, and managers should meticulously set the span of control to reflect the resources allocated to each position and unit that plays an important role in delivering customer value. This setting, like the others, is determined by how the business creates value for customers and differentiates its products and services. Managers should also examine the entrepreneurial behavior of the recruits, and measure the creative tension by fixing accountability to handle tasks (Simons 2005). Though there is a global influence on HRM practices, as multinational companies are spread across the geo-demographic segments in the world, the human resources practices in Eastern Europe appears to be less mature as compared to the USA and Canada. Commonly the different industrial regions focus more on personnel administration than the integration of human resources (HR) with corporate strategy. However, some companies like General Electric, General Motors, Toyota, and IBM have developed talent search and selection systems, which are also followed by other companies. Despite the new recruitment models used by the multinational companies, there is still some resistance to compensation patterns such as performance-based pay and value-added economic benefits. Most training to employees varies according to on-the-job requirements, and often job commitment remains low due to the mismatch of convergence of training with the job requirements. One of the major global concerns in HR today has emerged as talent relocation to relatively economically lucrative destinations. This is causing immigration pressure and the concern for replacing native employment at the destinations. Hence, companies at international destinations should focus on extrinsic rather than intrinsic rewards, build trust, use local managers to construct HR systems that employees will accept as fair, and adapt to the suggested shifts in the HR patterns. Changes in HR practices are evolving slowly, but managers in western hemisphere including North American countries must recognize the trans-culture effects and adapt their practices if they are to attract, motivate, and retain high-quality workers (Kiriazov et al. 2000).

Human resources managers should consider the job attraction parameters to drive good candidates. Some studies have identified that compensation is one of the important factors attracting the candidates for jobs followed by fringe benefits, career advancement prospects, category of employment, job autonomy, and supervision method. The organizational culture comprising the task, thrust, time, target and territory of work is also considered as a vital decision variable for the prospects to choose jobs. Another behavioral dimension that appears to be critical in determining the employer and employee relationship is the opportunity of sharing knowledge and skills of the employees for developing a harmonious workplace culture. Often firms succeed in convincing highly talented candidates to accept lower positions assuring that they will be promoted to the position that has a close match with their qualification and experience, but employees under such situations succumb to frustration, as they do not find an appropriate platform to share their knowledge and implement skills. The four factors that make higher impact on the recruits include intangible job context, employee development and skill utilization, remuneration packages and workplace, culture and rewards (Qu et al. 2001). It has been observed that in many industrialized countries there is a concern among growing firms about skills shortages and mismatches appearing in the labor market. Human resources managers are aware of recruitment difficulties and skill shortages that affect the market competitiveness of both small and large firms. However, there is a growing awareness among recruiters that education and training systems can influence the skill and occupational mix of a locality and local economic well-being. In services industry like tourism and hospitality, with their reliance on the secondary job market and high rates of employee turnover, there is a strong tendency to have high levels of recruitment and low levels of training (Bradley and Taylor 1996).

Employment in manufacturing has fallen in most major manufacturing countries over the past quarter-century. In the USA, manufacturing employment has declined since 1990 in line with the changes in Western Europe and Japan, although the timing of the decline has differed from country to country. The strong improvement in US labor productivity in manufacturing relative to other countries has several causes. One is US manufacturers' large investments in automation, which have eliminated many routine assembly jobs. Only two out of five workers in US manufacturing establishments are now directly engaged in production. A related factor is the rapid increase in education levels among US manufacturing workers, some 29% of whom possess college degrees. US labor productivity grew particularly fast in computer, electronic, and optical products (+337% between 2002 and 2015), motor vehicles (+65%), textiles, apparel, and allied products (+74%), and basic metals (+58%). All of these sectors experienced very steep declines in employment over that period. Average compensation per employee in US manufacturing was US$37.71 per hour in 2015, against US$5.90 of compensation paid in Mexico (Levinson 2017). The relative hourly compensation in the manufacturing industry in North American countries has been exhibited in Table 5.1.

Most firms intend to retain high performers by providing economic and relational incentives like determining the career path, and organizational patronage. The high performers have larger task plan (list of tasks to be performed), higher returns on their position (cost to firm), and transparency in the job description. On the contrary, the average

Table 5.1 Hourly compensation in manufacturing industry in North America (At US dollars-2015)

Country	*Direct pay*	*Total compensation*	*Change relative to the USA, 2000–2015 (%)*
Canada	24.64	30.94	12
Mexico	4.14	5.90	(−)17
USA	28.77	37.71	NA

Source The conference board, "international comparisons of hourly compensation costs in manufacturing 2015," https://www.conference-board.org/ilcprogram/index.cfm?id=38269 Retrieved on Feb 25, 2017

performers struggle at the edge of revalidation of contract as firms may look into hiring new people in lieu of average performers (Rajagopal and Rajagopal 2010). It has been observed that good salespeople possess a balance of cognitive and normative behavior. A study on comparing behavior with performance revealed that top sales performers focus the conversation with clients and manager simultaneously to draw a balanced judgment on selling the products and services while weak sales performers allow customers to control the dialogue. One of the attributes of a good salesperson is to be cost effective by performing the tasks on time so that productivity and returns to time ratio may increase. Persuasiveness is another important cognitive attribute of the salesperson that attracts customers and helps them stay with the firm for long term. Sales managers should not only try to hire only those who will become top performers, but also nurture their salespeople with potential (Gellarman 1990).

The globalization and growing technological developments in management of business organizations have dramatically reshaped the employment landscape. Most companies in North America have rapidly increased their international operations and moved into the competitive market with advanced information technology applications, finance, and engineering professionals. The micro-market analysis reveals globally located pools of talents that businesses can adopt, and stay competitive in the marketplace. Accordingly, companies today tend to augment the skills pool and drive up wages. In a radical development of HR in twenty-first century, companies must acquire an itinerant attitude that will allow them to establish global and super talents to grow their organizations competitive. It is predicted that most industries will go for automation and full-scale robotics and artificial intelligence will turn in a broad-based, affordable, easily justifiable way, but still, quality HR would be a predominant requirement for industrial growth and business performance. Most emerging companies are developing a workforce strategy to put multiple work models through crowdsourcing, distant manufacturing, and production sharing (Joerres and Bernstein 2016).

Except in some sectors where high-volume recruitment is the norm, organizations may face unexpected requirement situation for an unusually large number of new recruits at short notice. Such situations are generally managed by the outsourcing specialist within the firm, or an external recruiter is contacted to manage the point-to-point resourcing program. Recruiting people in executive and senior management levels demands acquisition of 'high-potential' recruits. In order to search high-potential recruits, firms need to look for candidates having long-standing and successful track record. Human resources department of such firms may start their search in association with wide range of 'search and selection' or 'headhunting' consultancies. Such recruits may be identified typically form long-standing relationships with client organizations. Certain organizations with sophisticated recruitment practices have identified that there is a strategic advantage in outsourcing people. In this process, complete responsibility for all workforce recruitment may be delegated to external agencies. In such arrangements the external recruitment services providers may not only physically locate talents or 'embed' their resourcing team(s) within the client organization's offices, but also collaborate with the senior human resource management team in developing the longer-term resourcing strategy and human resources plan.

In the global competitive business environment today, most companies tend to adapt a cosmopolitan approach to lead the market and concentrate more on local markets. It has various other implications as well. HR patterns are being tested in industrial organizations in developing countries including the USA and Canada to better manage external distances and develop leaders with capabilities to bridge international and national differences. The economic benefit-driven HR strategy in an organization can be developed by minimizing the global–local socio-economic differences and cultures. However, such strategic vision might limit a country-specific perspective towards the amount of industry services that need international talents and the extents of political ideology that allow to the share the domestic rate of employment (Ghemawat 2011).

Talent Search Organizations

The Talent Search Organizations (TSO) function as third-party recruiters that seek out candidates on demand of client firms. These organizations are generally more aggressive in searching best candidates than in-house recruiters. They use advanced sales techniques, such as initially posing as clients to gather employee contacts, as well as visiting candidates' offices. In order to attract good candidates, TSOs need strong brand equity of client firms. A desirable brand affiliation in conjunction with inspirational leadership appeals to talented young candidates, who show potentials and interest in an accelerated career track and acquisition of skills and experience at a fast pace. The TSO can successfully search talent if the client firm has a meritocratic culture and value. For instance, talent strategies that work at the home company may probably need extensive tailoring to gain competitive advantage. In some job markets, proficiency in English may impede spotting talent. It's critical to develop a core of local talent and to embrace and leverage diversity. In the talent race, a local company that creates genuine opportunities and exhibits the desired cultural conditions will often win out over a Western multinational offering higher pay (Ready et al. 2008). TSOs generate their own lists of candidates, and sometimes also buy databases of prospects. They may prepare a candidate for the interview, help negotiate the salary, and conduct closure to the search. TSOs hold memberships in industries and trade associations. They operate on a small scale with high margins on the candidate placements.

Firms can fill the talent gap in their company through various low cost and high benefit strategies instead of engaging external TSOs in the recruitment process. It is suggested that by talking to employees before they make their retirement plans, firms can optimize chances of finding mutually beneficial work arrangements such as flexible hours, telecommuting, part-time or temporary work, and job sharing. In a way, smart companies build loyal workers and look around for new challenges to contribute their time and talent (Cynthia 2008). Niche Placement Agencies (NPA) are the specialized firms in a talent search for professional and scientific sectors like health care, marine engineering, energy production, petroleum, and aviation industry. Because of their focus, these firms produce superior results and drive resources for developing specific skills. The specialization of NPAs in staffing allows them to search for better candidates within predefined demographic segments, develop large proprietary databases, and cater to the demand of client firms in short notice. These Niche firms are focused on developing long-term relationships with their candidates. A larger number of employers tends to undertake their own in-house recruitment, using human resources department of the firm. The front-line hiring managers and recruitment personnel, who handle targeted functions and prospecting candidates, support these operations. In addition to coordinating with the external agencies mentioned above, in-house recruiters may advertise job vacancies on their own websites, coordinate internal employee referrals, work with external associations, trade groups and focus on campus graduate recruitment of reputed institutes. While job postings are common, networking is by far the most significant approach when reaching out to fill positions.

Most hybrid firms[1] in the manpower placement industry attempting to combine the research aspects (discovering passive candidates) of recruiting, training, and developing a strategic fit between the candidates and job designs to hire them for their clients. These firms provide competitive passive candidate intelligence to support company's recruiting efforts. However, recruitment of people in sales organizations should be taken as an asset building exercise in the firms. Companies should balance develop-versus-buy decisions on human resources by using internal development programs to produce optimum needed talent. However, resource gaps can be filled in with outside hiring. Firms can reduce the risks in forecasting the demand for new positions by sending smaller batches of candidates through better modularized training systems. This process may be similar to the practices of manufacturers, deploying people in just-in-time production and operation lines. Sales organizations can also improve their returns on investment in development efforts by adopting innovative cost-sharing programs and seek to protect their investments by generating internal opportunities to encourage newly trained managers to stick with the firm. Taken together, these principles form the foundation for a new paradigm in human resource management and a talent-on-demand system for the competitive and fast growth business firms (Capelli 2008).

It has been argued over time that more than hiring human resources, retaining them in the firm is a difficult proposition. This appears to be true for the sales firms where every recruit builds his own contribution in terms of market share, client relationship, prospecting strategies and contributing revenue to the firm. If a salesperson leaves the firm, his walking away is considered not only as a gap in the human resources but also loss of market share and of his personalized efforts that contributed to the firm. Fast-moving markets require fast-moving organizations that are continuously refreshed with new talent. None of the firms would like to experience their talents to leave but as said earlier, when a good employee quits, the business is adversely affected. However, a market-driven approach to retention is based on the assumption that long-term, across-the-board loyalty is risk averse. By considering the long-term association with employees, firms need to develop useful retention mechanisms. It is possible to redesign jobs to reduce employee turnover and promote loyalty through particular work teams. Firms can team up with other companies to offer cross-company career paths and when there is no effective way to prevent attrition, firms may resort to the alternative of outsourcing, strengthening recruitment, standardizing jobs, cross-training employees, and organizing work around short-term generalized projects (Capelli 2000).

Organizational Structure

In the *international business division structure*, the firm's activities are separated into two units comprising domestic and international operations. The main function of such an international division is to draw a distinction between its domestic and international business. A worldwide *geographic organization* can overcome the problems associated with the international division structure. In this structure, foreign and domestic operations are not isolated, but are integrated as if foreign boundaries did not exist. Worldwide markets are segregated into geographic areas. Operational responsibility goes to area line managers, whereas corporate headquarters maintain responsibility for wide planning and control. Major attributes of the geographic organizational design of multinational companies are as below:

- Product lines are less diverse
- Products are sold to end users
- Marketing is a critical variable
- Similar channel is used for marketing of all products
- Products are based on the local consumer needs

This organizational design has various advantages markedly delegation of line of authority and explicit responsibility. Specifically, the merits of this system include:

- Responsibility and delegation of line of authority
- Manufacturing and product sales coordination
- Large number of executives
- Conflicts of roles and responsibilities
- Lack of specialists in the product sales line

An important disadvantage in geographic organizational design may be seen when a large number of top-level executives involve in operational tasks, which leads to the conflict in power play and command execution in the organization. Besides the agglomeration of top management personnel, the individual products may suffer, as responsibilities cannot be fixed easily on the operational executives.

A product organization design is different from geographic design wherein a worldwide responsibility is assigned to product group executives at the line management level and emphasis is placed on the product line rather than on geographic differences. The coordination of activities in a geographic area is handled through specialists at the corporate staff level, whereas focus is laid on the performance of product-mix in a given area in the product organization. Multinational companies operating within this structure have a variety of end users, handle diversified product lines with high technological capability, and logistics cost are diverted to the local manufacturers. This type of organizational design has several benefits including:

- Decentralization of authority
- High motivation of the divisional heads
- Adding or dropping new products have marginal impact on operations
- Control of product through the product life cycle.

In this organizational structure, a firm is segregated along product lines considering each division as a separate profit center with the division head directly accountable for profitability. Decentralization of operations is critical in this structure and more decisions are likely to be left to the local manager, who is then usually more highly motivated.

Decentralization of authority is a prime advantage of this structure where division heads are highly motivated. This structure allows the product managers to add new products and product lines, and withdraw the old ones with only marginal effect on the overall operations. Another advantage of this structure is that the control of a product through the product life cycle can be managed more readily and securely. However, firms following this organization structure often face the problem of coordination among product and territory managers. In addition, it is felt that executives quickly turn biased towards the regional and corporate staff in managing any product process.

In recent years, a synergy of all the above organizational structures defined as *matrix structure* has emerged among the multinational companies. The matrix structure offers greater flexibility than the single line of command structures and reconciles this flexibility with coordination and economies of scale to keep the strength of large organizations. The attributes and advantages of matrix organization include:

- Multiple command line
- Product and geographic coordination
- Product lines in a national setting
- Organization design reacts quickly to the local environment demand.

For the multinational firm, the matrix organization is a solution to the problem responding to both economic and political environments. General Electric Company in Asia operates with matrix structure, which has been successful. A matrix organization can encompass geographic and product-management components. However, some of the disadvantages in following this organizational design are power struggles among the supervisory personnel and parallel decision-making.

Besides the above organizational structures, an evolved organization structure blends value systems and action logics of various sectors of the society involving public, private, and voluntary sector in carrying business operations. A multidimensional model of a hybrid organization can be constructed consisting of structure and activities, values and strategy, and governance and politics. Lateral organizations, top-down organizations, and other types of organizational structures can all be combined into a hybrid structure. The hybrid organization can be defined as a complex organizational structure in which more than one organizational design is used. Some of the disadvantages of the hybrid organization include slow decision-making process, bureaucracy, disrupted work cultures, conflict of interest in business operations, and lack of competence in task management and individual accountability.

Despite cross-cultural organizational and power controlled organizational designs, often operationalizing a predetermined organizational system for manufacturing companies at international destinations has been challenging. A variety of factors account for poor productivity and cost outcomes as discussed below (Changali et al. 2015):

- Poor organization due to political and economic policy limitations in the international destination has one of the pertinent problems in managing the manufacturing platforms. In view of the above often, decision-making and manufacturing processes do not converge with the speed and scale of manufacturing planned for. The manufacturing and logistics teams typically negotiate the project, and this is usually dense and complicated. When a problem comes up, project managers may not understand how to proceed. There are different levels of planning, from high-end preparation to day-by-day programs. If the daily work is not finished, schedulers need to know but often do not, so that they can update priorities in real time.
- Inadequate communication among the policy makers, manufacturers, and employees in managing the company. Inconsistencies in working with subcontractors and contractors in manufacturing and marketing process. Often the manufacturing companies face off-industry and off-market stream operational issues as owners of the company in international destinations have cross-cultural management concerns and do not have a common understanding of how the project need to carried out or how it is performing at any given time. Companies periodically review the needs for improvement in various functions ranging from manufacturing to marketing and develop communication plans accordingly with the respective teams of employees. The result is that necessary equipment may not be in place. Companies defer to familiar people and teams rather than asking where they can find the best people for each job.
- Due to the communication gap within the manufacturing organization and their contractual counterparts, the performance on production and trade practices are often questionable in the

international destinations. Consequently, unresolved issues stack up because of lack of communication and accountability.

These problems are serious, systemic, and often common. However, some companies do manage to succeed. Design-to-market and Design-to-value are two distinguished touch points in an international market that manufacturing companies try to achieve rigorously. The design-to-market phenomenon is based on understanding and minimizing the elements that matches the consumer preferences, customization, and market competitiveness while the design-to-value concepts on one hand explain customer satisfaction and the minimal technical solution necessary value-added requirements on the other. These two concepts are used to justify capital investments to what extent it is required no more, no less. Consider the example of two utility companies who needed to build a similar substation building. According to the common economic observation, low-paying, low-skilled jobs that most American companies do not want or let other nations such as China to fabricate on offshore contracts, compete largely in the global market on cost parameters. Offshoring has driven the economy of the USA to focus on business services and advanced technology products where its comparative advantage truly lies. Manufacturing employment losses could be explained as a resultant of low-cost production abroad, productivity gains decreasing the need for labor, and a natural shift away from manufacturing toward a knowledge-based service economy (Nager and Atkinson 2015).

In recent years, many concepts for organizational excellence have put greater emphasis on employees making the recruitment process more goal oriented. This refers to the need for increased participation human resource personnel in the recruitment process for change on one hand, and drives more intensive approaches on choosing appropriate methods of selecting potential employees to augment the productivity and organizational growth. In view of low budgetary provisions, firms focus on single aspects, such as recruitment process design and evaluating various human resources concepts by short-term cost factors, which does not yield encouraging results in many cases. Therefore, more holistic concepts are needed to realize a sustainable success in the organization. Among others factors, demands for the development of organizational culture are crucial to acquire and retain potential employees (Zink 2008). It has been argued that to build a highly competent organization of highly skilled employees, firms may not simply engage human resources in hiring the best and brightest candidates, and then turn them loose into a Darwinian competition of survival of the fittest. Organizations need to provide and maintain the right environment for these employees to flourish, which indicates avoiding a number of common pitfalls, such as, often mistakenly believing that one individual can single-handedly turn around an entire department or organization, and overestimating the importance of pay as compared to the talent. Firms often commit mistakes by providing employee autonomy to achieve goals, which makes them carry overload of tasks. Such tendency of achieving goals in short span may cause various functional risks. However, achievements under such practices may appear by chance and not by design. Many firms may also be biased assuming that high performers need efficient colleagues throughout the organization in order to continuously improve talent in the organization (Groysberg et al. 2010).

Innovation, Technology, and Research and Development

Innovation is the critical dimension of economic change in a macro perspective and business growth within the micro perspective. At the macro level, economic change revolves around innovation and catalyzes entrepreneurial activities that lead to drive market power. As the market competition is continuously increasing in the global marketplace, the innovation-driven market power could provide better results than the conventional wisdom like price and promote competition. Alongside product design and strategy innovation, technological innovation often creates ad hoc monopolies in the market allowing abnormal profits in a short life cycle. Such temporary monopolies are sometimes necessary to provide incentives for firms to develop new products and processes (Pol and Carroll 2006). Increasing public debt and social entitlement outlays in some countries increase trade and economic commitments to generate additional space for near-term financial support through various forms of investments in innovation and technology. In order to attract better investment opportunities, fiscal policy of the country should concentrate on enhancing market demand and longer-term potential growth in key business and economic indicators. More broadly, accommodative macroeconomic policies must be accompanied by structural reforms that can counteract waning potential growth including efforts to boost labor force participation, improve the matching process in labor markets, and promote investment in research and development and innovation. Economies with large and rising non-financial debt, unhedged foreign liabilities, or heavy reliance on short-term borrowing to fund longer-term investments must adopt stronger risk management practices and contain currency and balance sheet mismatches (International Monetary Fund 2016).

Globalization has prompted many sources of growth open to the firms operating in mature markets, which has stimulated them in launching unique, superior products with a compelling value proposition to gain the competitive advantage. However, few companies bring their bold innovation to the market, while improvements and modifications to existing products are taken up by most of the firms. Improvement in the existing products and services is not an innovation as such change serves the firm to only maintain existing market share, rather than growing business. Innovations can be successful if the following strategies are meticulously adopted by the firms (Cooper 2012):

- Linking innovation strategy with the development efforts by exploring opportunities in potential markets as Apple managed its innovation of *i*-phone and *i*-pad,
- Nurturing the right workplace ambiance and culture for innovation under the leadership of senior executives, as found at General Electric Company and 3M,
- Setting up stage for seeding proactive ideas, carrying them through a system of innovation evolution as Swarovski and Swatch built their market though continuous efforts on innovation and branding, and
- Stepping into the idea launch process and managing the large and complex processes of driving an innovation to market.

It is necessary for the firms to adopt a right project selection method to cater to an innovation requirement. Thinking of an innovation is easy but making the same work is a challenging task. A cost-effective innovation is creeping to its popularity in developing countries and BRICS (Brazil, Russia, India, China, and South Africa) emerging markets where entrepreneurs face global challenges amidst paucity of resources but hold high market potentials. Such innovations offer low-cost solutions but exhibit attributes of being robust, consumer-friendly and high target potential at large and bottom-of-the-pyramid demographics. Such innovations are grown locally and are positioned initially in a niche. Scaling low cost innovations gives rise to various financial and managerial challenges. However, once such innovations are successful in large-scale operation they could pose major threats to the established commercial brands of the multinational company as a disruptive innovation. Bringing local innovations to commercial scale is subject to successfully managing various operational factors including cost, active demand, developing a sustainable business model, diffusion of innovation, social networking and demonstrating use value, effective entrepreneurial leadership, and managing corporate reputation (Soman et al. 2012).

Successful innovation leads to customer involvement and profits, which can be achieved through the co-creation by aligning consumers and market players in the innovation process. Some multinational companies have invested resources taking advantage of social media to diffuse new ideas and stimulating co-creation of innovative products and services. For many companies, developing new products does not occur as a chance or coincidence but innovative products emerge through careful attention to many important criteria. Firms should analyze their innovation practices and capabilities to become more effective in driving innovation as breakthrough and gain the competitive advantage. The contribution of employees towards innovation in products, services or strategy signifies the value and quality of innovation portfolio of an organization and projects the innovation effectiveness curve of the company (Kandybin 2009). Firms may involve in innovation process routinely understanding various perspectives in generating and managing innovative ideas. Firms need to understand some issues concerning the following tools to carry out the innovation process:

- Ideas come from anywhere. Everyone in the organization needs to be alert to catch and process it,
- It is necessary to stay democratic during churning ideas and developing innovative concepts,
- Brainstorming is the right way to steer the innovative ideas and filter them through the measures of economic viability and technological feasibility in order to take the innovation process to next level,
- One idea at a time is an ideal proposition to handle the innovation process analysis,
- Listening actively to others to analyze their standpoints and insights is an essential requirement for the innovation managers. This would

also help in borrowing insights and building concepts on social debates,
- Innovation activists in an organization should be open to criticism. They can further analyze constructive criticism and discard carefully the destructive comments,
- Innovation is a spontaneous impetus and voluntary effort. So organizations should refrain from making any sanctions to the employees involved in innovation process, if not successful,
- Initiatives in innovation process should be driven by strong organizational leadership and develop a sense of belongingness in carrying out such innovation,
- There is an immense need to maintain the information base during the innovation process as the innovation of products or services is an evidence-based and largely data-driven approach.
- The new phenomenon of product innovation is co-creation, which requires subject matter experts and customers to get involved and stay abreast during the process, and
- Carrying innovation though diverse groups is a boon as well a risk leading to behavioral conflicts and less proven facts.

Breakthrough innovations in markets are a continuous process, which is backed by the distribution, retailing, and services industry. Innovations leading to commercial breakthroughs demonstrate a highly skewed distribution of use value of inventions explaining that some are useless, a few are of moderate value, and there is rarely one that qualifies as a breakthrough. Those breakthroughs embed the long tail of innovation, and distribution plays a key role in the breakthrough process. It is necessary for firms to account for the total number of inventions a company generates, the average score out of the mean value of those inventions, and to count the number of successful breakthrough inventions. Such corporate awareness may help in developing a strategic balance between individual innovation workers and teams. Greater team diversity stimulates in generating higher involvement in working with breakthrough innovations. Thus, it is first and foremost requirement for the companies to introspect within the organization and identify how they want to improve their innovation process, take appropriate measures to drive the innovative products and services as breakthrough, and contrary to that, address any deficiencies in the process. Such dynamism in innovation process would allow the companies to improve their competencies and capabilities to innovate in ways that make the best sense for the organization and market (Fleming 2007).

Innovation and enterprise integration are two compelling sources of growth in a dynamic competitive marketplace. The ability to coordinate across organizational boundaries largely appears as a critical factor in determining the speed and life cycle of a market-driven innovation. Innovations need to be integrated into the larger operations of the corporation at sufficient level of scale to show a prolific impact on business and sustainability in the marketplace. Many large businesses spend resources on innovations but fail to capitalize on them. However, some organizations use innovations to optimize local operations than integrating them to create consumer value and corporate image. Large organizations spread the innovation tasks among two groups comprising innovation facilities group (IFG) and an innovation assimilation group. The IFG members provide organizational support on the techniques to carry out innovations and applications for the new technology. Firms also engage the innovation facilities group to explore new developments in the marketplace on the concept, prototypes, or breakthrough of the innovation and impart expert services for in-house initiatives to nurture the innovation within the organization. The innovation assimilation group acts as policy support unit to drive innovation to market. The members of this team provide resources to launch innovation and integrate operations into the business model of the firm. Firms need the above support teams to diffuse innovation and make it more (Cash et al. 2008).

The innovation assimilation group should help in developing the task map for the innovation team and integrate the process map by identifying the goal from the perspectives of consumers. By mapping out every step of the innovation task, companies can effectively manage the innovation process (Bettencourt and Ulwick 2008). A firm that engages simultaneously a high degree of both innovation quality and operational efficiency, gains a higher competitive advantage in the market in reference to prescribed and perceived quality of the innovation. Few firms are able to balance innovation quality and operational efficiency. Such management skills are referred as ambidextrous strategy, which differentiates firms and their products from the competing products and helps them enjoy a temporary monopoly in the market (Sarkees and Hulland 2008). Firms must ensure that all innovations should encompass attributes of four A's comprising awareness, acceptability, availability, and affordability to diffuse innovation in the overall market.

Innovation should always be customer-centric. For example, innovation in consumer health evolves through novel options around dietary products, consumer convenience, higher perceived value, and improved delivery mechanisms. Consumers intend to seek quick and effective solutions to prevent and treat minor ailments and provide low fat-high fiber diet products. Improved formulations provide relief via novel delivery mechanisms that make drugs easy to swallow or apply. New product development concepts have shifted towards herbal and quasi-traditional products, and dietary supplements as regulatory procedures are being revised in various markets across the destinations in the world. In case of consumer products in developed markets, health is one common theme for many soft drinks new products. Other areas of innovation are in creating products that combine the characteristics of two categories, and using packaging to create a product with unique benefits. There is a different set of opportunities for new products in developing markets than in developed markets. Global new product development in soft drinks was driven in 2012 by manufacturers' desire to add value to their products across developed and emerging markets alike. Key drivers for these products included the continued demand for beverage functionality, the consumer search for healthier soft drinks, and the expansion of both exotic and traditional flavors.

Since the beginning of the twenty-first century, the growth in investments toward Global Research and Development (R&D) is being driven in Asian countries in general and China in particular. Asian countries including China, Japan, India, and South Korea now account for more than 40% of overall global R&D investments, with North American investments now less than 30% and European investments slightly more than 20%. However, North America comprising the USA, Canada, and Mexico continue to lose global R&D share values on a yearly basis. The R&D investments in China had shown the annual growth of over 10% since the 1990s but has slowed down to less than 7% during 2016, which is still several times the growth rates of both the USA. and Europe whose annual growth rates are in the 2–3% bracket. The rest of the world accounts for a combined 8.8% of the global R&D investments with combined average growth of only about 1.5% annually. R&D investments during 2015–2016 in the USA continue to face restrictions on total federal government spending on R&D and the slow increase in industrial

R&D spending. Despite these problems on R&D support, the USA continues to be the largest single country in R&D investments with slightly more than a quarter of all global R&D spending. These R&D programs are supported by industrial investments (66%), federal government supported investments (25%) and academic/non-profit investments (7%).

In general, R&D is funded by the federal government, industry, academia, and non-profit organizations who perform varying levels of that research along with FFRDC (Federally Funded R&D Centers). There are substantial changes that are being seen in the character of the USA's industrial R&D makeup. Life science R&D, for more than ten years, has been the largest sector in the industrial technology arena. In other industrial areas, most global automotive companies are expected to grow their R&D programs due to strong technology shifts from internal combustion to electric propulsion systems, manual to automated driving systems and increasingly integrated electronic systems.[2] In terms of innovation quality and the international dimension of patent applications, the USA holds the top place among the developed countries, followed by the UK, Japan, Germany, and Switzerland. Top scoring middle-income economies are narrowing the gap on innovation quality: China leads this group, followed by Brazil and India, fueled by an improvement in the quality of higher education institutions. Innovation achievers seem to perform strongest in market sophistication, and knowledge and technology outputs. At low-income levels, countries that outperform their peers focus on removing structural obstacles to innovation, such as poor access to finance and poor linkages within the innovation systems. Emphasis in emerging countries should be placed on gaining knowledge as much as on providing the right framework conditions that stimulate a process of innovation and knowledge diffusion in reference to gaining political stability and supportive institutions, and developing good and widespread technical education to enhance absorptive capacity. However, there is a growing concern among countries to develop stronger links and interaction between publicly funded research institutes and private companies (Cornell University, INSEAD, and WIPO 2015).

International Investments

Multinational enterprises are an important part of the international economy. Through international direct investment, they bring substantial benefits to home and host countries in the form of productive capital, managerial and technological expertise, job creation and tax revenues. The investment objectives of a multinational company should reflect the following issues:

- Ensure that the operations of enterprises are in harmony with government policies;
- Strengthen the basis of mutual confidence between enterprises and the societies in which they operate;
- Improve the foreign investment climate; and,
- Enhance contribution of the enterprise to sustainable development.

An investment proposal is a type of abridged business plan designed specifically to meet the information needs of potential investors. It focuses on the management, marketing and financial aspects of the company that would make it an attractive investment. There are two stages of an investment proposal—selling of the proposal, and its review. The process of selling and reviewing should go through a variety of formal and informal procedural follow-ups and negotiations. Successful international companies continue to be interested in growth prospects, evaluating a variety of proposals from different sources that could potentially lead to investments abroad. These sources include company employees, unknown host country firms, licensees, distributors, and joint venture partners.

Most companies aim at going global and choose to invest extensively through joint ventures, subsidiaries, or making foreign direct investments in potential destinations. The objective of corporate venturing is to gain a competitive advantage by responding quickly to changes in markets and managing local threats. Customer-centric investments in destination countries earn attractive returns. During their first 3 years as public companies, firms backed by corporate venture funds show better stock price performance than those companies backed by traditional venture capital. Most companies meticulously align their goals with the investment so that they can focus on right portfolios. Most companies streamline their decision process to optimize the returns.

Companies need to invest as much in learning from their start-ups as in making and overseeing deals (Lerner 2013). Some companies have seen their venture initiatives fail, and even firms with successful funds have struggled to make use of the knowledge gained from start-up investments. Multinational company must follow the guidelines given below while drafting and pursuing the investment proposals with the governments or organizations of the host countries:

- Focus the investment proposal specific to the requirements of the country or region
- Develop necessary convergence with the macro policies of the country
- Delineate the approval points and schedules
- Check with all the people whose approval is needed
- Define alternative goals and approaches
- Determine the key indicators for all business proposal
- Prospect for selling the proposal at reasonable bid to optimize long-term gains
- Establish priorities and develop activity schedule accordingly
- Be on the competitive edge along with participating bidders and draw defense for the project in terms of project execution and achievements
- Identify any potential competitors of the project and any points of potential resistance, and then establish strategies, or at least mental contingency plans to deal with them.
- Measure the proposal against all stated corporate policy objectives
- Write the proposal in the prescribed format with the required information only
- Prepare strong defense for all possible objections on the investment project
- Try to keep the project moving forward at a deliberate speed. Don't let it get stalled by excessive reviewing.

In measuring investment in North America, both the Middle East and Latin America and the Caribbean recorded strong growth in FDI in 2013. Ontario was the top state in the region with $7.23 billion invested in 2013. Quebec and North Carolina were the two fastest-growing states, with respective investments of $3.93 billion and $1.88 billion. FDI into North America declined by 1.36% in 2013, with the region attracting $58.06 billion over the year compared with $58.86 billion in 2012. The number of projects in 2013 decreased by 0.77%, falling from 1693 to 1680, and job creation rose by 4.48%, up from 135,385 new jobs in 2012 to 141,452 in 2013. In 2013, FDI into Latin America and the Caribbean more than doubled from $69.37 billion in 2012 to

\$139.81 billion. Project numbers increased 10.18% from 1198 to 1320, and the region experienced a 20.54% increase in jobs created. The top three source countries, Brazil, Mexico and Bermuda, all more than doubled their outbound capital investment in 2013, accounting for more than 70% of FDI from the region (FDI Report 2014).

The systematic appraisal and professional management of all capital projects helps to ensure that the best choices are made and the best value for money is obtained. It is not enough to be satisfied that the investment is justified; it is also necessary to ensure that it produces its planned benefits at minimum costs. These costs include the ongoing current costs generated by the use of capital asset, as well as the initial capital cost. The appraisal stage involves two separate tasks: preliminary appraisal and detailed appraisal. The preliminary appraisal aims to establish if there is a sufficiently good prima facie case for considering a project in depth. It leads to the recommendation, whether or not to proceed to the detailed appraisal stage. A detailed appraisal should only be carried out if justified by the outcome of the preliminary appraisal, and it leads to a recommendation on whether or not to proceed further with the project in principle. However, it is necessary for the multinational companies to carefully review their investment proposals before the appraisal at the government or sponsor's level. The review of the investment proposal may be undertaken on considering the following issues:

- Review and describe the financial sector. Append the basic statistics for each, including assets, deposits and borrowings, capital and reserves, and profits
- Describe the expected growth of internal rate of returns and its management criteria
- Describe the money and capital markets, the different instruments, their terms and conditions, etc. Estimate the total market value of each type
- Describe the foreign exchange regime. Find out which institutions are authorized to deal in foreign exchange rates during the last 5 years
- Explore credit allocated or directed by the government or regulatory authorities to particular market segments, and if there are any subsidized credit schemes in operation
- Describe how the project fits within government's development objectives and policies for the sector.

- Describe the market for the products and services. Provide historical data and forecasts.
- List the main competitors, both domestic and foreign. Give indications of their volumes and market shares. Explore if any of them are planning expansions. Also, find out what will be the likely reaction of competitors to this project
- Review the marketing strategy selected and its justification. Describe preparations for market research, product planning, pricing strategies, distribution, promotional programs, advertising, selling and so forth.
- Describe planned human resources management for the project, including the availability of personnel. There is also need to describe relevant laws, regulations, and practices. Indicate the cost of staff at all levels.
- Describe proposed training programs and programs for localization, if relevant.
- Provide detailed plans for raising the required capital. Provide assumptions and details of pre-operating expenses and how they will be funded and accounted for.
- Provide projected balance sheet, profit and loss account, and cash flow projections for the first 3 years of operation, stating detailed assumptions, especially rate and spread assumptions.
- Compute various measures of performance as appropriate, such as risk assets to capital, operating ratios, return on assets and return on equity.
- Compute sensitivity analyses at various levels of business relative to the base assumption, and
- Discuss realistically the risks involved in carrying out the project, including market, government regulations, management, labor, competition, system failures and so forth. Then review how these risks will be guarded against.

The review process of an investment proposal is determined by the perspectives of the management board of a company. Often the process and philosophy of the review is leader-centric and it changes dramatically with a new person at the helm. In any event, most companies have a comprehensive system for reviewing investment proposals and all strive to determine whether or not the investment will provide long-term, lasting benefits for the owners. A framework for evaluation can be laid out considering the variables suggested for review of the investment proposal. In the final analysis, the evaluation should provide the cost/benefit effects of the project for the host country, Parent Corporation, and foreign subsidiary.

The financial objectives of the multinational companies are aimed at measuring the performance of the capital employed. Capital employed is the sum of all assets along with the accumulated reserves for depreciation. The multinational companies may recognize while setting targets, that not all operations are directly comparable, and state that targets for area profit centers and operations the nature of the operations and performance plans must be taken into account. Emphasis on asset management by the multinational company at all levels is laid in reference to annual targets for cash generation, capital expenditures, and balance sheet items including inventory and receivables management. The finance managers of the company pay special attention to the differences between actual cash-generating capacity and book results. Each production group and profit center of product categories develop net cash-generating capacity for its own requirements, and also pools up sufficient funds for the company to meet its high-priority investment commitments and opportunities. Financial objectives constitute the foundation for making financial decisions for a company. The companies should be able to integrate the financial objectives for both domestic and international business. For example, in order to protect against exchange rate fluctuations, a firm might require managers in the overseas subsidiaries to regularly forecast the exchange rates month-by-month. Based on these forecasts, corporate funds in a currency likely to be substantially depreciated would be utilized before funds in stronger currencies. Fluctuations in the foreign exchange rates adversely affect the domestic and international investments due to uncertainty in economy and returns on investments in the long term. The foreign direct investment in the USA by North American countries is exhibited in Table 5.2.

Among various sectors, foreign direct investment in the USA mining sector tripled from $8 billion in 2013 to $25 billion in 2014. Professional, scientific, and technical services were the second fastest-growing sectors, more than doubling to $14 billion in 2014 from $5 billion in 2013. Manufacturing ranked third in growth, received an additional $52 billion more in foreign direct investment in 2014 over the previous year. Foreign direct investment in the USA was down in several key sectors in 2014 from a year earlier, including banking, information,

Table 5.2 Foreign direct investment in the USA: contributions of Canada and Mexico (In million dollars)

Country	*2009*	*2010*	*2011*	*2012*	*2013*	*2014*	*2009–2014 (%)*
Canada	30,366	7357	18,790	16,398	24,153	21,116	−30
Mexico	2469	123	2432	776	3508	2421	−2

Source Foreign direct investment in the USA, organization for international investment, Washington, DC

and in finance and insurance. By far, the largest decline was in holding companies. The industry's $2 billion inward investment in 2013 was followed by a massive $125 billion disinvestment the following year 2014. The divestment by British Vodafone of Verizon was largely responsible for this. International firms engage heavily in US manufacturing. Chemicals, with $340 billion in cumulative foreign direct investment by the end of 2014, represented a third of all foreign investment in manufacturing. Foreign companies spend billions annually in the US chemicals industry because it boasts a highly educated workforce, excellent research centers, strong intellectual property protections, and a robust regulatory system. About half of all foreign investment stock in US chemicals was in the pharmaceuticals and medicines sector through 2014 (Organization for International Investment 2016).

Exchange rates are volatile and can lead to sizeable losses in business. The foreign exchange rate measures the price of one currency in terms of another. A convertible currency can legally be exchanged for another convertible currency at a given rate of exchange. A currency is partially convertible when it can be legally used to purchase foreign exchange to finance only certain transactions. An increase in the exchange rate of a country may be expressed as a depreciation of the value of US dollars to buy one unit of the other currency. During the era of gold exchange standards, the exchange rates between the currencies were determined by the ratio of weights of gold defining the currencies. The exchange rates are of two categories spot exchange rate and forward exchange rate. The spot exchange rates are quoted for delivery of the currency purchased within a period of 2 days while the forward exchange rate quotations are for the prices agreed today that sustain for delivery at one of the future dates—maybe 1–3 months ahead. These quotations are usually made by commercial banks and other customized maturities may be negotiated.

The foreign currencies are bought at the spot for many reasons that include finance for imports, buying foreign assets such as bonds and real estate etc. Most users of the forward market engage in swap transactions, in which the same currency is bought and sold simultaneously but is delivered at two different points of time. Swift movements in the exchange rates occur with changes in the international economic and diplomatic relations between the countries. Change in the expectations of the market participants also affects the exchange rates. In the long-run interaction among the currencies is shaped by the political and economic conditions. For example, the long-standing stability in the political and economic systems over decades in Germany and USA makes their currencies safe These currencies are thus viewed as safe. On the contrary, the currencies of Brazil, Israel, and Mexico lost their purchasing power as they faced hyperinflation in the recent past (Rajagopal 2007).

Arbitrage and Hedging

In reference to the literature on economics and finance, arbitrage may be explained as the practice of taking advantage of a price difference between two or more markets at the same time. In arbitrage, companies strike a combination of matching deals that could capitalize profit exploiting the difference between the prices of identical financial instrument across the markets. In financial management context, an arbitrage may be understood as a transaction that involves risk-free profit at low transaction costs. For instance, an arbitrage could be exercised when there is the opportunity to instantaneously buy low and sell high of identical financial instruments across the markets. This is a very common practice followed by the multinational companies through their financial agents or corporate fund managers.

The securities, futures, and derivatives industries are among the most regulated businesses in many countries. At the same time, professionals in these markets have to adjust to a business environment transformed and made more competitive by new technologies, where once-reliable businesses have abruptly become unprofitable and novel business models unimagined only a few years ago are viewing for competitive footholds, and by the globalization of the financial markets. The arbitraging activity may be also be explained as the purchase or sale of an instrument and the simultaneous taking of an equal and opposite position in a related instrument to exploit mispricing. The simultaneous purchase and sale of an asset in order to profit from a difference in the price have emerged as one of the significant activities of companies in the financial markets. Most private sector companies having public equities are engaged in arbitrage to enhance profit and stakeholder values by playing with their financial instruments across the primary markets. Arbitrage is a trade that profits by exploiting price differences of identical or similar financial instruments, in different markets or in different forms.

Arbitrage is followed by public equity companies as there is always a risk in the financial markets as a result of market inefficiencies, and this strategy provides a mechanism to ensure the prices do not deviate substantially from fair value for long periods of time. As the financial markets in the twenty-first century have grown along the technology support, arbitrage has turned as a computerized trading system set to monitor fluctuations in similar financial instruments. Any inefficient pricing set-ups are usually acted upon quickly and the chances of trading at low or unyielding prices are eliminated in a matter of seconds. For example, if the same index contract is traded in two different exchanges, it should trade at the same price in both exchanges. If the prices are not the same, an arbitrageur will buy at the cheaper price and immediately sell at a more expensive price in the other market, making a guaranteed profit. The arbitrage channel is an area which exists both above and below the fair value of a future, within which no arbitrage will take place. This is because additional costs, such as exchange fees, bid/offer spreads, and commissions will exceed arbitrage profits within this channel. Thus, the width of the channel depends on the costs incurred by the participant in the marketplace.

Globalization has driven the capital markets open up for large and emerging companies to work with a powerful mechanism for arbitrage across national financial markets to augment their profits. However, to gain a competitive advantage in the internal markets companies need to balance the opportunities in the financial markets with the challenges of operating financial instruments in multiple markets. To minimize competition, companies choose to stay constrained and underinvest in the arbitrage unless banks have sufficient reputational capital. This problem arises when mispricing of financial instruments is large. More competition among financiers, higher arbitrageur wealth, and allowing for explicit contracts affect the sustainability of corporate finance and primary financial markets. Buying and selling the financial instruments largely depends on stakeholder relations with the company and trust of stakeholders on the financial markets that would be valuable for mitigating the risk in arbitrage (Kondo and Papanikolaou 2015).

Often the assets being arbitraged are identical in a more complicated way, for example, they are different sorts of financial securities that are each exposed to identical risks. Some kinds of arbitrage are completely risk-free—this is pure arbitrage. For instance, if euros are available more cheaply in dollars in London than in New York, arbitrageurs can make a risk-free profit by buying euros in London and selling an equal of them in New York. The scope of absolute arbitrage has become unusual in recent years, by the increasing concern on the globalization of financial markets. Today, a lot of so-called arbitrage, much of it done by hedge funds, involves assets that have some similarities but are not identical. Hedging involves deliberately taking on a new risk that offsets an existing one, such as your exposure to an adverse change in an exchange rate, interest rate or in a commodity price. Hedging is most often done by commodity producers, traders, and financial institutions. More recently, firms have hedged using financial instruments and derivatives. Hedging sounds prudent, but some economists reckon that firms should not do it because it reduces their value to shareholders. The arbitrage pricing theory says that the price of a financial asset reflects a few key risk factors, such as the expected rate of interest, and how the price of the asset changes relative to the price of a portfolio of assets. If the price of an asset happens to diverge from what the theory says it should be, arbitrage by investors should bring it back into line (Rajagopal 2007). Hedging may be defined as a strategy to reduce the risk of investments from adverse price movements of financial instruments. Normally, a hedge consists of taking an offsetting position in a related security, such as a futures contract.

Hedging is an investment intended to offset potential losses and gains that may be incurred by the investment. In simple language, a hedge investment is used to reduce any substantial losses suffered by an individual or an organization. A hedge fund can be constructed from many types of financial instruments, including public equity, exchange-traded funds, insurance, forward contracts, swaps, options, many types of over-the-counter and derivative products, and futures contracts. Public futures markets were established in the nineteenth century to allow transparent, standardized, and efficient hedging of agricultural commodity prices. They have since expanded to include futures contracts for hedging the values of energy, precious metals, foreign currency, and interest rate fluctuations. Companies generally delegate responsibility for managing a derivatives portfolio to in-house financial experts and the company's financial advisers because the inventiveness of modern financial markets makes it possible for companies to double or even triple their capacity to invest in their strategic assets and competencies.

Notes

1. A *hybrid company* can be identified whose responsibility is limited by guarantees of its stakeholders and amount of contributed capital. The hybrid companies enjoy the status of private, public, and voluntary sector domains. Such companies blend elements, value systems and action logics like social impact and profit generation) of various sectors of society. Shareholders and Warrantors build the hybrid companies. The first category of members belong to public domain. The second category of members is not in the public domain, although many sport clubs or voluntary organizations determined by guarantees of their members, and new members joining these companies become warrantors.
2. R & D Magazine. 2016 Global R & D Funding Forecast, Winter, 2016(file:///D:/Academic%20documents/Books/Palgrave%20 Book%206/Material/R&D%202016.pdf Retrieved on February 26, 2017)

References

Bettencourt, L. A., & Ulwick, A. W. (2008). The customer-centered innovation map. *Harvard Business Review, 86*(5), 109–114.

Bradley, S., & Taylor, J. (1996). Human capital formation and local economic performance. *Regional Studies, 30*(1), 1–14.

Capelli, P. (2000). Market driven approach to retaining talent. *Harvard Business Review, 78*(1), 103–111.

Capelli, P. (2008). Talent management for the twenty first century. *Harvard Business Review, 86*(3), 74–81.

Cappelli, P. (2001). Market-driven approach to retaining talent. *Harvard Business Review, 83*(1), 25–32.

Cash, J. I., Earl, M. J., & Morison, R. (2008). Teaming up to crack innovation and enterprise integration. *Harvard Business Review, 86*(10), 90–99.

Changali, S., Mohammad, A., & Nieuwland, M. (2015). *The construction productivity imperative*. New York: McKinsey & Co.

Cooper, R. (2012, March 15). *Creating bold innovation in mature markets, IESE-Insight Magazine*.

Cornell University, INSEAD, & WIPO. (2015). *The global innovation index 2015: effective innovation policies for development*, Fontainebleau, Ithaca, and Geneva.

Cynthia, M. P. (2008). *How to close the talent gap*. Harvard Business School, Boston, MA: Harvard Business Publishing Newsletter.

FDI Report. (2014). *Global greenfield investment trends*, The FDI Report, The Financial Times Ltd., London. Retrieved on February 26, 2017 from http://ftbsites.ft.com/forms/fDi/report2014/files/The_fDi_Report_2014.pdf.

Fleming, I. (2007). Breakthroughs and the "Long Tail" of Innovation. *Sloan Management Review, 49*(1), 69–74.

Gellerman, S. W. (1990). Tastes of a good salesperson. *Harvard Business Review, 68*(3), 64–65.

Ghemawat, P. (2011). The cosmopolitan corporation. *Harvard Business Review, 89*(5), 92–99.

Groysberg, B., Lee, L. E., & Abrahams, R. (2010). What it takes to make 'Star' hires pay off. *Sloan Management Review, 51*(2), 57–61.

International Monetary Fund. (2016). World economic outlook, subdued demand: Symptoms and remedies, International monetary fund.

Joerres, J. A., & Bernstein, A. (2016). Globalization. *Robots, and the Future of Work, Harvard Business Review, 94*(10), 74–79.

Kandybin, A. (2009). Which innovation efforts will pay? *Sloan Management Review, 51*(1), 53–60.

Kiriazov, D., Sullivan, S. E., & Tu, H. S. (2000). *Business success in eastern Europe: Understanding and Customizing HRM*. Business Horizons.

Kondo, J. E. & Papanikolaou, D. (2015). Financial Relationships and the Limits to Arbitrage, *Review of Finance, 19*(1), 2095–2138.

Lerner, J. (2013). Corporate Venturing, *Harvard Business Review, 91*(10), 86–94.

Levinson, M. (2017). *U.S. Manufacturing in International Perspective*, Congressional Research Service, CRS Report 7–5700, Washington, DC.

Nager, A. B., & Atkinson, R. D. (2015). *The myth of America's manufacturing renaissance: The real state of U.S. manufacturing*. Washington, DC: The Information Technology and Innovation Foundation. Retrieved online on February 26, 2017 from http://www2.itif.org/2015-myth-american-manufacturing-renaissance.pdf.

Organization for International Investment. (2016). *Foreign Direct Investment in the USA*. Washington, DC: Organization for International Investment. Retrieved on February 27, 2017, from http://ofii.org/sites/default/files/Foreign%20Direct%20Investment%20in%20the%20United%20States%202016%20Report.pdf.

Pol, E. & Carroll, P. (2006). An Introduction to Economics with Emphasis on Innovation (2nd ed.). *Thomson Learning*, NY.

Qu, H., Ryan, B., & Chu, R. (2001). The perceived importance of job attributes among foodservice employees in Hong Kong hotel industry. *International Journal of Hospitality and Tourism Administration, 2*(2), 57–76.

Rajagopal. (2007). *Dynamics of International Trade and Economy: An Inquiry into Emerging Markets.* Hauppauge, New York: Nova Science Publishers Inc.

Rajagopal and Rajagopal, A. (2010). Measuring performance of sale force: Analysis of administrative and behavioral parameters. *International Journal of Economics and Business Research,* 2(5), 399–413.

Ready, D. A., Hill, L. A., & Conger, J. A. (2008). Winning the race for talent in emerging markets. *Harvard Business Review, 86*(11), 62–70.

Rowly, C., & Benson, J. (2002). Convergence and divergence in Asian human resource management. *California Management Review, 44*(2), 90–109.

Sarkees, M., & Hulland, J. S. (2008). Innovation and efficiency: It is possible to have it all. *Business Horizons, 52*(1), 45–55.

Schweitzer, L., & Lyons, S. (2008). The market within: A marketing approach to creating and developing high-value employment relationships. *Business Horizons, 51*(6), 555–565.

Simons, R. L. (2005). Designing high performance jobs. *Harvard Business Review, 83*(7), 54–62.

Soman, D., Kumar, V., Metcalfe, M., & Wong, J. (2012). *Beyond great ideas: A framework for scaling local innovations.* Rotman School of Management.

Sparrow, P. (2007). Globalization of HR at function level: four UK-based case studies of the international recruitment and selection process. *The International Journal of Human Resource Management, 18*(5), 845–867.

Zink, K. J. (2008). Human resources and organizational excellence. *Total Quality Management & Business Excellence, 19*(7), 793–805.

CHAPTER 6

Market Volatility and Risk Factors

Volatility in consumer markets is different from volatility in primary markets. It largely depends on the functional factors in the market such as demand, consumer preferences, supply chain efficiency, innovation and technology, and pricing strategies. The chapter argues that as the thinking is changing, increasing globalization of the markets and technological interventions in business are both pragmatic and philosophical shifts in the international trade models. As such, the products, services life cycles, and investment benchmarks in the international trade are changing frequently causing the volatility in business models. While addressing these factors, this chapter also analyzes the risk factors in international business towards new product development, brand equity, price volatility, and the ubiquitous role of consumer credit in doing business at the destination markets. The chapter argues that the market volatility and evolution of international market space is governed by the forces beyond the control of any company or investor that include government policies, availability of capital, international economic indicators such oil price volatility, and geopolitical conflicts.

Public policy issues in product development and marketing are growing with political concerns towards the customer welfare, competition regulation, and efforts towards bringing balance between the business and society. Customer-oriented governments regulate companies to use marketing tools to match their products policy with civil requirements. The concept of public policy marketing could enable governments to intervene and control the corporate marketing policies in the interest

Rajagopal and V. Zlatev, *Business Dynamics in North America*,
DOI 10.1007/978-3-319-57606-0_6

of citizen. Companies need to develop their product policies based on non-commercial marketing outcomes specific to the context of public administration. They should also analyze the social behavior of products and market policies in reference to the public policies advocated by the government in the destination markets. Thus public policy marketing, though tested in narrow perspectives with ecological, public health, and advertising concerns, both in developed and emerging countries, is expected to grow extensively by the mid-twenty-first century and improve the implementation of the public policy in accordance with the public charters laid jointly by the public–private partnerships (Buurma 2001). New product developers need to be aware of the emerging public policy concerns and consider their impact on product development and launch. Public interventions on new products include the concern about the environment, the results of climate policy, government mandates on fuel emission, and ecological sustainability. Consumer concerns have made the public policy interventions towards the product discount advertising, rebate redemption disclosures, rebate redemption processes, and discounted payment processes in the USA. With respect to the above public policy, federal guidelines have been laid for announcing discounts and discount related complaints of consumers (Pechmann and Silk 2013). The product-related public intervention policies envelop various social and public concerns but more prominently look into the following areas:

- Product liability
  - Guarantees and warrantees
  - Returns and recall policies
  - Defects in manufacturing
  - Services liabilities
- Design defects
  - Dangerous Condition
  - No Safety Device
  - Inadequate Materials
- Product vulnerability
  - Product packaging
  - Manufacturing defects
  - Adequate instructions
  - After-use dangers
  - Legal issues

- Environmental concerns
  - During manufacturing process
  - Exploiting natural resources
  - Disposal of industrial waste

Various product related matters like breach of product liabilities, user issues due to defects in product design, product vulnerability due to packaging and non-compliance to the legal standards, and environmental concerns of products towards manufacturing and disposal draw government intervention through implementing the public policies. Socio-political concerns for environmental improvement impose regulations on the companies engaged in developing new products that can conflict with market operations and shareholder values. Differentiating products along environmental lines is a conceptually straightforward way of reconciling corporate strategies with public policies. Since the last decade of the twentieth century companies have been complying with various requirements for successful environmental product differentiation. These requirements include developing willingness in consumers to pay for public goods, dissemination of credible information about the environmental attributes of their products, and defending themselves against imitation and market disruption. More broadly, all companies are made to comply with the environmental public policies, and to develop corporate business strategies accordingly. The appropriate environmental strategy depends on the fundamental economics of the industry and the internal capabilities of the company (Reinhardt 1998).

The labor market in the changing global economic order plays a significant role in determining the production patterns across the regions in reference to the concerns of companies over the cost effectiveness and profit making. Accordingly, the trend of production sharing, by ways of getting the parts of products manufactured at different locations and assembled at another place, has become popular among the companies in developed countries, in order to take advantage of the low wages of skilled and unskilled labor. The labor market effects on international fragmentation of production in the USA and Europe has shown the increasing trend of increase in relative labor wages and demand in industrial production since 1980s. Models of trade due to fragmentation of production indicate that with international fragmentation, a change in the relative factor intensities of the affected industries can be seen. However, the shift in intensity of labor usage is observable in the USA and Europe, which relates to the production sharing activity. For example, General Motors established its automobile manufacturing plants in Mexico, Brazil, South Korea, and India, on the basis of labor cost effectiveness and location advantages in manufacturing. However, theoretical models indicate that the sign of the effects of fragmentation on labor demand is a priori ambiguous (MEANING???), as it depends upon the relative factor intensity in reference to manufacturing resources, technology, and targets to cater demand. Most companies engaged in production sharing are delocalized, and integrate their operations with trade and economic policies of the region. Therefore, the effects of fragmentation on labor markets turn out to be a profit-centric concern for the companies than the local political concerns of generating domestic employment (Helg and Luica 2005).

The global electronics contract manufacturing industry reached a staggering $360 billion revenue in 2011, expanded to $426 billion by 2015. This included American companies, contracting outside firms largely in third-world countries with cheaper labor costs to manufacture their products. While this figure is not exclusive, large US corporations such as Apple Inc., Google, IBM, and Microsoft, who conduct all of their manufacturing on foreign shores, and Nike Inc., which subcontracts all of its footwear production to independently owned and operated foreign companies, lead the trend. It has been observed that labor cost savings is one of the three most important drivers leading to overseas outsourcing. Nevertheless, the cost gap between the USA and China has shrunk nearly 50% since 2009 and stood about 16% by 2013. Labor costs in China and elsewhere are rising and coupled with rising fuel prices and rising shipping costs, the economic argument for sending jobs overseas may be becoming less persuasive (Lach 2012). Although re-shoring for the USA companies have been benefitting economically to reduce cost and increase market competitiveness, the political philosophy is changing in 2017 with an emphasis to enhance the domestic employment. However, there are many companies that have already re-shored or are in the process of re-shoring is growing. Of these, some companies include General Electric (Water heaters), Master Lock (Locker and room locks), Windstream Technologies (Windmills), National Cash Register-NCR (ATM machines), and Michigan Ladder (Heavy duty ladders).

Multinational companies keep launching new products frequently to maintain the competitive differentiation and to lead in the marketplace. Continuous introduction of new products and line extensions add complexity throughout a company's operations, and as the costs of managing that complexity multiply, margins shrink. In addition, such strategies are often difficult for the companies to assure quality as per the legal requirements as described below:

- Negligence
  - Manufacturer lets the product be injurious
- Warranty
  - A promise from manufacturing, retailing, services companies
  - Express warranty—a statement of fact about a product
  - Implied warranty—arises when product is made available for a given use
- Strict Liability
  - Seller is responsible for not putting a defective product on the market
  - Defenses—assumption of risk; unforeseeable misuse; not defective
- Misrepresentation
  - Implied use of product, even if not defective

In order to maximize profit potential, a company needs to identify its innovation fulcrum, the point at which a product extension becomes risk averse as it destroys more value than it creates. The usual ways to manage the product line complexities in a company appear to be difficult as the problem is often treated on the factory floor rather than in the market in reference to the real consumer bound situations (Gottfredson and Aspinall 2005).

Product Life Cycle Management

Most firms build their marketing strategies around the concept of the product life cycle. However, by positioning their products in non-conventional ways, companies can extend the span of product life cycle in reference to how customers perceive them. In doing so, managers can shift products lodged in the maturity phase back and propel new products forward into the growth phase. Some non-conventional positioning strategies firms can use to shift consumers' thinking include reverse positioning, breakaway position, and furtive position. The reverse positioning strategy holds products in a particular stage of the life cycle for a longer period while adding new ones. Breakaway positioning associates the product with a radically different category, like Trendy, a brand of Swatch Company associated its watches in the category of fashion accessory. The furtive positioning strategy offers consumers, who are not confident in the products of the company, a new offering by concealing the product's true nature. A company can use these techniques to go on the offensive, and transform a category by demolishing its traditional boundaries (Moon 2005). Detailed knowledge on how innovation, market performance, and competition serves as the basis for decisions of firms and policy makers about determining the life cycle of a product. Managers should consider consumer preferences and product knowledge as significant drivers in the course of changing market conditions. In order to model the market evolution and the resulting changes, technological regimes of products need to be integrated into the process of determining the product life cycle (Werker 2003).

Driving quick marketing results within shorter product life cycles are pushing companies to introduce new products more frequently. Though new products can offer tremendous value, the subsequent product introductions and their transitions in the marketplace pose enormous challenges to managers. A common problem faced by many companies in the process of developing new products frequently has been the lack of a formal process to guide managerial decisions. Drawing from research at Intel and examples from General Motors and Cisco Systems, a process to facilitate decision-making during new product transitions may be illustrated. The proposed process analyzes the risks affecting a transition, identifies a set of factors across departments tracking those risks, monitors the evolution of these factors over time, and develops playbook-mapping scenarios of risks and responses. This process helps level expectations across the organization, reduces the chance and impact of unanticipated outcomes, and helps synchronize responses among different departments. It assists managers in designing and implementing appropriate policies to ramp up sales for new products and ramp down sales for existing products, balancing the supply and the demand for both so that combined sales can grow smoothly (Erhun et al. 2007). A marketer has to make more crucial decisions at the growth stage of the product. The major strategies are drawn at this stage to provide adequate support to the product in the market in reference to:

- Rationalizing the product line and width
- Innovative promotional approaches
- Identifying new market segments

- Evolving comprehensive distribution policy
- Changing the strategy of product awareness, advertising to the product preference and launching advertising campaigns accordingly

It is essential at this stage of PLC to rationalize the product portfolio in the company and develop strategies to promote only the categories of product, which had gained considerable response from the consumers. Such product categories need to be promoted through innovative promotion approaches, giving more emphasis on the advertisements and advertising campaigns based on product preference. However, the possibilities of exploring new market segments and comprehensive coverage of distribution also need to be worked out in the same stage of PLC. The stage of maturity is the sustainable stage in the PLC. As there will not be encouraging growth in the profit through the product marketing, there is enormous scope for developing the business relationships and renovating the product attributes. At the last stage of PLC—stage of decline, the strategies need to be built to re-launch the product in the same or new market segments. The most important need at this stage of PLC is to sustain the brand image and rebuild the same through product and institutional advertising.

It has been observed that amidst global competition, increasingly heterogeneous markets, together with shorter product life cycles are forcing many companies to simultaneously compete in the three domains of product, process, and supply chain. Dependencies among decisions across these domains make this competitive situation of companies very complex in the marketplace. Managers should consider building the existing product characteristic concepts such as component commonality, product platforms, and product modularity based on the three-dimensional concurrent engineering. This framework can be used to focus advice for product design on product architecture dimensions critical for a given operational strategy, to assess advantages and limitations of operational strategies in conjunction with given product architectures, or to develop dynamic capabilities such as planning effective product and operation strategy combinations (Fixson 2005). Firms should understand that focusing on the manufacturing process gives a new dimension to strategy. The "process life cycle," related to but distinct from the product life cycle, facilitates the understanding of strategic options available. Most companies occupy a particular region on a natural, diagonal matrix of the stages of the product life cycle and the choices of production process for that product. A company may seek competitive advantage off the diagonal, but should understand the implications of each move (Hayes and Wheelwright 1979).

The product life cycle measures the likelihood, character, and timing of competitive and market events. A product strategy that includes some sort of plan for a timed sequence of conditional moves provides an offensive rather than a reactive move. Most successful products pass through certain recognizable stages. Awareness of these stages affects decisions on marketing factors such as pricing, product identity, and sales and distribution networks. New uses and new customers extend the product life cycle. Planning in the early stages for product life extension helps to guide the direction of ongoing technical research in support of the product (Levitt 1965).[1]

Microeconomic Technology Drivers

In a given perspectives of microeconomic environment new technologies intending to operate marketing activities, firms may perform an opportunity analysis to determine the suitability to seek market advantage in terms of economic cost-benefit ratio. A conceptual scheme for analyzing economic environment in reference to innovation and technology may be drafted and implemented by the firm in order to evaluate the existing and potential marketing opportunities. Many other microeconomic variables may be selected for industry or market analysis in the launch innovation and technology depending upon the specific requirement of the firm. The microeconomic foundations of productivity rest on two interrelated areas, the sophistication with which companies compete, and the quality of the innovation and technology developed by the firm. The careful examination of variables of business drivers as discussed above would also help the firm to know the supply and demand situation, free markets, the price system, and government policy. Microeconomic analysis of business drivers for innovation and technology would help firms in determining the projected growth of new products in competitive and non-competitive markets. In addition, the analysis of the most relevant microeconomic variables may also help in assessing the issues of strategic decision-making like market breakdown, income redistribution, role of government, trade and tariff regimes, and anticipated gains from international trade over short and long run. The major microeconomic factors can substantially influence trade forecasts. This can include shortages, strikes, supply problems, product defects, capital problems, splitting and integration of innovation and technology, and a wide variety of other factors. The cost-benefit criteria should respond to a series of questions towards the efficiencies of markets, competition, and the financial implications of doing business. In view of the microeconomic environment, the firm may determine the consumer preferences on products by available segments. More significantly, the firm may determine the consumer price sensitivity, propensity of consumption, and whether the consumer has enough to pay a price that will yield a profit to the firm in reference to the innovation and technology led products. The size of the market for the new products may also be known by analyzing the microeconomic variables. It is necessary to build the strategic business mind-set to outwit the competitors and gain competitive advantages over the segmented markets. The following factors need to be considered for achieving the strategic business leadership:

- Develop a plan capable of delivering outcomes that will add significant value to a state of affairs.
- Explore internal and external fit for the innovation and technology led products.
- Capitalize on market needs and behavioral change in the markets in order to turn them to advantage.
- Stay future-focused
- Plan implementation of business strategy in both sequential and parallel direction to accomplish goals and sustain the impact thereof
- Develop win-win platform at an acceptable cost to launch the technology led innovation products

Making decision on the innovation and technology products involves rigorous benefit-cost analysis (BCA). Benefits of new products in a market are measured by the propensity of consumers to pay for the product and services of the firm. The proper calculation of costs is the amount of compensation required to offset negative consequences. The dynamic markets and technologies today have called into question the sustainability of competitive advantage under pressure to improve productivity, quality, and speed of operations. Managers should also work with the techniques of total quality management, benchmarking, and reengineering while developing new products. A company's profitability on the new products depends on the structure of the industry in which it competes and operates within five basic forces of competing: the intensity of rivalry among existing competitors; the threat of new entrants; the threat of substitute products or services; the bargaining power of suppliers; and the bargaining power of buyers. Industry structure is relatively stable, but industries are sometimes transformed by changes in buyer needs, regulation, or technology. Companies can shape industry structure instead of passively reacting to it. Many factors determine the nature of competition including not only rivals, but also the economics of particular industries, new entrants, the bargaining power of customers and suppliers, and the threat of substitute services or products. A strategic plan of action based on this might include positioning the company so that its capabilities provide the best defense against the competitive forces and anticipating shifts in the factors underlying competitive forces.

Market competition and growth of innovation and technology have always featured the unpredictable, the surprising, and the unexpected in the global marketplace. However, the increasing deployment of information technology in the firms has developed hyper-connectivity on one hand and complexity in business management on the other. Market competition and growth of technology are now intertwined and interdependent as market need has become the principal driver of innovation and technology. The new products are embryonic to the consumer need and market demand, and are grown largely on predicting outcomes. There are too many continuously changing interactive elements in play that create complexities in managing the marketing of technology led innovative products in different market segments. Managers looking to handle these difficulties need to adopt strategic approaches than tactical for sustainable results, and to overcome conventional wisdom by using the models that simulate the behavior of the market players including consumers in order to make the technology led new products sustainable. They should also make sure that their strategies are future-oriented and can manage the market risk. Firms introducing new products rapidly in the marketplace should minimize the need to rely on predictions and work with the user-oriented product design and applications. They can list the complexity factors in a system and build to minimize the consequences of failures in the business system. Firms can also develop strategic alliances to share the unforeseen risks in the innovation and technologies led products, and to enhance organizational capabilities and competencies (Sargut and McGrath 2011).

Administrative complexities play a significant role in explaining new technology drive. Process simplification, zero defect products, cost and profit, and overall governance of new products development have many odds to be either eliminated or managed within the organizational system. Most managers who exert developing new strategies for setting up competitive business, think about the odds and complexities or critically examine the process and give up the innovation process. Such behavior is also affected significantly by the perception of administrative complexity (van Stel and Stunnenberg 2006). Firms engaged in rapid development of new products find the gap between diffusion and adoption. It is expensive for companies to manage piled up inventory of obsolete products unless they can be improved and revert to the active demand. Expensive downtime for production-line changeovers and merchandise languishing on retailers' shelves or in their showrooms also cause serious concerns to the firms engaged in developing new products. For service companies, though, complexity is much harder to spot and root out, largely due to the ease with which new products can be created and marketed (Gottfredson and Schwedel 2008). Large organizations are complex by nature and face new business challenges such as globalization, innovative technologies, and regulations over the period. Market uncertainties and competitive threats add layer upon layer of complexity to corporate structure and management.

The technology marketing grid has several factors that pose conflicts and challenges to the innovation and technology development firms during different levels of the process. The complexity grid comprises twelve commonly observed points of conflicts, which has independent effects of each point as well as in a matrix form. The conflict points in the grid include ideation, resources management, process management, capabilities and competencies, technology marketing, growth and next-generation innovation and technology issues, involvement, organizational policies, operational efficiency, competitive decision, business environment, and organizational culture, all of which nurture the innovation and technology development projects in the firm. In the complexity grid ideation process, the extent of involvement of employees, consumers, and market players stage cognitive and organizational conflicts and challenges, while management of resources and organizational policies raise various challenging issues during different phases of innovation and technology development. Similarly, the process and operational efficiency commonly drive various issues of concern in reference to capabilities and competencies and work culture of the organization. Firms face many conflicts during the innovation process on marketing of the technology led products and the existing business environment. Moving the innovation and technology to the next generation is also not an easy step-up as firms often get snared in the unwise competitive decisions in an effort to push the innovation and technology led products in the marketplace.

Large firms have been the driving force behind the market economies in the developed countries. Traditional theories suggest that new products not consistent with the existing demand retard economic growth, hence classical theories suggest that serving products to the existing market demand is safer than creating demand in the market to position the products. However, the global competition and the changing consumer behavior on experimenting new products have raised new theoretical concepts on the relationship of launching new products with the market demand. Large firms are engaged in continuously developing new products and could benefit, in contrast to small firms, from economies of scale and scope. Many economists believed that more large firms would lead to more economic growth and that the share of small firms eventually would disappear or reduce to only a small fraction. Globalization has induced extensive cross-culture working ambience and driven most firms to multi-dimensional manufacturing and marketing operations to sustain in the competition marketplace. Hence, most firms have become increasingly complex and ungovernable causing decline in performance, unclear accountability, and opaque decision process that raise questions about the sustainability of the firm. To avoid frustration and inefficiency, executives need to address systematically the causes of complexity using a simplicity-minded strategy in their companies by streamlining the structure, pruning non-responding products before introducing new products to create space, building disciplined processes, and improving managerial behavior (Ashkenas 2007).

Firms operating in niche environment have tried to secure against risks by focusing on potential threats outside the organization like competitors, shifts in the strategic landscape, natural disasters, or geopolitical events. They are generally less skillful at detecting internal vulnerabilities that creep into organizations through various interrelated systems. Indeed, as firms increase the complexity of their systems, they often tend to fail drawing sufficient attention to the introduction of new products and strategies and manage growing system flaws. The possibility of random failure rises as the number of combinations of factors that can go wrong increases, while the opportunity for competitors to counter the strategies also goes up. Firms should meticulously assess the risks in technology marketing and stay aware of market information to guard against market uncertainties and make appropriate decisions. It is also necessary for technology marketing firms to identify vulnerabilities in the marketplace and fix them before competitors or disruptive innovation products attack the new technology products (Bonabeau 2007).

Business leaders have expressed that previous assumptions and business models developed to cater regional oligopolistic market requirements are inadequate to help managers in understanding the strategic needs for global markets. Management practices guided by complexity science will lead to a highly human-oriented approach to business that not only brings greater purpose and fulfillment to people's lives but steers organizations to greater financial success (Hoe 2001). In today's increasingly competitive global marketplace, companies create value and ensure survival based on their ability to manage the complex web of suppliers and customers comprising their value chain. At the heart of this process is the accurate, timely, and complete disclosure of information between value chain partners to enables the types of coordinated action mandated by exchange partners (Hausman et al. 2005).

NAFTA Status

Mexico's first step in opening its closed economy was focused on reforming its import substitution policies in the mid-1980s. Further reforms were made in 1986 when Mexico became a member of the General Agreement on Tariffs and Trade (GATT). As a condition of becoming a GATT member, for example, Mexico agreed to lower its maximum tariff rates to 50%. Mexico went further by reducing its highest tariff rate to 20%. Mexico's trade-weighted average tariff fell from 25% in 1985 to about 19% in 1989. At the time that NAFTA was implemented, the US–Canada FTA was already in effect and US tariffs on most Mexican goods were low, while Mexico had the highest protective trade barriers. Under the agreement, the USA and Canada gained greater access to the Mexican market, which was the fastest-growing major export market for US goods and services at the time.[2] NAFTA also opened up the US market to increased imports from Mexico and Canada, creating one of the largest single markets in the world. Some of the key NAFTA provisions included tariff and non-tariff trade liberalization, rules of origin, services trade, foreign investment, intellectual property rights protection, government procurement, and dispute resolution. Labor and environmental provisions were included in separate NAFTA side agreements.

Over the twentieth century, global business players were obsessed with achieving sustainable competitive advantage and secure a position within an industry that allowed them to be the business leaders for the long term. Some organizations like General Electric Company and Unilever have succeeded with this approach. However, in the current competitive market and politico-economic edge, most companies with tactical strategies do not last long to rule the global marketplace. The forces driving the global marketplace today include innovation, technology, consumer value, digital revolution, and regional trade agreements that relax the barriers to entry like North American Free Trade Agreement (NAFTA) between USA, Mexico, and Canada, in force since 1994. The global marketplace is becoming uncertain due to frequent political, economic, social, technological and legal changes. Hence, companies need a portfolio of multiple transient advantages that can be built within the resilient determinants such as customer value. Transient advantages call for a whole new playbook involving business strategies that are more customer-centric than market-oriented or industry bound. Companies that adapt to this shift could set broad strategic themes and then let consumers experiment them, and social media may be activated to share the experience. Companies with such strategy bent adopt decision metrics that support entrepreneurship and develop resistance to disruptive innovations that tend to prove shifts in consumer behavior (McGrath 2013).

The NAFTA trade across the US partners has grown since 1994 benefited to USA and Canada proportionately more than the Mexico. There were various political and economic reasons that fluctuated the trade conditions among the NAFTA partnering countries. US trade with Canada more than doubled in the first decade of this agreement (1989–1999) from $166.5 billion to $362.2 billion. US exports to Canada increased from $100.2 billion in 1993 to $312.1 billion in 2014 and then decreased to $266.8 billion in 2016. US imports from Canada increased from $110.9 billion in 1993 to $349.3 billion in 2014 and then decreased to $278.1 billion in 2016. The US merchandise and services trade with Canada and Mexico during 2000–2015 is exhibited in Table 6.1.

It can be observed from the above Table that US merchandise trade balance with Canada and Mexico has been under deficit as against the services trade with these countries during (2001–2015). The market

Table 6.1 US Merchandise and Services Trade in NAFTA Marketplace (In Billion US Dollars)

Year	*Canada*			*Mexico*			*NAFTA*		
	Exports	*Imports*	*Trade balance*	*Exports*	*Imports*	*Trade balance*	*Exports*	*Imports*	*Trade balance*
2001	163.4	216.3	−52.8	101.3	131.3	−30.0	264.7	347.6	−82.9
	(24.7)	(17.8)	(6.9)	(16.7)	(10.9)	(5.8)	(41.4)	(28.7)	(12.7)
2005	211.9	290.4	−78.5	120.2	170.1	−49.9	332.1	460.5	−128.3
	(32.8)	(22.6)	(10.2)	(22.5)	(14.4)	(8.1)	(55.3)	(37.0)	(18.3)
2010	249.3	277.6	−28.4	163.7	230.0	−66.3	412.9	507.6	−94.7
	(53.1)	(27.4)	(25.7)	(24.6)	(14.0)	(10.6)	(77.7)	(41.4)	(36.3)
2015	280.6	296.2	−15.5	235.7	296.4	−60.7	516.4	592.6	−76.2
	(56.4)	(29.0)	(27.4)	(31.5)	(21.9)	(9.6)	(87.9)	(50.9)	(37.0)

Figures in parentheses indicate the US private services trade with NAFTA partners
Source Villareal and Ferguson (2017)

opening provisions of the agreement gradually eliminated all tariffs and most non-tariff barriers on goods produced and traded within North America over a period of 15 years after it entered into force. Some tariffs were eliminated immediately, while others were phased out in various schedules of 5–15 years while tariffs in most industrial sectors were phased out within 10 years. US import-sensitive sectors, such as glassware, footwear, and ceramic tile, received longer phase-out schedules. The agreement included safeguard provisions in which the importing country could increase tariffs, or impose quotas in some cases, on imports during a transition period if domestic producers faced serious injury because of increased imports from another NAFTA country. It terminated all existing drawback programs by January 1, 2001. Most of the market opening measures from NAFTA resulted in the removal of tariffs and quotas applied by Mexico on imports from the USA and Canada. Because Mexican tariffs were substantially higher than those of the USA, it was expected that the agreement would cause US exports to expand more quickly than imports from Mexico (Villareal and Fergusson 2017).

The macroeconomic factors of the neighboring countries also govern the cost drivers. When a new automobile plant is set up, it aims at designing, manufacturing or assembling, and delivering a particular model by penetrating into the neighboring markets to gain the advantages of economies of scale. The automobile plant of Toyota at Kentucky manufactures the Camry model to cater to the markets of NAFTA group of countries. The high market share multi-domestic companies derive gains from spreading their production activities across multiple product lines or diversified business lines to achieve an advantage through the scope of economies. The manufacturing and marketing activities of Proctor and Gamble, Unilever, and Colgate-Palmolive may illustrate this global attribute explained by the cost drivers. The other cost drivers include global sourcing advantages towards low cost global communications and automation processes. The location of strategic resources in relation to the production plants, cost differences across the countries, and transport costs are also some important considerations of the cost drivers. The US unemployment rates until the recent economic crisis (2007–2011) were much lower in the decades following NAFTA than before the agreement came into effect, even at a time when the US labor force was growing steadily. The exports of corn and other agricultural products under the NAFTA have led to a surge of displaced Mexican farmers drifting northward. Recent research has found that, on average, for every 100 jobs the US manufacturers created in Mexican manufacturing, they added nearly 250 jobs at their larger US home operations and increased their US research and development spending by 3% (Posen 2014).

NAFTA phased out all duties on textile and apparel goods within North America meeting specific NAFTA rules of origin over a 10-year period. Prior to NAFTA, 65% of US apparel imports from Mexico entered duty-free and quota-free, and the remaining 35% faced an average tariff rate of 17.9%. Mexico's average tariff on US textile and apparel products was 16% with duties as high as 20% on some products. NAFTA phased out Mexico's restrictive auto decree. It phased out all US tariffs on imports from Mexico and Mexican tariffs on US and Canadian products as long as they met the rules of origin requirements of 62.5%. Some tariffs were eliminated immediately, while others were phased out in periods of 5–10 years. NAFTA rules of origin for textiles and apparel define when THE imported textile or apparel goods qualify for preferential treatments. For most products, the rule of origin is "yarn forward", which means that goods must be produced from yarn made in a NAFTA country to benefit from preferential treatment. Prior to NAFTA, the USA assessed the following tariffs on imports from Mexico on automobiles (2.5%), light-duty trucks (25%), and trade-weighted average of

3.1% for automotive parts. Mexican tariffs on US and Canadian automotive products were as follows: 20% on automobiles and light trucks, and 10–20% on auto parts. NAFTA set out separate bilateral undertakings on cross-border trade in agriculture, one between Canada and Mexico, and the other between Mexico and the USA. As a general matter, US–Canada FTA provisions continued to apply on trade with Canada. Regarding US–Mexico agriculture trade, NAFTA eliminated most non-tariff barriers in agricultural trade, either through their conversion to Tariff-Rate Quotas (TRQs) or ordinary tariffs. Tariffs were phased out over a period of 15 years with sensitive products such as sugar and corn receiving the longest phase-out periods. TRQ allowed NAFTA partners to export specified quantities of a product to other NAFTA countries at a relatively low tariff, but subjected all imports of the product above a pre-determined threshold to a higher tariff. Approximately one-half of US–Mexico agricultural trade became duty-free when the agreement went into effect. Prior to NAFTA, on average, most tariffs in agricultural trade between the USA and Mexico were low, though some US exports to Mexico faced tariffs as high as 12%. However, approximately one-fourth of US agricultural exports to Mexico (by value) were subjected to restrictive import licensing requirements (Villareal and Fergusson 2017).

Opening up of markets can play an important role in weakening the vested interests and reducing economic rents associated with long-standing economic and institutional arrangements. Trade can thus spur improvement in domestic institutions that otherwise would not have been possible. In addition, international agreements can be an important external anchor and catalyst for institutional change by breaking through domestic impediments to reforms. Chile and Mexico provide important role models for the region. Institutional strengthening in both countries has allowed them to establish a successful inflation-targeting framework, lower the public debt, open the trading regime, and build a strong regulatory and oversight framework for the banking system. However, in order to achieve significant results of trade openness measures in Mexico, further institutional reforms are necessary with a focus on reducing macroeconomic instability, improving the investment climate, institutional framework, scope for prolific corporate venturing and putting in place business education and innovation system capable of fostering technological advancement and productivity growth. In addition, regional trade integration needs to be supplemented with multilateral actions on other trade sectors to maximize the gains from trade liberalization and reduce the possible operational costs. Dramatic changes in trade policy in emerging economies have made a significant impact on the degree with which the emerging economies are being integrated into the world economy. The market openings around the world have created considerable opportunities for these countries to expand trade and to stimulate the growth of their economies. Trade liberalization has also done much to improve the competitiveness and as a result, the growth of trade has often been much faster than the growth of domestic output.

The deeply integrated North American economy depends on efficient freight transport systems. Cabotage[3] is restricted by cross-country regulations in North America that remain pervasive and continue to impose significant restraints on freight transportation. Liberalizing Cabotage could improve efficiency and productivity, increase trade opportunities and regional economic integration. Open Cabotage could also reduce greenhouse gas emissions. However, reform is difficult because these regulations are linked to tax, immigration, and other customs issues and because they protect the interests of domestic transport industries (Blank and Prentice 2015).

Business Partnering and Market Competition

The business partnership strategies should be developed keeping in view the heterogeneity in economic development, culture and institutional modalities that exist in both regions while seeking globally balanced relations. The relationship should be based on fundamental shared principles and values, which in turn can be translated into clear political messages and a general sustained process of dialogue and cooperation. Relationships can be strengthened at the bi-regional, regional or bilateral levels, taking advantages of the special circumstances of country groupings. Building relationships should proceed at different levels and speeds among the countries of the region. Considering the multiplicity of forums it is necessary to focus the trade partnering negotiations at bilateral and multilateral levels and avoid overlap between distinct dialogues and similar initiatives taken at other forums. Bilateral negotiations should be strategically pursued in removing/reducing the non-tariff and investment barriers. The trade-related negotiations among the Latin America–East Asian countries should also focus on the technical norms and standards; rules of origin, antidumping, subsidies, countervailing measures; other liberalization and deregulation measures (privatization);

sub-regional, regional and hemispheric integration processes; and convergence and divergence between regional integration and multilateral trade regimes. The negotiations should also be dealt by simplifying the customs rules and procedures, including non-transparent and inefficient infrastructures; differing customs; improper application of rules of origin, customs valuation, pre-shipment inspection and import licensing. Customs problems can be especially difficult for small and medium enterprises that have less experience and fewer resources for handling these problems.

NAFTA removed significant investment barriers, ensured basic protections for NAFTA investors, and provided a mechanism for the settlement of disputes between investors and a NAFTA country. NAFTA provided for "non-discriminatory treatment" for foreign investment by NAFTA parties in certain sectors of other NAFTA countries. The agreement included country-specific liberalization commitments and exceptions to national treatment. Exemptions from NAFTA investment provisions included the energy sector in Mexico, in which the Mexican government reserved the right to prohibit foreign investment. It also included exceptions related to national security and to Canada's cultural industries (Villareal and Fergusson 2017). The US foreign trade investment with Canada and Mexico during has been encouraging bidirectional during 2001–2015 period despite the business adverse situations during the economic recession (2007–2011). The position of the US towards foreign direct investment (FDI) with the NAFTA partnering countries is exhibited in Table 6.2.

The above Table shows that FDI has been an integral part of the economic relationship between the USA and Mexico for many years, especially after NAFTA. Two-way investment increased rapidly after the agreement went into effect. The USA is the largest source of FDI in Mexico. The stock of US FDI in Mexico increased from $15.2 billion in 1993 to $104.4 billion in 2012 (587%) and then decreased to $92.8 billion in 2015. Mexican FDI in the USA, while substantially lower than US investment in Mexico, has also increased rapidly, from $1.2 billion in 1993 to $16.6 billion in 2015.

Regional or bilateral agreements may bring faster results than the multilateral process, may enable parties to conclude levels of liberalization beyond the multilateral consensus, and may be able to address specific issues that do not register on the multilateral menu. The resulting achievements in trade liberalization can be substantial complements to

Table 6.2 Foreign direct investment in NAFTA Region (in million dollars)

Year	*Canadian FDI in the USA*	*FDI of the USA in Canada*	*Mexican FDI in the USA*	*FDI of the USA in Mexico*
1993	40,373	69,922	1244	15,221
2001	92,420	152,601	6645	52,544
2005	165,667	231,836	3595	75,687
2007	*201,924*	*250,642*	*8478*	*91,046*
2010	*192,463*	*295,206*	*10,970*	*85,751*
2011	*205,225*	*330,041*	*12,500*	*85,599*
2015	268,972	352,928	16,597	92,812

The *italics* in the table show the patterns of FDI during the economic recession (2007–2011) in the USA
Source Villareal and Ferguson (2017)

the WTO system, and they can be the important building blocks for future multilateral liberalization. The most powerful economic arguments against regional and bilateral trade agreements are that they can cause trade diversion and trade distortions and ultimately undermine the multilateral system because of their discriminatory nature. In some cases, preferential rules of origin have proven to stifle technological developments, networks and joint manufacturing, and to restrict third-country sourcing unduly, leading to trade diversion. Moreover, they can create obstacles to trade facilitation by increasing administrative complexity at customs. One specific example is the proliferation of different preferential rules of origin a prominent source of trade costs and complexity in today's global marketplace in which companies depend on the rapid delivery of products and components from multiple overseas sources. Such effects are costly to business and detrimental to the regional trading areas. Harmonization and simplification of preferential rules of origin and the accumulation of origin could alleviate some of these obstacles to trade facilitation.[4]

The area of operation or the size of the market also determines the consumer responsiveness and the effectiveness of the delivery of the goods and services. Thus alternatively, a follower in the large market may be the leader in the small market or niche. Smaller firms normally avoid competing with the larger firms. However, it has been observed that there is an increasing interest of big companies to serve the small area of operation or niche by setting up small business units. The niche strategy would be profitable to the firms with low shares of the total market. The main reason is that the niche strategy provides total knowledge about the customer segment to the company to enable it to serve better through value addition. As a result, the niche company can change a substantial markup over cost because of the value addition. The niche marketing strategy provides *high margin* to the company while the mass marketing strategy may provide the advantage of *high volume* to the company. The niche market should have the following strategies:

- Adequate size of the market
- Purchasing power of the segment to the tune of profitability
- Potential for growth
- Negligible interest to the competing companies
- Appropriate skills and resources to serve the niche in a superior fashion
- Well-knit defensive strategy to counter the competitors attacks.

The most important issue in the niche marketing is specialization. There are three major tasks to be attended by the companies looking for developing the niche marketing strategy. They are creating a niche, expanding the niche and protecting the niche markets. It is also highlighted that for a further expansion of supplies, developing countries are in need of assistance in complying with foreign standards and in establishing international equivalency. However, the niches are always risk averse to the attacks of the competing companies. The market niche also helps in encouraging the FDI with specific focus on the product and services. FDI is to some extent firm-specific as each firm specializes in a particular niche of the market.

Globalization has also induced regional growth of markets as a springboard for firms to go global. In this process, firms grow out of their niche with the support of technology and customer relation strategies. Many firms serving the niche move to the regional marketplace as the Internet and related technologies vastly expand the variety of products that can be produced, promoted and purchased. Although this revolution is based on a simple set of economic and technological drivers, its implications are far-reaching for managers, consumers, and the economy as a whole. In this process, customers derive value from an important characteristic of Internet markets and the ability of online merchants to help consumers locate, evaluate, and purchase a far wider range of products (Brynjolfsson et al. 2006). Developing new competencies in the niche firms requires constant experimentation. However, the innovation-imitation-equilibrium cycle suggests that industry leaders teach customers what to demand by defining the current state of the art in performance, price, service, and other dimensions; firms learn to judge competitive offerings against these standards, and the learning effect is cumulative (Werther and Kerr 1995).

A strong market-oriented strategy of the firm alleviates the possibility of using coercive influence strategies by the competitors and offers an advantage to the customers over competitive market forces (Chung et al. 2007). Market orientation is an organization-wide concept that helps explain sustained competitive advantage. Since many manufacturing firms have linked their marketing strategies with services delivery attributes, the concept of market orientation is expanding as a system in global corporate settings. The route to market is the multi-channel retailing strategy that caters to the wide preferences of shopping to the customers at a varied price, delivery and services options. A company may set more than one routes for its products and services to facilitate consumer convenience in buying. It is necessary that sales people should know these routes to markets and prospect consumers at their most convenient route. In multi-channel selling strategy, salespeople can prospect consumers for offering superior products, typically accompanied by superior service outputs, to be sold at higher prices for the premium market segment while low-price strategy is followed for mass-market retail locations (Jindal et al. 2007). However, luxury goods are not commonly sold through catalogues, e-bays or call centers and differentiated products usually need relatively more intermediary support to be delivered satisfactorily to the end customer. However, urban shoppers incur higher search costs when searching for a product across retailing channels and gathering information on prices as the urban shoppers are more guided by the value for money considerations in shopping. It is observed that price-sensitive customers always intend to strike a beneficial deal over the costs they incur during searching for such bargain through various channel options (Rajagopal 2007). A route to market is a distinct sales process followed by salespeople towards prospecting customers for a selected product or service through a specific market channel. Agents of call centers, representatives of e-bay, and personal selling representatives engaged in prospecting consumers may be assigned to manage sales in different routes to market. Globalization and innovative selling practices have introduced multiple channels selling strategies to improve customer satisfaction and strengthen customer–retailer dyadic loyalty (Wallece et al. 2004).

Strategic thrust has a significant magnitude and direction in sailing the business through turbulent situation. The factors associated with the competitive advantage and business investments uphold the strategic thrust to achieve the business objectives through the positive channel efforts. The competitive advantage may be assessed in reference to the superior consumer value and the lowest delivered cost. Such combination of the strategies may be termed as competitive superiority that explains the cost effective delivery strategy to enhance the consumer value. An overall edge is gained by performing most of the activities at a lower cost than competitors. This would enable the company to optimize its cost of delivery of the new products and simultaneously enhance the consumer value to uphold the strategic thrust of the company.

International Trade Risks

Political, economic, religious and other tensions can shift at a moment's notice and disrupt business operations for exporters, traders, investors, banks and other organizations involved in international commerce. Companies can be subject to the discriminatory actions or inaction of foreign governments and third parties, potentially leading to forced shutdowns, relocations and other unexpected expenses. The political risks in international business are developed with illegitimate use of political power. The way political power is exercised determines government action and the degree of risk that threatens a firm's value. For example, a dramatic political event may pose little risk to a multinational enterprise, while subtle policy changes can greatly impact a firm's performance. Firm-specific political risks are the risks directed at a particular company in reference to its country of origin, nature of activities in the host country, social and economic goals etc. and such risks are by nature discriminatory. The risks specific to the firms may be concerned with the governmental policies as well as due to the instability in the political system governing the country.

The policy risks broadly include administrative controls on prices, investments, and transfer of funds that affect the international business in the country. Besides, the policies on nationalization and domestication of identified industry segments, and changing macroeconomic policies of the country carry a major risk for the international business. The political instability, civil unrests, bureaucracy, and corruption are also of concerns to the inefficiency of the internal governance in a country that seriously affect the investments, manufacturing, and marketing operation of multinational companies targeting to do business in the destination country. International diplomacy also affects the exchange rates, investments, and international trade at the destination country. The political risks may be identified by analyzing contextually the political and social system of a country, its degree of openness to international trade, efficiency of the product markets, labor market dynamics, and its capital markets. By critically examining these contextual areas, companies can map the business contexts of any country and match their strategies to each of these contextual points, They can take advantage of strengths of destination markets. However, firms need to weigh the benefits initially against the anticipated costs (Khanna et al. 2005).

On the contrary, the country-specific political risks are not directed at a firm, but are countrywide, and may affect firm's performance. An example in this context may be the decision of the government to forbid currency transfers on the outbreak of a civil war within the host country. The political risks also include government risks and stability risks. The government risks are those arising from the policies of a governing authority, in reference to the use of authority. A legitimately enacted tax hike or an extortion ring that is allowed to operate and is led by a local police chief may both be considered as government risks. Indeed, many government risks, particularly the firm-specific ones, contain an ambiguous mixture of legal and illegal elements. Instability risks, on the other hand, arise from political power struggles. These risks could be the conflicts between members of a government fighting over succession or mass riots in response to deteriorating social conditions. The country level risk in reference to the government policies and political instability may vary in its intensity.

As the global economy has recovered after the initial twenty-first century economic recession during 2007–2012, multinationals have reverted to weigh their options for investment in the less politico-economic risk destination countries. Companies look for positive impact destinations where government policies are pro-international business and no contradictory economic trends are observed. It is not easy to locate such destinations on the global map for doing political and economic risk-free manufacturing business operations as while potential emerging markets—Brazil is planning to expand its business across the countries, Indonesia is attempting to pull down inflation by keeping the interest rates low. Companies need a way to cut through the political chaos and find out the right options that could optimize benefit minimizing the risk. The business consulting organizations prepare a matrix to select a right destination on the basis of their macroeconomic conditions and foreign investment policies. Such indicators serve as a practical guide for determining the potential growth destinations where governments are encouraging foreign investment and developing pro-business opportunities. Globalization and its impacts have profound implications for a broad range of issues important to the funding community. These issues range from the sustainable use of the worlds' resources and the protection and preservation of the environment to the need to improve living standards, safeguard human rights, promote and protect cultures, and ensure democratic and responsive global governance. While the idea of globalization has only recently captured public attention, globalization has been occurring for centuries. Globalization of market opportunities was observed as the outgrowth of the above factors and the scope of such marketing opportunities has increased with the continued deregulation of the significant functional sectors like financial services, leisure industry, information technology etc.

As multinational companies of the western hemisphere tend to penetrate into the developing regions and bottom of pyramid market segments in search for growth, they have no choice but to compete in the big emerging markets of Brazil, Russia, India, China, Indonesia, and South Africa. The dynamism for globalization has been spread across the political thinkers and business managers hitting dual perspectives of building diplomatic relation. The first is by narrowing down trade and economy barriers across the countries in the world and equalizing the power play among the nations, and the second is by giving more space for multinational companies to do business in the far reachable markets. Breaking the social, cultural, economic, and political barrier for moving the business in various destination markets is a tough challenge for the multinational companies. Though globalization of business has become the lifeline of most companies, creating a sustainable corporate strategy in tune to the local market conditions is difficult. Thus, most companies do not stay competitive in the local markets and lose their market share to the low cost customer-centric companies.

The act of exporting a product by an international firm at a price lower than the price it normally charges on its own home market is defined as dumping the product. Dumping is a type of pricing strategy for selling products in foreign markets below cost, or below the price charged to domestic customers. Such strategy is adapted to capture a foreign market and to damage rival foreign national enterprises. The legal definitions are more precise, but broadly the World Trade Organization (WTO) agreement allows governments to act against dumping where there is a genuine (material) injury to the competing domestic industry. In order to do so, the affected country's government shows that dumping is taking place, calculates the extent of dumping as how much lower the export price is compared to the exporter's home market price, and shows that the dumping is causing injury or threatening to do so. The subsidies that require recipients to meet certain export targets, or to use domestic goods instead of imported goods are prohibited under the WTO agreement because they are specifically designed to distort international trade, and are therefore likely to hurt other countries' trade. The agreement further specifies to the member countries that the countervailing duty, which is parallel to antidumping duty, can only be charged after the importing country has conducted a detailed investigation similar to that required for antidumping action. The argument against dumping is largely on the price differentials intended strictly to weaken competition and over the long run uproot the native products from the market. Hence, all countries pass antidumping laws to secure their home markets from any undue foray by foreign firms.

Though dumping is commonly not regarded as a healthy business strategy for the foreign forms, there are sometimes good management reasons for doing so. A typical case describing the positive side of this strategy may be to survive in a large competitive market by selling at very low prices. Another case is when a company has overproduced and wants to sell the product in a market where it has no brand franchise to protect. However, if the firms have implemented dumping, they can well reverse it. The "reverse dumping" refers to the less-common practice of selling products at home at prices below cost. This would be done in extreme cases where the share at home needs to be protected while monopolistic market positions abroad can be used to generate surplus funds. Regardless, dumping is considered to be illegal since it is destructive to trade, and competitors can take an offender to court to settle a dumping case. The usual penalty for manufacturers whose products are found to violate the antidumping laws is a countervailing duty, an assessment levied on the foreign producer that brings the prices back up over production costs and also imposes a fine.

Global market competition has driven the large companies to operate on economies of scale by reducing the cost and stay competitive in the market with reference to price and services. When low-cost competitors emerge in a given marketplace, one of the toughest decisions to be made by firms with premium products and brands is whether to respond to such competitive threats. For example, Ryanair has emerged as a low cost airliner and its entry into the European aviation market has been a huge success against the large airliners. Likewise, the world's leading telecommunications companies are highly active competing with one another to recognize the threat from the Chinese low-cost competitor Huawei, now a leader in fixed-line networks, and mobile telecommunications networks. The example of Vizio, a little-known LCD TV supplier may also be cited that overtook the premium brands in 5 years to become the North American market leader in large-format TVs. Complacency and arrogance produce blind spots that delay a response and leave incumbents vulnerable (Ryans 2010). The initial impact of low-cost players on incumbent companies may not be the most important consideration. In many markets, if they are relatively easy to enter, a number of low-cost competitors may do so. There might be enough business for everybody at first, with little direct competition between the low-cost players. Economic geography in an era of global competition exhibits many inconsistencies in the marketplace. The theoretical understanding reveals that location is no longer considered as a source of competitive advantage. Open global markets, rapid transportation, and high-speed communications allow any company to source anything from any place at any time. Geographic, cultural, and institutional proximity provides firms with special access, closer relationships, better information, powerful incentives, and other advantages that are difficult to tap from a distance. Competitive advantage lies increasingly in the local business hub, customer relationships, and motivation that distant rivals cannot replicate (Porter 1998).

Global retailing firms build their strategies to resolve the regional disparities in their strategies by coordinating and integrating the strategy implementation activities that involve centralization, standardization, delegation of authority and local responsiveness. In the global marketplace, India and China have made significant progress in economic and commercial sectors. China has emerged as a manufacturing base for the world in providing quality products at low prices, and leading the retailing operations in domestic and international markets. As more firms turn their attention to compete in the emerging markets, they strive towards developing a viable alternative to sustain competition (Saran and Guo 2005).

In the highly competitive and global marketplace of today, the pressure on organizations to find new ways to create and deliver value to customers grows ever stronger. The Asian economies other than Japan have grown over six percent consistently during 2005–2006. Positive forces at work in retail consumer markets today include high rates of personal expenditures, low interest rates, low unemployment and very low inflation. Negative factors that hold retail sales back involve weakening consumer confidence (Rajagopal 2006). In the last two decades, technological innovation, logistics, and supply chain have moved to the center stage. There has been a growing recognition that it is through an effective management of the logistics function and the supply chain that the goal of cost reduction and service enhancement can be achieved. The global marketplace may be described as a spatial network of markets across the countries comprising homogenous and customized segments.

In a contemporary global market competition, new and intermediate firms coevolve around shifts in consumer demand, innovation, working cooperatively and competitively to support new products, and satisfying customer needs. In an increasing market competition, several firms may compete for survival and dominance. Hence, it is necessary for firms to develop generic competitive strategies to sustain the market rivalry. Managers of these firms may thus develop competition matrix and plan appropriate marketing strategies to survive against the threatening firms. A competitive matrix is an analysis tool that helps in establishing the competitive advantage of a firm. It provides an easy-to-read portrait of the competitive landscape of firms and positions them in the marketplace. This can be just a two-dimensional matrix, the main features of firms in one axis and competitive advantages across firms on the others.

There are some common strategies adopted by retailers to overcome the competitive threats such as price-slashing by competitors and switching behavior of consumers. Such wishful thinking holds that sales promoters will thrive if only they communicate better with consumers during pre-purchase situations, and assist in product demonstrations involving consumers to help their purchase decisions using self-reference criterion. The competitive strategies whether effective or ineffective, moderate the market effect in sales and market share (Berry 2001). The firms need to ascertain a continuous organizational learning process with respect to the value creation chain and measure performance of the new products introduced in the market. In the growing competitive markets, the large and reputed firms are developing strategies to move into the provision of innovative combinations of products and services as 'high-value integrated solutions' tailored to each customer's needs than simply 'moving downstream' into services (Davies 2004). With the emergence of virtual shopping and liberalization of economic policies in the developing countries all over the world, competition has become like a traditional derby in which many companies participate for the neck to neck race. In this business game, the rules are subject to change without notice, the prize money may change at short notice, the route and finish line is also likely to change after the race begins, new entrants may join at any time during the race, the racers may form strong alliances, all creative strategies are allowed in the game and the state legislature may change without notice and sometimes with retrospective effect. Hence, to win the race any company should acquire the strategies of outwitting, outmaneuvering and outperforming the competitors. In this process, a company must understand thoroughly all the moves of the rival firms from various sources. In the scenario of growing competition, retailer firms can also establish how a customer relationship management and monitoring system ensures the buying decision-making process through the use of joint project teams and facilitating technology. Development and innovative applications of e-commerce transactions, as well as the integration of available technology, can provide an organization with a unique opportunity to remain competitive within today's global business environment. Although technology plays an important role in gaining competitive advantage for organizations worldwide, information technology professionals, consumers, and e-retailers ensure proper security measures to overcome the harmful impact of the misuse of these technologies (Medlin et al. 2008).

Large firms operate on economies of scale in the market with low cost and high differentiation of products and services. Such strategy leads the firms in the mass market and drives them to gain high market share. Many firms operate at the same time in a given marketplace and competition among the firms turns fierce. Some firms operate at a high cost but also go for high differentiation of products and services. Firms with such attributes locate themselves in the premium market and struggle for achieving high brand equity. On the contrary, firms that have low differentiation of products and services and low cost of marketing, operate in niche by following defensive marketing strategies. In case the firms have low differentiation of products and services at a high cost of marketing, the business growth turns slow affecting the brand equity of the firm. If this situation prevails for a long time with such firms, it may cause disaster in the long run. Many small firms that emerge with high cost and low differentiation stay out of market competition and become extinct over a period either by shutting down operations or merging with stronger firms. There are many attributes of the competition—some of which are simple to manage while some stay complex, as discussed below:

- Well-informed buyers and sellers
- Identical products
- Independent buyers and sellers
- Geo-demographic monopoly
- Economies of scale
- Collusion
- Profit maximization
- Product differentiation
- Interdependence among firms
- Independence among firms

It is difficult for the companies to develop a geo-demographic monopoly in business as it is unusual to get a large homogenous consumer segment in an overseas destination. As overseas firms enter the destination markets, there are chances of collisions with the local or other multinational companies dealing with similar or identical products and services. As the competition grows in the destination markets product differentiation turns more complex, as companies may not be able to stick to the same price line with innovative products and services. To survive in a competitive marketplace it is important for the firms to have an obvious sense of advantage and to drive the business to achieve its predefined objective. Defining the objective, scope, and advantage requires them to manage the trade-offs amidst market competition. If a firm pursues growth or size, profitability is jeopardized, which may ignore retail customers in case the firm chooses to serve institutional clients. Hence, trade-offs in the marketplace will bounce if appropriate decision is not taken by the firms. On the contrary, a firm may derive its competitive advantage from economies of scale and it may not be able to accommodate idiosyncratic customer needs. Accordingly, the growth of local firms may emerge with high brand equity in niche amidst the threats of large firms while large firms can follow a combination of long-run and short-run strategies to outwit regional firms.

Notes

1. Levitt, T. (1965), Exploit the product life cycle, *Harvard Business Review*, 43 (6), 81–94.
2. United States International Trade Commission, Potential Impact on the US Economy and Selected Industries of the North American Free-Trade Agreement, USITC Publication 2596, January 1993.
3. Trade operations through sea, air, or surface transport services within or into a particular country to that country's own transport services.
4. International Chamber of Commerce: Regional Trade Agreements and the Multilateral Trading System, Document # 103, 2002.

References

Ashkenas, R. (2007). Simplicity minded management. *Harvard Business Review, 85*(12), 101–109.

Berry, L. L. (2001). The old pillars of new retailing. *Harvard Business Review, 79*(4), 131–137.

Blank, S., & Prentice, B. E. (2015). NAFTA at 20: Time to open the internal borders of North American to Cabotage. *Research in Transportation Business & Management, 15*(3), 4–14.

Bonabeau, E. (2007). Understanding and managing complexity risk. *MIT Sloan Management Review, 48*(4), 62–68.

Brynjolfsson, E., Hu, Y. J., Smith, M., & Smith, M. (2006). From Niches to Riches: Anatomy of the Long Tail. *MIT Sloan Management Review, 47*(4), 67–71.

Buurma, H. (2001). Public policy marketing: Marketing exchange in the public sector. *European Journal of Marketing, 35*(11), 1287–1302.

Chung, J., Jin, B., & Sternquist, B. (2007). The role of market orientation in channel relationships when channel power is imbalanced. *The International Review of Retail, Distribution and Consumer Research, 17*(2), 159–176.

Davies, A. (2004). Moving base into high-value integrated solutions: A value stream approach. *Industrial and Corporate Change, 13*(5), 727–756.

Erhun, F., Concalves, P., & Hopman, J. (2007). Art of managing new product transitions. *Sloan Management Review, 48*(3), 73–80.

Fixson, S. K. (2005). Product architecture assessment: A tool to link product, process, and supply chain design decisions. *Journal of Operations Management, 23*(3–4), 345–369.

Gottfredson, M., & Aspinall, K. (2005). Innovation versus complexity: What is too much of a good thing? *Harvard Business Review, 83*(11), 62–71.

Gottfredson, M., & Schwedel, A. (2008). *Cut complexity and costs, Harvard Business Publishing Newsletters, August 01*. Cambridge, MA: Harvard Business School Press.

Hausman, A., Johnston, W. J., & Oyedele, A. (2005). Cooperative adoption of complex systems: A comprehensive model within and across networks. *Journal of Business & Industrial Marketing, 20*(4), 200–210.

Hayes, R. H., & Wheelwright, S. C. (1979). Link manufacturing process and product life cycles. *Harvard Business Review, 57*(1), 133–140.

Helg, L., & Luica, T. (2005). *Patterns of International fragmentation of production and implications for the labor markets*. Working paper # 503, Bocconi University, Milano, Italy.

Hoe, S. L. (2001). Weaving complexity and business: Engaging the soul at work. *Leadership & Organization Development Journal, 22*(6), 301–303.

Jindal, R. P., Reinartz, W., Krafft, M., & Hoyer, W. D. (2007). Determinants of the variety of routes to market. *International Journal of Research in Marketing, 24*(1), 17–29.

Khanna, T., Palepu, K. G., & Sinha, J. (2005). Strategies that fit emerging markets.*Harvard Business Review, 83*(6), 63–76.

Lach, A. (2012). 5 facts about overseas outsourcing, Center for American Progress, Washington, DC. Retrieved March 03, 2017 from (https://www.americanprogress.org/issues/economy/news/2012/07/09/11898/5-facts-about-overseas-outsourcing/).

Levitt, T. (1965). Exploit the product life cycle. *Harvard Business Review, 43*(6), 81–94.

Medlin, B., Dawn, D., & Romaniello, A. A. (2008). The cost of electronic retailing: Prevalent security threats and their results. *International Journal of Electronic Marketing and Retailing, 2*(1), 80–96.

McGrath, R. G. (2013). Transient advantage. *Harvard Business Review, 91*(6), 62–70.

Moon, Y. (2005). Break free from the product life cycle. *Harvard Business Review, 83*(5), 86–94.

Pechmann, C., & Silk, T. (2013). Policy and research related to consumer rebates: A comprehensive review. *Journal of Public Policy & Marketing, 32*(2), 255–270.

Porter, M. E. (1998). Clusters and the new economics of competitions. *Harvard Business Review, 76*(6), 77–90.

Posen, A. (2014, July 22). The errors of conservatives obscure the case for trade, *Financial Times*, (News Paper).
Rajagopal. (2006). Where did Trade Liberalization Drive Latin American Economy: A Cross Sectional Analysis. *Applied Econometrics and International Development, 6*(2), 89–108.
Rajagopal. (2007). *Dynamics of International Trade and Economy: An Inquiry into Emerging Markets*. Hauppauge, NY: Nova Publishers.
Rajagopal. (2008). Point of sales promotions and buying stimulation in retail stores. *Journal of Database Marketing and Customer Strategy Management, 15*(4), 249–266.
Reinhardt, F. (1998). Environmental product differentiation: Implications for corporate strategy. *California Management Review, 40*(4), 43–73.
Ryans, A. (2010, June). When companies underestimate low-cost rivals. *McKinsey Quarterly*.
Saran, A. & Guo, C. (2005). Competing in the global marketplace: The case of India and China. *Business Horizons, 48*(2), 135–142.
Sargut, G., & McGrath, R. G. (2011). Learning to live with complexity. *Harvard Business Review, 89*(9), 68–76.
van Stel, A., & Stunnenberg, V. (2006). Linking business ownership and perceived administrative complexity. *Journal of Small Business and Enterprise Development, 13*(1), 7–22.
Villareal, M. A., & Ferguson, I. F. (2017). *The North American Free Trade Agreement*. Congressional Research Service, 7-5700, February 22, pp 1–42.
Wallace, D. W., Giese, J. L., & Johnson, J. L. (2004). Customer retailer loyalty in the context of multiple channel strategies. *Journal of Retailing, 80*(4), 249–263.
Werker, C. (2003). Innovation, market performance, and competition: Lessons from a product life cycle model. *Technovation, 23*(4), 281–290.
Werther, W. B., Jr., & Kerr, J. L. (1995). Shifting sands of competitive advantage. *Business Horizons, 38*(3), 11–17.

CHAPTER 7

International Trade Policies and Development

The role of government in promoting international trade is more significant than the entrepreneurial efforts. The diplomatic relations, fiscal and monetary policies, and public economics strategies largely affect international trade dynamics. Governments of developing nations have become cautious of opening more industries to multinational companies. This chapter discusses the role of government from macro to micro perspectives in reference to the North American region countries. Most developing nations prioritize national security more broadly, narrow the scope foreign companies from entering the domestic marketplace, and often favor promoting state-owned enterprises. The chapter argues that the rise of capitalism in international trade has driven globalization's new risks in managing trade-related public policies in most emerging markets. The political ideology in regional and international economy, USA–Mexico trade support policies, potential conflicts and bilateral conflict resolutions, and the role of international organizations such as WTO, OECD and the like in bilateral trade development have been discussed critically in this chapter.

The development of trade and economy during the post-economic recession (2007–2011) period in North America has exhibited many political and economic changes that have affected the international trade dynamics to a large extent. Consequently, the global economy in 2016 has turned into a fragile state, with the declining growth trend as compared to that registered in both 2014 and 2015. However, the average performance of developed countries since the 2008–2009 economic and

Rajagopal and V. Zlatev, *Business Dynamics in North America*,
DOI 10.1007/978-3-319-57606-0_7

financial crisis is set to continue with the added threat that the loss of momentum in developing countries over the past few years is able to register growth greater than previously anticipated. Developed countries dominated by a change in the international trade diplomacy, the external environment facing trade flow from developing countries to the developed countries looks upset with potentially damaging results for their prosperity and stability of international trade growth in the short and medium run. In addition, more widespread contagion from unforeseen shocks appears to be disturbing off and on the mobility of the trade concerning manufactured goods and services, knocking global growth back even more sharply. The decision by the United Kingdom electorate to leave the European Union (EU) is such a shock. Beside the Brexit referendum of United Kingdom, recovery in the euro zone has lagged behind that of the USA due to more narrow use of monetary policy while by very tight fiscal stances in some other developed countries. The tentative pick-up of growth from 2015 seems likely to stall in 2016 due to the international trade uncertainties across North America, Europe, United Kingdom, and the Pacific Rim.

Politically, Free Trade Agreements (FTA) are viewed as a means of cementing "strategic" relationships, especially with the major powers such as the US, China, and the European Union. Also in terms of the economy, there is the prospect of extra export market access and greater foreign investment. Furthermore, they are devices to ward off future protectionist pressures and manage trade tensions in an orderly manner. Therefore, from the above information, it can be deduced that Mexico's decision to enter into trade liberalization would help it to attain the goals set to reestablish the economy. However, not all that glitters is gold, it has been known that there are also quite a few risks involved in creating FTA's, some of which, if not managed adequately could be more detrimental to a country than beneficial. Among these, the spaghetti bowl effect[1] exists. This refers to the complexity that can develop due to having too many, crossing and conflicting trade agreements with too many countries. It becomes difficult to efficiently manage trade with any of the partners and the risk of falling into incompliance is much greater. In extreme cases, hub countries may force weaker countries into agreements that negatively affect them, lowering wage rates or forcing production of quantities that simply cannot be attained due to lack of technology or raw material.

The production sharing practice followed by the multinational companies in Mexico because of the globalization process also helped in gearing up the export competitiveness of the country. The business linkages between global companies and local manufacturers are influenced by NAFTA and provide opportunities for some contract manufacturing clusters to upgrade their operations beyond the assembly export role traditionally associated with Mexico's *maquiladora* plants (Bair 2002). Evidence of industrial upgrading includes expanded employment opportunities in activities such as textile production, the generation of linkages to local suppliers, and improved working conditions in plants producing for brand-name clients. Some counter arguments generated over post-NAFTA period state that paradoxically the intense liberalization in recent years has made it less likely that such agreements would be beneficial except for agreements between some countries and Brazil, Mexico, or (to a lesser extent) Argentina (Catao and Falcetti 2002). The trade policy can be used for protection even without high tariffs or quantitative restrictions through antidumping measures, countervailing duties, and safeguard measures, which would limit, rather than promote, competition (Rajapatirana 1994). It has also been argued that unstable political ideologies and power disequilibrium in the Mexico historically evidenced that policy makers have relaxed economic policies during booms and restricted them during busts. This might be explained for the reason of weak institutional framework, unfavorable political-economic equilibrium, and volatile access to international capital markets. The most common pattern of financial reforms in Mexico has been towards radical liberalization and implementation of prudential norms that moderated the initial process of liberalization. However, growth has been inadequate in the post-reforms period not because of the failure of reforms to yield the expected growth payoff because of international experience, but because of the combination of an unfavorable external environment with the insufficient depth and breadth of reforms (Igor 2000). The openness-growth connection is still an open question in the empirical literature. Although some studies have found that openness has a positive impact on economic performance, others have seriously questioned the significance of this result. One of the studies on Latin American trade issues emphasizes that openness involves more than just trade liberalization (Cuardos et.al. 2004). The increasing importance of international capital flows and especially foreign direct investment (FDI) seems to be another relevant component of outward-oriented policies.

The expansion of international relations in Mexico has accelerated the economic growth of the country since the establishment of the North America Free Trade Agreement with the USA and Canada. This advancement is attributed to the practices of transnational corporations and the democratization process that motivates openness, greater professionalism and the expansion of public relations across diverse trade associations. More and more evidence is indicating the pitfalls of aggressive tactics of international trade expansion, but most of the books do not present the convergence of traditional and contemporary thoughts on the international trade and sectoral growth in the economy of Mexico. The rapid expansion of Mexico's trade took off prior to NAFTA accompanied by a marked change in its trade composition and led Mexico to become a net exporter of machinery. During this sweep of international trade negotiations, substantial changes were noticed prior to actual implementation of the preferential trade agreements reflecting lagged effects of the trade reforms. Among various macroeconomic factors level of bilateral trade, growth in gross domestic product, political risk, geographic expansion of trade, and exchange rates affect the performance of international trade. At the same time, relationships between FDI and country-of-origin factors including market size and cultural distance also drive the competitiveness of the home country to enhance the performance of international trade and develop sustainable trade relations in the emerging market context. Improved competitiveness is at the top of the agenda for Mexico as it moves to leverage economic progress made over the past decade. The analysis indicates that Mexico has a large scope for trade promotion from trade facilitation reform as overall increments from domestic reforms are expected to be implemented effectively in future (Rajagopal 2011).

Political Ideologies

Systems of government vary considerably throughout the world and are always associated with particular values or principles. Absolute monarchies are based upon deeply established religious ideas, notably the divine right of kings. The political systems in most contemporary western countries are founded upon a set of liberal-democratic principles. Western states typically respect the ideas of limited and constitutional government, and believe that government should be representative, based upon regular and competitive elections. In the same way, traditional communist political systems have conformed to the principles of Marxism–Leninism. Communist states were dominated by a single party, a ruling Communist Party, whose authority rested upon Lenin's belief that the Communist Party alone represents the interests of the working class. Even the fact that the world is divided into a collection of nation-states and that government power is usually located at the national level reflects the impact of political ideas, in this case of nationalism and, more specifically, the principle of national self-determination. Political ideologies have commonly been associated with particular social classes such as liberalism with the middle classes, conservatism with the landed aristocracy, socialism with the working class and so forth. These ideas reflect the life experiences, interests and aspirations of a social class, and therefore help to foster a sense of belonging and solidarity. However, ideas and ideologies can also succeed in binding together divergent groups and classes within a society. A unifying set of political ideas and values can develop naturally within a society. The values of elite groups such as political and military leaders, government officials, landowners or industrialists may diverge significantly from those of the masses. Ruling elites may use political ideas to contain opposition and restrict debate through a process of ideological manipulation (Heywood 2007).

The focus of marketing has shifted from knowing everything about the market for products and services to knowing the customer in the context of competition, and the broader economic, social and political macro forces to cocreate marketing strategy for the mutual benefit of consumers and firms. Such marketing philosophy emphasizes the benefits of consumers, stakeholders, and firms. Globalization has become a functional dynamics of emerging firms in the business environment today. Most firms believe that globalization is a synonym for business growth, and invest perennial resources in developing a strategy for going global. It has become one of the most pertinent issues for managers of growing firms around the world (Svensson 2002). Many forces drive local enterprises to globalize by expanding their brand reach and participating in foreign markets through various modes of entry. In developed countries, domestic markets have turned matured and firms are demanding to seek international markets, while in some countries like Brazil, Russia, India, and China, firms are born global. A large number of companies in the USA are nourished by the huge domestic market, but they typically lag behind their European and Japanese rivals in internationalization. Born Global firms maintain dynamic growth in the competitive marketplace and achieve substantial international sales from an early stage of development despite economic and technological constraints. They internationalize rapidly as the period from domestic establishment to initial foreign market entry is often 3 years or less. Born global firms are emerging in sizable numbers worldwide. Until recently, international business was mainly the domain of large, well-resourced multinational enterprises. The appearance of large numbers of born global firms is revolutionizing the traditional character of the international business and helping to reshape the global economy (Cavusgil and Knight 2009). Companies intending to go global exhibit two apparent objectives- to take advantage of opportunities for growth and expansion, and survival in the business amidst growing competition. However, firms that fail to pursue global opportunities will eventually lose their domestic markets and will be pushed aside by stronger and more competitive global firms. In the process of going global, firms need to adopt innovative marketing strategy to withstand competing firms. Most firms follow a global perspective to expand their business across the destinations instead of adopting a country-by-country or region-by-region perspective in developing a marketing strategy.

Globalization has moved through several phases from capitalistic philosophy to democratic business notions involving stakeholders in the process of business growth. Before the recent economic recession in the western hemisphere (2007–2011), going global seemed to make sense to every company in the world to expand their scope of business. However, as the globalization entered a different phase following the recent economic recession, the nature of globalization changed to guarded globalization that made companies secure their global movements observing the political and economic trends in the destinations. The scope of carrying business in emerging destinations has become wary due to protective regulations laid by governments, which allows opening more industries to multinational companies as the political philosophy for business development is leaning toward both pro-globalization and pro-localization. This conception has driven the Darwinian dynamics of 'struggle for existence' and 'survival of the fittest' among the companies leaving the international business in a fix. They are defining economic security more broadly and perceiving more and more sectors to be of strategic importance such as energy, agribusiness, media marketing, and defense products and services. The new phase of globalization has prompted the rise of state capitalism in some of the world's most important emerging markets, and has altered the business fields for the multinational companies.

Hence, most companies focus on the strategic importance of their industry to both the host and home governments in order to manage risk, and choose to establish alliances with local players like Walmart established an alliance with Bharati Enterprise in India. The multinational companies seeking global advantage in the emerging markets look for several new ways to add value abroad and enter multiple sectors to carry business or stay home (Bremmer 2014).

Globalization can be described as the combined influences of trade liberalization, market integration, international finance and investment, technological change, the increasing distribution of production across national boundaries, and the emergence of new structures of global governance. However, globalization in its radical sense should be taken to mean the development of a new economic structure, and not just conjectural change toward greater international trade and investment within an existing set of economic relations (Hirst and Thompson 1996). The globalization thought process broadly includes the following attributes:

- Global marketplace
- Wide marketing opportunities
- Social and economic welfare
- Diversity and cross-culture focus
- Theory of Comparative Advantage

Global marketplace equipped with global communications has become the focus of the global business arena that enables the world markets to remain open and involve in the fair competitive practices. At the same time, the anti-globalization moves in the process of development protest against the hazards of suppressive strategies of the global companies affecting the regional trade entities. The efficient multinational companies from the leading countries enter the secured country markets and drain out the regional players from the benefit market segments (Rajagopal 2007). Globalization not only entails the economic process and free markets in relation to trade and competitiveness but also envelopes the quality of life, ecological concerns, corporate power of multinational companies, human rights and needs, and so on. Such complexity embraces also the social, political and cultural dimensions doing business beyond boundaries in the globalization process. Thus, globalization encompasses a spread of the complex dynamics of general culture evolution and diffusion of consumer cognition on a global scale (Brinkman and Brinkman 2002).

Over the twentieth century, global business players were obsessed with achieving sustainable competitive advantage and secure a position within an industry that allowed them to be the business leaders for the long term. Some organizations like General Electric Company and Unilever have succeeded with this approach. However, in the current competitive market and politico-economic edge, most companies with tactical strategies do not last long to rule the global marketplace. The forces driving the global marketplace today include innovation, technology, consumer value, digital revolution, and regional trade agreements that relax the barriers to entry like North American Free Trade Agreement (NAFTA) between USA, Mexico, and Canada, in force since 1994. The global marketplace is becoming uncertain due to frequent political, economic, social, technological, and legal changes. Hence, companies need a portfolio of multiple transient advantages that can be built within the resilient determinants such as customer value. Transient advantages call for a completely new playbook involving business strategies that are more customer-centric than market oriented or industry bound. Companies that adapt to this shift could set broad strategic themes and then let consumers experiment them, and social media may be activated to share the experience. Companies with such strategy adopt decision metrics that support entrepreneurship and develop resistance to disruptive innovations that tend to prove shifts in consumer behavior (McGrath 2013).

Operating in the global environment requires mastered skills to penetrate in the host countries, particularly when the trade barriers and government protections have been removed and business policies have been restructured. The concept of the global customer is gaining in importance every day and so is the global-customer-centric organization. The theory of comparative advantage suggests that firms may choose a destination to expand their marketing operation that offers a relative economic advantage on factors of production (land, labor, and capital), technology, and managerial expertise. The comparative advantage in business may be defined as the ability of a firm to produce a particular good or service at a lower marginal and opportunity cost over another. Even if one country is more efficient in the production of all goods (absolute advantage in all goods) than the other is, both countries will still gain by trading with each other, as long as they have different relative efficiencies.

Going global is an easy process for firms. Firms need to simulate the impact of their business in the global market in reference to their resources, target markets, and operational efficiency. Most firms concentrate on product markets considering the customers who seek the same benefits or to be served with the same products, services, innovation, and technology regardless of the geo-demographic differences and cognitive behavior. There are a number of paradoxes in communicating the product-marketing strategies in the global marketplace. For example, paradoxical values may emerge within and between cultures while advertising products and services in the global marketplace. It is necessary for the firms evolving to a global scale to understand that markets are people, not products. There may be global products, but there are not global people; hence firms need to adopt the consumer-centric marketing approach in the global marketplace rather than going rampant in employing strategies to outmaneuver or outperform the competitors in the marketplace (Svensson 2012).

The manifold impact of globalization during the twentieth century has not only shifted the market patterns but has also made remarkable structural changes in the economy of developed and developing countries. The globalization effects apparently lean towards the capitalistic economic system advocating the liberal trade practices. Countries following socialistic economic patterns are yet unable to receive the global market benefits to the full extent. The increasing liberalization of markets has driven companies to create new markets in the potential destinations to expand their production and business operations. Corporate efforts of companies and business-friendly initiatives of various governments are offering destination level competitive advantage for the firms. However, often companies find that it is difficult not only to create markets and but also to cope with the state requirements to do business in the new destinations despite their potential to generate competitive advantage. Walmart, a global retail giant experienced turbulent landing in India, though it had evaluated Indian market as a high-potential market in Southeast Asia. According to the foreign corporate investment policy, FDI is not allowed in the retail sector in India. Walmart had to collaborate with Bharti Enterprises- an Indian retail company to get into the business in Indian market. However, the Walmart management was determined to serve India and its people through its cash and carry business. Management believed that the company had the supply chain infrastructure, direct farm program, and supplier development that enabled it to make good investments and provide good returns for its shareholders. The Indian government requires retailers to source 30% from small suppliers, which might restrict the procurement operations for Walmart and might raise a challenge to comply with such requirement (Loeb 2013). Such politico-economic ideology largely grows in the democratic destinations that largely lean towards protecting the domestic industries and markets against the penetration of multinational companies. Business in new destination markets sometimes appears more as a compromise than a promise due to political and economic pressures.

Most companies discretely develop strategies to master the market environment by understanding market competition and anticipating the political and economic shifts in the destination countries. Companies gain competitive advantage through privileged access to customers in the destination markets and overpower the competitors to build their unique posture. For instance in the markets with relatively fewer competitors, companies focus on customer-centric strategies to build loyalty and gain sustainable market share. Thus, competitive advantages need to be architected in view of corporate goals and the macro environment comprising politico-economic conditions and market competition. If local or domestic companies have even brief success in earning greater than normal returns on investments, new entrants cloud to grab a share of profits by developing competitive differentiation. For firms operating in such markets, a better option is to build sustainable strategy and run the business as efficiently as possible than trying to gain short-run advantages through untenable tactics. Developing countries with large demographic and complex socio-economic structure often build barriers for multinational companies to enter into local markets and drive them competitive. The two most powerful competitive advantages the multinational companies tend to achieve by overriding the politico-economic policies in the potential destination countries are—customer captivity and economies of scale. However, in the developing countries where the open market economy is encouraged, intensive market competition outgrows and establishes capitalist business philosophy. Companies entering such markets take the maximum unforeseen risk to drive the advantages by securing niche markets initially and later reaching the complex playing fields (Greenwald and Kahn 2005).

Broadly, three politico-economic ideologies including communalism, democracy, and capitalism are fostered across the countries with their confined merits and demerits in the society. However, there have been continuous shifts in these ideologies, which tend to transform to the ideology closest to better economic advantages. Communism emerged with the ideology of Karl Marx in the mid-nineteenth century. It focused on the concepts of equality of income and wealth in the society and common ownership of good and services. This ideology portrayed the state as a powerful entity to govern the production and marketing activities and encouraged state ownership, controlled trade, and nationalization of companies. Theocracy emerged over a period as a diversified school of thought, which allowed governance of the state as an act on behalf of the God. Marxism led ideology subsequently gained support across much of Europe, and a communist government seized power during the Russian Revolution, leading to the creation of the Soviet Union, the world's first Marxist state, in the early twentieth century. Some countries like Russia and China adopted communism as a politico-economic convention, and nurtured largely domestic markets by discouraging the international companies to penetrate until the late twentieth century. As the globalization whirled over the western hemisphere in the mid-twentieth century, and as industries across the countries have experienced the benefits of capitalist business, the communist ideology dominated in some countries tended to blend with capitalism (Mintzberg 1996).

The growing capitalistic concerns among multinational companies encourage privatization of manufacturing and services, free trade, and driving market competition. Capitalism has grown in the twentieth century within two major philosophies—managerial capitalism and shareholder value capitalism. The managerial capitalism emerged in early twentieth century, which is defined by the then radical notion that firms ought to have professional management while the second school of thought in business was evolved over 1970s emphasizing shareholder value capitalism. The governing premise of the shareholder value capitalism is that the purpose of every corporation should be to maximize shareholders' wealth. Theoretically, if firms pursue this goal, both shareholders and society will be benefited. However, in reality, shareholders often experienced faced dissatisfaction in realizing their due values. Consequently, in the twenty-first century customers became the center of the business universe (Martin 2010).

Democratic political and economic system is largely woven around the people of the country and it advocates protectionism in support of the public interest. The business environment in democratic economic systems encourages localization, partial privatization, and public–private partnership. Governments in democratic countries build strong public sector industries with state control and lean towards nationalization and domestication of companies. Five rising democratic countries at different stages of democratic consolidation and economic development, comprising India, Brazil, South Africa, Turkey and Indonesia collectively known as IBSATI, illustrate the positive correlation between political governance, and economic and social progress. These countries excel in blending local business with global industries and are increasingly asserting themselves as important international players in the fields of governance, economics, and peace and security. The democratic governance philosophy allows international companies to collaborate with the local business houses and offer a win–win market conditions. The IBSATI democratic countries have made distinct choices in the twenty-first century to transition towards greater openness both politically and economically by setting them on a path towards renewed business and economic growth (Piconne and Miller 2013).

International Trade Policies

The USA has been an active partner with developed and developing countries since the end of World War II, Its trade policy has evolved significantly through conventional trade practices between the partnering countries since then. The passage of the landmark 1934 Reciprocal Trade Agreements Act (RTAA) is one of the notable trade developments. Since the beginning of the twentieth century, the USA and its trading partners had high import tariffs in place. In the initial years, there was no multinational international agreement that set out rules of trade between nations, and the few trade agreements that existed had generally been negotiated on a bilateral basis. Trade negotiations, when they occurred, were focused on manufactured goods and the elimination of tariffs. Over the years, the USA has gained in conducting international trade through several means. Liberalization and globalization of trade and investment since the mid-twentieth century have made the country wealthier than the conditions of protected economy. Opening the US market to imported goods has strengthened US foreign policy by improving living standards in allied countries in Europe, Asia, and Latin America. Such liberalized imports policy has fostered not only long-term engagement with many countries but also reciprocated the exports for the USA to countries across the globe. It has also promoted core US beliefs about how societies are best structured to benefit their citizens, including free enterprise, democratic governance, open markets, respect for workers' rights and the environment, and transparent regulation.

Over the globalization movement backed by the developed countries, US economic growth has slowed down significantly despite strong economic push, and consequently imports have fallen. In response, monetary policy has been made flexible with fiscal policy to promote the trade. The changed economic environment had an impact on US trade policy implementation, with a slowing economy likely to increase pressures for greater border protection and government support. The USA continues proposed antidumping and countervailing measures, and the initiation of investigations increased between 1998 and 2000. Such initiations may have an alarming effect on trade, with preliminary duties applied in most cases. A large percentage of investigations in the past two years involved steel products. The USA applied four safeguard measures in 1998–2000, involving agricultural or steel products, and initiated a global safeguard investigation covering certain steel products in June 2001. The USA has strongly advocated reductions in subsidies affecting competition in international markets. Consistent with this position, US federal export subsidies have declined, and government export financing is relied upon for a comparatively low share of exports. However, given the size of the US economy, domestic support has also appreciably impact world markets. In this respect, the largest recipient of government outlays is the U.S. agricultural sector. These outlays nearly tripled between 1997 and 2000, exceeding the decline in the value of agricultural output. In 2000, nearly US$30 billion was made available in direct payments to farmers and ranchers.[2]

The international trade of the USA during 2008–2010 has been dominated by the financial crisis, which resulted in the economic recession on a global scale causing a deep contraction of trade flow with the partnering countries. As the prompt action by the USA through financial and macroeconomic policies to restore liquidity to its financial system and to boost domestic demand have made an important contribution to global economic recovery, the US share has risen to 18.6%, the largest share since 2009. However, a part of the decline in the US share in manufacturing to the world performance was due to the decrease in the value of the dollar between 2002 and 2011. The international value of US dollar has been on the rise since 2011, which is attributable to a stronger dollar and better international trade performance. The USA is continuing to play its historical leadership role in fostering a strong, multilateral trading system, inter alia by maintaining and reinforcing its resistance to protectionist pressures (Levinson 2017). However, with the change in political ideology in 2017 onwards, the intensive focus of trade policies on the domestication of manufacturing and services industries might cause the derailment of international trade dynamics and global economic order established since mid-twentieth century integrating global resources.

The USA remains one of the most transparent and open economies in the world. Import tariffs are low, and a significant proportion of imports enter the USA duty-free under zero-level MFN tariffs or preference programs. Nonetheless, it was also noted that significant tariff peaks remained in certain sectors, such as footwear, leather, textiles and clothing, and in agriculture where there is also a considerable number of non-ad valorem duties. However, the 2008 Farm Bill continues to provide domestic support related to prices, and in many cases, to production as well, which will lead to subsidies rising again automatically as world prices fall from their current high levels.[3] The Import substitution industrialization model came to be the iconic commercial model and the defining policy during the mid-twentieth century, coming to its height during the 1960s. It led to the growth of national industrial production at an average annual rate of 8.9%, yet its closed and overprotected character led to the decline in overall productivity (Basave and Gutiérrez-Haces 2011). During this period, foreign firms benefited from this protected scheme and its high growth rates and expanding the internal market. Import substitution has been an integral part of Mexico's development strategy, but has had disappointing results. Two particularly persistent problems have been the geographic concentration of new ISI industries and their capital-intensive nature. This high degree of capital intensity has caused the new industries to have little effect on Mexico's chronic unemployment problem. These problems, coupled with the tendency of ISI to produce inefficient plants which require continued protection, have led to a search for alternative policies. One such policy is the export promotion scheme which appeared in the 1960s. Such programs appear to contain the most promise for Mexico's future. An empirical study reveals that increasing exports caused output growth in Mexico, which is a possible confirmation of the Export-led growth paradigm. However, no effect of FDI on GDP is found. The inclusion of NAFTA's potential impact confirms the positive effect of exports and reveals that GDP and exports drive FDI. The evidence suggests that export promotion and liberalization in Mexico had the potential to attract greater flows of foreign capital and induce economic growth (Galan and Oladipo 2009). However, this entire transition gives way to the most important commercial adjustment in recent Mexican history, the NAFTA. It is in this agreement that the enveloping transition culminates as an instituted participation of Mexico in foreign markets. The analysis of the impact of this FTA on Mexican commercial policy follows, highlighting its specific effect on the main exports industry, the manufacturing industry or *maquiladoras*.

Shifting production capacity to exports was one way many companies attempted to cope with the crisis generated by the peso devaluation and the collapse of the domestic market. This shift was facilitated by the implementation of the NAFTA in 1994. While the government hoped that the Agreement would stimulate investment from American and other foreign companies anxious to use Mexico as an export platform to the US market, the debate about NAFTA's implications for development focused on qualitative transformation in the relationship between Mexico's maquiladoras and the rest of the economy. The supporters of NAFTA argued that this treaty would integrate the maquiladoras into the domestic industrial sector (Piaget and Niembro 2011), while others critically viewed that NAFTA would perpetuate with low-wage syndrome, and eventually result in the economy of contract manufacturing (Castañda 1993).

The triadic FTA among the USA, Canada, and Mexico, NAFTA, commenced in 1994 in order to improve the regional trade in North America. The overall economic impact of NAFTA is difficult to measure since trade and investment trends are influenced by numerous other economic variables, such as economic growth, inflation, and currency fluctuations. The agreement appeared to have accelerated and encouraged trade liberalization that was already taking place in Mexico, but many of these changes may have taken place without an agreement. Nevertheless, NAFTA is significant, because it was the most comprehensive FTA negotiated at the time and contained several groundbreaking provisions. However, in view of the new governance (2017 onwards) in the USA, there are possibilities of renegotiating positions of Canada and Mexico in the NAFTA. Mexico has stated that, if NAFTA is reopened, it may seek to broaden negotiations to include security, counternarcotics, and transmigration issues. Mexico has also indicated that it may choose to withdraw from the agreement if the negotiations are not favorable to the country. Congress may also wish to address issues related to the US withdrawal from the proposed Trans-Pacific Partnership (TPP) FTA among the USA, Canada, Mexico, and nine other countries. Some observers contend that the withdrawal from TPP could damage US competitiveness and economic leadership in the region, while others see the withdrawal as a way to prevent lower cost imports and potential job losses. NAFTA phased out Mexico's restrictive auto decree and opened the Mexican auto sector to foreign investment from the USA. It has liberalized North American auto trade and has been instrumental in the integration of the North American auto industry. The role of the Internet in international commerce has expanded dramatically since NAFTA's implementation over 20 years ago. While technological advancements have fundamentally changed how firms trade and do business across international borders, some companies argue that new barriers have also emerged, which existing trade rules fail to address (Villareal and Ferguson 2017).

NAFTA countries comprise USA, Canada, and Mexico. Canada and the USA have one of the world's largest investment relationships. The USA is Canada's largest foreign investor, and Canada is the fifth largest foreign investor in the USA. US investment is primarily in Canada's mining and smelting industries, petroleum, chemicals, the manufacture of machinery and transportation equipment, and finance. Canadian investment in the USA is concentrated in finance and insurance, manufacturing, banking, information and retail trade, and other services. US corporate ownership is divided among large institutions and individual investors that own small stakes in many corporations. Corporate goals in USA are relatively of short-term and attempt to maximize the return to shareholders, and financial relationships with banks and access to capital are influenced by government regulation that have significant effects on a nation's competitiveness. Access to international capital in USA has increased due to the globalization of financial markets, technological advances, and national financial deregulation.

In the past several years, the business environment in Canada has been quite resilient compared to the economies of many industrialized nations. Commodity prices have remained high and interest rates have continued to be low, creating a favorable investment environment for the resource companies that are so important to the Canadian economy. A combination of rigorous regulation, strong capitalization, and the conservative practices of Canadian banks has distinguished and insulated the Canadian banking system from the more dramatic losses experienced by banks in other industrialized countries. Of the various forms of business organization mentioned above, the corporation with share capital is the entity most often used to carry on commercial activities in Canada. Partnership, trust or a wide variety of legal arrangements may be used to carry on business activity in Canada.

NAFTA Conflicts and Settlements

A wide array of trade in North America now takes place in accordance with the clear and well-established rules of the NAFTA and the World Trade Organization (WTO). Nonetheless, in such a large trading area, disputes are bound to emerge. Accordingly, the NAFTA directs the governments concerned to seek to resolve their differences amicably through the NAFTA's Committees and Working Groups or other consultations. If no mutually acceptable solution is found, the NAFTA provides for expeditious and effective panel procedures. One of the principal elements of the NAFTA is the establishment of a clear set of rules for dealing with the settlement of disputes. Dispute settlement provisions for countervailing duty and antidumping matters are covered under Chap. 19. Chapter 20 of the NAFTA includes provisions relating to the avoidance or settlement of all disputes regarding the interpretation or application of the NAFTA. There are also special rules for disputes under Chap. 11 (Investment) and Chap. 14 (Financial Services). Administrative support to dispute settlement panels is provided by the Canadian, US and Mexico national sections of the NAFTA Secretariat as required.

There is an established mechanism under Chap. 11 of the agreement for the settlement of investment disputes that assures both equal treatment among investors of the Parties to the Agreement in accordance with the principle of international reciprocity and due process before an impartial tribunal. A NAFTA investor who alleges that a host government has breached its investment obligations under Chap. 11 may, at its option, have recourse to one of the following arbitral mechanisms:

- World Bank's International Centre for the Settlement of Investment Disputes (ICSID);
- ICSID's Additional Facility Rules; and
- Rules of the United Nations Commission for International Trade Law (UNCITRAL Rules).

Alternatively, the investor may choose the remedies available in the host country's domestic courts. An important feature of Chap. 11 arbitral provisions is the enforceability of final awards in domestic courts by arbitration tribunals. Article 1904 establishes a mechanism to provide an alternative to judicial review by domestic courts of final determinations in antidumping and countervailing duty cases, with review by independent binational panels. A Panel is established when a Request for Panel Review is filed with the NAFTA Secretariat by an industry asking for a review of an investigating authority's decision involving imports from a NAFTA country.

In Canada, the Canada Border Services Agency (CBSA) makes dumping and subsidy determinations, while the Canadian International Trade Tribunal (CITT) conducts injury inquiries as to whether or not the dumping or subsidy has caused injury or retardation (material retardation of the establishment of a domestic industry), or is threatening to cause injury to the domestic industry. In the USA, the Department of Commerce, International Trade Administration makes dumping and subsidy determinations, while the United States International Trade Commission conducts injury inquiries. In Mexico, the Secretaría de Economía, Unidad de Prácticas Comerciales Internacionales makes both the dumping/subsidy and injury determinations. These agencies are referred to as investigating authorities. The dumping, subsidy and injury determinations of the investigating authorities can also be appealed, in Canada to the Federal Court of Canada, in the USA to the Court of International Trade and in Mexico to the Tribunal Fiscal de la Federación. Although, panel decisions are binding on the NAFTA partners on their claims for settlement, there is also possibility of reconsideration through the review of binational panel decisions that governments of NAFTA countries may initiate in extraordinary circumstances. This is known as the Extraordinary Challenge Committee (ECC) procedure.[4] The challenge is not an appeal of right but a safeguard to preserve the integrity of the panel process. If either government believes that a decision has been materially affected by either a panel member having a serious conflict of interest, or the panel having departed from a fundamental rule of procedure or having exceeded its authority under the Agreement, either government may invoke review by a three-person, binational Extraordinary Challenge Committee, comprised of judges and former judges. ECC decisions, like binational panel decisions, are binding as to the particular matter addressed.[5]

All disputes regarding the interpretation or application of the NAFTA in Chap. 20 are intended to resolve disputes by agreement, if possible. The process begins with government-to-government (the Parties) consultations. If the dispute is not resolved, a Party may request a meeting of the NAFTA Free-Trade Commission (comprised of the Trade Ministers of the Parties). If the Commission is unable to resolve the dispute, a consulting Party may call for the establishment of a five-member arbitral panel. In order to analyze the trade disputes and claims of the NAFTA partnering countries, scientific review boards which may be selected by a panel, in consultation with the disputing Party, to provide a written report on any factual issue concerning environmental, health, safety or other scientific matters to assist panels in rendering their decisions. As well, disputes relating to the following chapters may be referred to dispute settlement procedures.[6]

The juridical relationship between the NAFTA and WTO Agreement is of considerable interest from the standpoints of policy and technical analysis of legal norms. As a matter of policy, a decision by NAFTA negotiators whether to accord legal priority to the NAFTA or WTO would appear to involve a choice whether to accord a greater degree of attention and concern to more narrow regional economic and political interests, or to broader multilateral interests. In light of the importance, the trade policy makers have ascribed to the potential for conflict between the regional and multilateral integration models, NAFTA negotiators might have been expected to make a clear choice in this hierarchy of interests. Evidence from the text of the NAFTA and from the early NAFTA dispute settlement panel reports suggests that no such overarching policy determination was made or that, if it was made, the determination was implemented in an uncertain manner. The NAFTA is politically justified by its attention to interests which are more difficult to address at the WTO multilateral level. If the results of NAFTA negotiations are placed beneath WTO Agreement norms, then in theory, this attention to regionally specific interests might be jeopardized by the superiority of more generalized WTO norms. There are, therefore, political and social motivations for advocating priority for the NAFTA. Though the NAFTA–WTO hierarchy of norms is uncertain, and while such uncertainty is bound to lead to or exacerbate future NAFTA disputes, the political and social forces, which impelled the initial state of ambiguity have not dissipated. While interests in political stability and economic efficiency might enhance the dispute settlement matters within or through the external bodies like WTO, the partnering countries may be in no more favorable position to agree on such a clarification during the post-NAFTA execution period (Abbot 1999).

Globalization and Business Analytics

Globalization has driven tremendous entrepreneurial dynamism in the marketplace down to the bottom of the-pyramid of the market strata causing bidirectional movements of business forces. Most multinational companies are aiming at expanding their business activities in the local markets, while the enterprises operating in the niche are trying to go beyond territorial boundaries. Consequently, the marketplace today has been congested with the overflowing brands, corporate interventions, instability in demand, and chaos in making business decisions. Every company, irrespective of its operational size and investment, is competing today for improving its performance and stay competitive in the marketplace. Decision-making has turned complicated for the companies as the uncertainties in the market increased discretely across the destination in the world. The term *decision-making* has become more stakeholder-oriented among the firms since the mid-twentieth century. Indeed decision terminology was imported from public administration into the business world as it was needed to treat decision-making more bureaucratically to manage the result oriented strategies of the companies to gain the competitive lead. Further decision-making incorporated the terms like resource allocation and policy making, shifting the managerial thought process, and the role toward a series of interlinked actions that envelopes any decision in a company. Yet, decision-making in business emerges out of a conventional process to a broad competitive market pursuit, putting the managers of a company on pretest to implement the decision in a controlled situation, measure the results, and take the business decisions at the macro level across the markets and consumer segments. All business decisions need to be calculated meticulously for the potential risks along with an indulging human behavior. The advances in technology that support the cognitive processes have improved the decision-making in complex business situations. The business decisions today are largely supported by scientific data analytics than subjective judgments. The data-based decision support systems are reliable, provided the quality of data is acceptable and has passed the reliability tests. Such information analysis could lead executives to make well-enough decisions and test the decision-response matrices before implementing the decisions at macro level (Buchanan and O'Connell 2006).

Making an appropriate decision in the changing market environment is an uphill challenge for most companies especially when there is a paucity of information, and the available data is not of adequate quality. Market information analysis for decision-making is subject to the quality of the data and when it comes to supporting business decisions, it is difficult to build the value of managers' experience and intuition around the business analytics process as they are based on qualitative parameters. The Internet has given the sporadic access to the market information system in small quantities, which attracts most researchers and managers to use the information for making arbitrary decisions. However, it would be reckless to make a business decision based on isolated information without attempting to draw some meaningful inferences from the larger data sets spread across the temporal and spatial parameters. As the intensive use of cross-company spatial and temporal data in decision-making is growing among the companies since the last decade of the twentieth century, this process leads to better decisions and improved business performance. One academic study cited in this report found that controlling for other variables, firms that emphasize decision-making based on data and analytics have performed 5–6% above the average performance. However, still many regional and small firms rely on conventional measures, managerial intuitions, and experience for decision-making. Though there is a direct connection between data-driven decision-making and firm performance, the quality of decisions largely depends on the size of the data sets and its reliability indicators. The approach to Big Data has provided the companies, opportunity to analyze and interpret the segments of information for decision-making. The Big Data is distinguished by its large volume, reliability, and availability across the information channels. The current trend in the global marketplace shows that companies have a growing preference for data analytics and data-driven decisions despite the problems of data accessibility and choosing the right analytics process. Some companies believe that management decisions based purely on intuition or experience are increasingly regarded as suspicious, while most companies consider that management decisions are increasingly based on hard analytic information to derive competitive strategies. A large number of managers feel that the decisions they have made in the recent past would have been better if they would have all the relevant data in hand as it would have helped to derive sustainable and strategic decisions in business focusing on a long-term business growth (Economist 2012).

The dependency on the data-driven decision-making among the companies has increased over the past decade (2001–2010), and they have used business analytics a tool to learn the competitor strategies. Business Analytics has helped the companies to make competitive and sustainable decisions through statistical and operations analysis, developing predictive models, and application for optimization techniques, using the large databases of corporate information over spatial and temporal dimensions. The business analytics results qualify companies on taking various high-value decisions like innovation and technology and to see that business is moving in the right direction in the competitive marketplace. However, the most common questions among the companies are, which best practices the managers involved in business analytics projects should employ, how they would advise their less experienced peers, and how they would be able to convince the top management of the company about a right decision emerging out of the business analytics. The use of business analytics in the corporate decisions has the following positive impact on the companies:

- Delivers clarity towards decision-making,
- Reduces biases towards execution,
- Provides value in learning competitor moves and market dynamics,
- Creates working abilities among managers to gain commitment,
- Builds managerial orientation towards intelligent experimentation, and
- Promotes smart use of information technology.

Most business analytics project managers offer opportunities to the strategic managers and explain market scenarios in conjunction with the information technology (IT) department. In good companies IT department acts proactively in the business analytics and decision process by pursuing opportunities to deliver faster implementation cycles, maintaining just enough process, and designing the business decisions process maps to ensure quality and professional support (Viaene and Van den Bunder 2011).

Business analytics in the twenty-first century has risen into prominence as it offers solutions that benefit a variety of disciplines in business like marketing, new product development, innovation, and customer services. Interestingly, business analytics is not just primarily an extension of information technology or business intelligence or a business function, but a convergence of IT capabilities and competencies, and business performance measures in a company. Business analytics demands an increased collaboration across organizations on issues relating to information selection and screening the data sets, as well as to warn managers about the data intricacies, risks, and teams for the information oversights. The software tools the companies consider as a part of business analytics span across various areas, including analytics, data integration, querying and reporting and managing information technology projects. As business analytics is designed to enable fact-based real-time decision-making, it might be one of the expensive tools to work with for the companies that have a paucity of resources.

In reference to the changing scenarios of market economy and information technology, most companies are leaning towards reaching the cost efficiencies, improving market competitiveness, and increasing revenues as the principal objectives of their companies. Driving through the business analytics experiences every organization gets different outcomes as the appropriateness of the decisions taken and implemented varies by companies towards realizing the benefits. The major challenges observed in acquiring and analyzing market information include data integration with multiple systems or information channels, data quality, and building integration with other enterprise applications. Data integration components provide business organizations with market and enterprise data access and processing across systems and platforms, as well as integrated data quality, which is critical to providing accurate and consistent information. In the global marketplace, companies tend to invest in business analytics to access the right information at the right time in order to empower fact-based real-time decisions at every level of the enterprise, to achieve key objectives and to gain maximum return using the IT tools appropriately. Business analytics is generally both historical and predictive, helping the companies take more proactive, fact-based decisions for building market competitiveness (Computerworld 2009). As the data flow continues to plunge the companies with the market information, more companies are under increasing pressure to develop systems that create both business value and competitive advantage by using the business analytics approached effectively. It has been observed that companies gain competitive value from analytics provided they have the right tools, technology and people, and organizational factors. The management support for analytics is essentially needed from top–down directions and engaging managers in using analytics to identify and address strategic threats and opportunities.

Managing the large data sets of market information in a company needs a new organizational culture, which should be able to shift the decision-making and performance reporting culture from top–down to bottom–up formats based on analyzing the real-time market situations rather than deriving decisions on the perceptional, emotional, or cognitive biases. In companies that compete through market information-based decisions, managers are made aware that business analytics stays central to strategy. Such companies launch multiple initiatives involving complex data and statistical analysis and manage quantitative approaches at the enterprise level. Shifting from conventional to business analytics based decision-making culture in business organizations requires a significant investment in technology, the accumulation of massive stores of data, and the formulation of companywide strategies for managing the data. However, transforming the decision-making culture in the companies also requires commitment and willingness to change to the analytics based thinking. A new breed of organizations like Amazon, Harrah's, Capital One, and General Electric Company have all dominated their fields by deploying industrial-strength analytics across a wide variety of activities. However, among companies that offer competing products and services and use comparable technologies, business processes used in decision-making serve as points of differentiation. Companies engaged in using business analytics hire talented employees and offer intensive training in analytics to improve their performance on managing quantitative tools and techniques for advising managers to take appropriate business decisions in marketing, logistics and operations, investments, and customer services. Consequently, business analytics appears to be the most contemporary tool for making the real-time business decisions (Davenport 2006).

New Dimensions of Competitive Growth

In view of the economic development of the countries involved, their political, social, legal and administrative systems, and with equal respect for the views of all participating countries, future business collaborating and economic cooperation North American countries may be guided by the following strategies:

- The countries of each region should exhibit multi-dimensionality by giving priority to strengthening their relations with one another, through efforts that carry forward on the political, economic and social dimensions, particularly in areas of trade, investment, social development, science and technology, education, culture and institutional development.
- The business partnership strategies should be developed keeping in view the heterogeneity in economic development, culture and institutional modalities that exist in both regions, while seeking globally balanced relations. The relationship should be based on fundamental shared principles and values, which in turn can be translated into clear political messages and a general sustained process of dialogue and cooperation. Relationships can be deepened at the bi-regional level, regional or bilateral levels, taking advantages of the special circumstances of country groupings. Building relationships should proceed at different levels and speeds among the countries of the region.
- Considering the multiplicity of forums, it is necessary to focus the trade partnering negotiations at bilateral and multilateral levels and avoid overlap between distinct dialogues and similar initiatives taken at other forums.
- In order to promote the private and public sectors in both regions to take advantage of trade and investment opportunities, Asia and Pacific and Latin American countries should have a framework for discussing and harmonizing common trade and investment interests.
- Economic issues should be a key part of the cooperation process between the two regions in view of the current low levels of economic exchange and the great potential for expansion. Close and growing economic ties are an important element for recovery and sustained growth in both regions. Both regions should work

together to develop priorities, policies and measures in economic cooperation and thus maximize inter-regional synergy, based on the following principles: (i) closer cooperation and dialogue between government and the private sector, with the latter as the engine of growth; (ii) non-discriminatory liberalization, transparency and open regionalism; and (iii) consistency and compliance with applicable international rules, particularly those of the WTO.

- Increased trade and investment based on open markets and firm adherence to applicable international rules would contribute to early restoration of broad-based economic growth in both regions. The policies should be framed to remove the existing bottlenecks such as information exchange and knowledge sharing to intensify the bi-regional/bilateral trade and investment flows.

Operational Issues in Business Partnering Model

Bilateral negotiations should be strategically pursued in removing/reducing the non-tariff and investment barriers. The trade-related negotiations among the Latin America–East Asian countries should also focus on the technical norms and standards; rules of origin, antidumping, subsidies, countervailing measures; other liberalization and deregulation measures (privatization); sub-regional, regional and hemispheric integration processes; and convergence and divergence between regional integration and multilateral trade regimes. The negotiations should also be dealt on simplifying the customs rules and procedures, including non-transparent and inefficient infrastructures; differing customs; improper application of rules of origin, customs valuation, pre-shipment inspection and import licensing. Customs problems can be especially difficult for small and medium enterprises that have less experience and fewer resources for handling these problems.

Bi-regional multilateral trade needs to be encouraged among the Latin America and East Asian countries which would enable them to promote liberalization which is conducive to increasing the traditional trade flows among the participating countries. The bi-regional diplomatic negotiations should be evolved towards developing an action plan aiming at reducing NTBs and transaction costs, as well as promoting trade and investment opportunities between the two regions. Such a plan could provide concrete goals to be achieved in identified priority areas such as: (a) customs procedures, standards, testing, certification and accreditation; (b) public procurement; (c) quarantine and SPS procedures; (d) intellectual property rights (IPR); and (e) mobility of business people. The detailed descriptions on the above issues are discussed below:

Customs Procedures

- Accelerated alignment and harmonization of tariff nomenclatures with the World Customs Organization (WCO) standards;
- Accelerated implementation of obligations under the WTO Customs Valuation Agreement;
- Endeavor to start negotiations on customs co-operation and mutual administrative assistance agreements between the Latin American and Asian business partners;
- Promotion of transparency through mutual access to existing databases such as customs duties and nomenclature, tariff quotas, import and export procedures and formalities, rules of origin, customs legislation, etc.;
- Improvement of predictability for the business community through publication, and clarification upon request, of customs regulations and procedures in force taking into account, where appropriate, the relevant international customs Conventions, such as the Kyoto Convention;
- Promotion of standardized and simplified documentation taking into account the existing international standards and the ongoing discussions in various international fora.

Standards, Testing, Certification, Accreditation and Technical Regulations

In supporting and enhancing the bi-regional trade-related cooperation in the areas of standards, testing, certification, and accreditation bodies, the deliverables which may need to be considered during evolving the trade policies or tenure agreements are discussed as below:

- Close consultation, where appropriate, in relation to the work of international bodies dealing with standards such as the International Organization for Standards (ISO) and the International

Electrotechnical Commission (IEC) and to the WTO—Technical Barriers to Trade (TBT) discussions;

- Work towards the improvement of mutual understanding of each other's systems of testing, accreditation and certification of conformity, and the development and dissemination of information materials on national standards, certification and accreditation procedures in SME friendly format;
- Accelerated alignment of national standards to international standards, ensuring that national standards thus aligned are embodied in national laws and regulations, and periodic reporting thereon;
- Identification of sectors of priority interest with a view to the consideration of entering into Mutual Recognition Arrangements (MARS); and
- Establishing cooperation in the promotion of technical and institutional capacity-building in relation to standards, testing, certification, accreditation and technical regulations, including the exchange of information on existing programs, the identification of possible gaps, and the enhancement of cooperation programs as appropriate.

Public Procurement

The governments of Latin America–East Asian countries may develop a Trade Facilitation Action Plan (TFAP) with a focus providing transparency in public procurement, in particular through exchanging information on public procurement procedures, statistics, and opportunities. The plan may include the exchange of information on central government procurement procedures and making them available in a format suitable for the business community; sharing inventory of existing database and promoting mutual cooperation on exploring the technical support on public procurement projects.

Quarantine and Sanitary and Phytosanitary (SPS) Measures

The bi-regional trade agreements should also discuss the issues related to promotion of simplification and rationalization in procedures and documentation considering international best practice, and enhancement of transparency on electronic media. This would help to enhance the trade among the partnering countries in plant genetic engineering and value-added trade of flora based products. Such negations would facilitate the enhancement of transparency in key quarantine and SPS areas including inspection and approval procedures, quarantine requirements and normal inspection processing time.

Intellectual Property Rights (IPR)

The TFAP should also focus on cooperation in technical, institutional and human capacity-building in relation to IPR awareness and enforcement including the exchange of information on existing programs, the identification of possible gaps in these programs, and their enhancement as appropriate.

Mobility of Business People

With a view to facilitating direct business-to-business contacts between the two regions, the negotiating countries should draw administrative measures to examine and report on concerns identified by the business community with respect to formalities for business travel and temporary stay.

Trade in Private Sector

The role of private sector organizations and chambers of commerce can be assumed in the creation of a private sector network linking Asian and Latin American companies. The integration process also involves mutual perceptions that are cultural, with an aim to replace the conventional agreements with contacts among actual business people and the possibility of creating common policies and benefits.

The political risks in international business are developed with illegitimate use of political power. The way political power is exercised determines government action and the degree of risk that threatens a firm's value. For example, a dramatic political event may pose little risk to a multinational enterprise, while subtle policy changes can greatly influence a firm's performance. Firm-specific political risks are the risks directed at a particular company in reference to its country of origin, nature of activities in the host country, social and economic goals etc. and such risks are by nature discriminatory. The risks specific to the firms may be concerned with the governmental policies as well as due to the instability in the political system governing the country. The country-specific political risks are not directed at a firm, but are countrywide, and may affect firm's performance. An example in this context may be given as the decision of the government to forbid currency transfers or the outbreak of a civil war within the host country. The political risks also include government risks and stability risks. The government risks are the ones that arise from the policies of a governing authority, in reference to the use of authority. A legitimately enacted tax hike or an extortion ring that is allowed to operate and is led by a local police chief may both be considered as government risks. Indeed, many government risks, particularly the firm-specific ones, contain an ambiguous mixture of legal and illegal elements. Instability risks, on the other hand, arise from political power struggles. These conflicts could be between members of a government fighting over succession, or mass riots in response to deteriorating social conditions. The country level risk in reference to the government policies and political instability may vary in its intensity.

However, market access has also been improved by the growing trade blocks at regional levels. Such accessibility to the markets is further reinforced by reducing the trade barriers through far-reaching business communication strategies, product and market development programs, and customer relations. This situation has given a boost in determining the market opportunities as narrowing the trade barriers helped in deregulating certain sectors of trade such as financial services. However, there may be some exceptions to this common pattern. The global marketplace equipped with the application of global communications has become the focus of the global business arena that makes the world markets remain open and involve in the fair competitive practices. At the same time, the anti-globalization moves also exist in the process of development that protests against the hazards of suppressive strategies of the global companies affecting the regional trade entities. The globalization moves have opened up high comparative advantages in many manufactured goods through partnership deals to explore the business in the emerging economies. They generally display an increasing specialization trend and high consumer values. The leading alliances between the major multinational enterprises may be seen in reference to production, finance, and technology and supply chain along with other complementary activities.

Notes

1. The spaghetti bowl phenomenon is concerned with the international economic policy that refers to the embedded complexities which arises from the application of domestic controls in the executing the free trade agreements within the group of countries. The complex rules of origin often push high administrative costs and implementation problems.
2. World Trade Organization, Trade Policy Reviews: First Press Release, Secretariat and Government Summaries, United States: September 2001, Press Release Press/Tprb/17217 September 2001(https://www.wto.org/english/tratop_e/tpr_e/tp172_e.htm Retrieved on March 07, 2017).
3. World Trade Organization, Trade Policy Reviews: United States, Concluding remarks by the Chairperson, September 29 and October 1, 2010(https://www.wto.org/english/tratop_e/tpr_e/tp335_crc_e.htm. Retrieved on March 08, 2017).
4. NAFTA Secretariat: Overview of the Dispute Settlement Provisions, Chap. 11, Washington DC(https://www.nafta-sec-alena.org/Home/Dispute-Settlement/Overview-of-the-Dispute-Settlement-Provisions.Retrieved, March 8, 2017).
5. Ibid Chapter. 19.
6. Ibid Chapter. 20.

References

Abbot, F. M. (1999). The North American integration regime and its implications for the world trading system, Jean Monnet Center for International and Regional Economic Law and Justice, New York University. Retrieved March 8, 2017 from (http://www.jeanmonnetprogram.org/archive/papers/99/990201.html).

Bair, J. (2002). Beyond the Maquila model—NAFTA and the Mexican apparel industry. *Industry and Innovation, 9*(3), 203–205.

Basave, J. & Gutiérrez-Haces, M. T. (2011). Striving to overcome the economic crisis: Progress and diversification of Mexican multinationals; EMGP report, Mexico; IIEc/Vale Columbia Center; Mexico City and NY. (http://www.vcc.columbia.edu/content/emerging-market-global-players-project retrieved November 20, 2016).

Bremmer, I. (2014). The new rules of globalization. *Harvard Business Review, 92*(1), 103–107.

Brinkman, R. L., & Brinkman, J. E. (2002). Corporate power and the globalization process. *International Journal of Social Economics, 29*(9), 730–752.

Buchanan, L., & O'Connell, A. (2006). Brief history of decision making. *Harvard Business Review, 84*(1), 32–41.

Castañda, J. (1993). Can NAFTA change Mexico. *Foreign Affairs, 72*(4), 66–80.

Catao, L., & Falcetti, E. (2002). Determinants of Argentina's external trade. *Journal of Applied Economics, 5*(1), 19–57.

Cavusgil, S. T., & Knight, G. (2009). *Born global firms: A new international enterprise*. New York: Business Expert Press.

Computerworld. (2009). *Defining business analytics and its impact on organizational decision-making*. Market Vibe, Austin, TX.

Cuardos, A., Orts, V., & Algnacil, M. (2004). Openness in growth: Reexamining foreign direct investment, trade and output linkages in Latin America. *The Journal of Development Studies, 40*(4), 167–192.

Davenport, T. H. (2006). Competing on analytics. *Harvard Business Review, 84*(1), 98–107.

Economist. (2012). *The deciding factor: Big data and decision making*. London: The Economist Intelligence Unit.

Galan, B. I. V. & Oladipo, O. (2009). Have liberalisation and NAFTA had a positive impact on Mexico's output growth? *Journal of Applied Economics, 12*(1), 159–180.

Greenwald, B. C., & Kahn, J. (2005). All strategy is local. *Harvard Business Review, 83*(9), 94–104.

Heywood, A. (2007). *Political ideologies: An introduction*. Basingstoke, UK: Palgrave Macmillan.

Hirst, P., & Thompson, G. (1996). *Globalization in question*. New York: Polity Press, Blackwell Publishers.

Igor, P. (2000). *Growth and reforms in Latin America and the Caribbean in the 1990s*, United Nations Economic Commission for Latin America and the Caribbean (ECLAC). Working paper, Economic Division, May.

Leon, I. (2001). *A market process analysis of competition policy in Latin America*. Catholic University of Adres Bellow (UCAB), Venezuela. Working paper.

Levinson, M. (2017). *U.S. manufacturing in international perspective* (pp. 1–19). Washington DC: Congressional Research Service, CRS Report-R42135.

Loeb, W. (2013, October 16). Wal-Mart: What happened in India, *Forbes Online*. Retrieved February 28, 2015 (http://www.forbes.com/sites/walterloeb/2013/10/16/walmart-what-happened-in-india/).

Martin, R. (2010). The age of customer capitalism. *Harvard Business Review, 88*(1), 58–65.

McGrath, R. G. (2013). Transient advantage. *Harvard Business Review, 91*(6), 62–70.

Mintzberg, H. (1996). Managing government, governing management. *Harvard Business Review, 74*(3), 75–83.

Piaget, K., & Niembro, S. (2011). *Liberal trade environment in Mexico: Competitiveness and challenges.* In Rajagopal (Ed.), *International trade relations of Mexico: A window to the world.* Hauppauge, NY: Nova Publishers.

Piconne, T., & Miller, A. (2013). The path to progress? How democratic development drives five rising leaders. *The Brookings Institutions*, December (http://www.brookings.edu/research/articles/2013/12/democratic-development-five-countries-piccone-miller. Retrieved on March 06, 2013).

Rajagopal. (2007). Dynamics of growth in Foreign trade in transitional economies: Analysis of European, Latin American and Asian Countries. *Journal of East-West Business, 13*(4), 37–64.

Rajagopal. (2011). *International Trade Relations of Mexico: A Window to the World.* Hauppauge, NY: Nova Publishers.

Rajapatirana, S. (1994). *The interface of trade, investment and competition policies: Issues and challenges for Latin America.* World Bank, Latin America and Caribbean Department, Report # 009.

Svensson, G. (2002). Beyond global marketing and the globalization of marketing activities. *Management Decision, 40*(6), 574–583.

Svensson, L. E. O. (2012). *Practical Monetary Policy: Examples from Sweden and the United States.* NBER Working Papers 17823, National Bureau of Economic Research, Inc.

Viaene, S., & Van den Bunder, A. (2011). The secrets to managing business analytics projects. *MIT Sloan Management Review, 53*(1), 64–70.

Villareal, M. A., & Ferguson, I. F. (2017). *The North American Free Trade Agreement* (pp. 1–42). Congressional Research Service, 7-5700, February 22.

CHAPTER 8

Functional Strategies in Managing International Trade

Corporate success depends on breaking through the clutter of market information and competitive intervention by meticulously conducting the marketing research facing consumers in the marketplace. As the competition is growing continuously in the global market, the risk on traditional decision-making tools and techniques are also falling in jeopardy. This chapter discusses the impact of advanced marketing-mix, operations and logistics, brand management, investments, and transfer of technology towards developing international trade in the North American marketplace. The discussions on approaches for cost-effective trade management, technology breakthroughs, and running real-time business decisions to gain a competitive advantage in the international marketplace are some of the significant contributions of this chapter.

Globalization has evolved over a long understanding of consumer behavior, needs, and matching competencies of firms to satisfy the consumers. It upholds the product, service, brand, and corporate values. In the twentieth century, the corporate philosophies of the companies were spinning around the conventional marketing maxims such as customer value, competitive advantage, and product focus. Such marketing dynamics have driven firms to study the market, develop products or services that satisfy customer needs and wants, develop the appropriate marketing-mix, and satisfy its own objectives as well as provide customer satisfaction on a continuing basis. However, it became clear in the latter half of the twentieth century that the functional definition of marketing was narrow with a focus on market and competition. The broad

Rajagopal and V. Zlatev, *Business Dynamics in North America*,
DOI 10.1007/978-3-319-57606-0_8

philosophy of marketing firms until 1980s was marketing to customers, which has shifted to marketing with customers by associating them in the evolution of the business of firms. Globalization is a continuous phenomenon involving manifold change dynamics from innovation to organizational culture, and consumer behavior to competition in the market. In the twenty-first century, globalization is growing within the triangle of challenges emerging from radical consumerism, digitization, and politicization. Corporate leadership has become critical, as the companies tend to increasingly invest resources, adopt the mind-set of experimenters to gain consumer attention and acquaintance, and orchestrate hybrid organizational models to harness diversity for gaining competitive advantage in the global marketplace (Ferraro and Cassiman 2014).

Integrating a global strategy involves five key dimensions: selecting markets of global strategic importance; standardizing products; locating value-adding activities in a global network; using uniform marketing techniques and integrating competitive moves across countries. Industry globalization drivers defined as the industry conditions that determine industry globalization potential and organization and management factors, largely determine the use of global strategy. Such drivers have the strongest influence in global trade. The application of global strategy in industries with high globalization potential improves business performance. Global companies constantly search for opportunities to achieve the benefits of globalization; take a zero-based view of existing activities; flout conventional wisdom and established practices; systematically analyze industry, strategy, and organizational linkages; and make multiple reinforcing changes in strategy and organization. They assume that strategy should be global but implemented locally (Yip and Johansson 1994).

In the growing competitive markets, the large and reputed firms are developing strategies to move into the provision of innovative combinations of products and services as "high-value integrated solutions" tailored to each customer's needs than simply "moving downstream" into services. Such firms are developing innovative combinations of service capabilities such as operations, business consultancy, and finance required to provide complete solutions to each customer's needs in order to augment the customer value (Rajagopal 2007). The market-driving behavior for innovations is different from a firm's market orientation, which emphasizes the competitive dynamics among firms conducting identical business viz. automobile sales. It is argued that the firm's market orientation on innovation-led products interacts with other strategic orientations, in the process determining how they are manifested and implemented. Furthermore, market orientation plays a critical role in determining transitions among various strategic orientations over time among the firms engaged in identical business of products and services. A strong market-oriented strategy of the firm alleviates the possibility of using coercive influence strategies by the competitors and offers an advantage to the customers over competitive market forces (Chung et al. 2007).

Managing Marketing-Mix

Demography, Society and production resources largely determine the consumption pattern of a region. A system of consumption depends on production and marketing activities in a region. Hence, every country exhibits a specific pattern of consumption potential and structure. The consumption level in a country can be measured in terms of volume and compared with other countries in the region. The structure of consumption in a country may be determined by analyzing the behavioral attributes of the consumers thereof. A country may emphasize producer goods over consumer goods in reference to economic factors; what is considered as a necessity in one economy may be considered as a luxury in another. In addition, consumption in advanced countries is characterized by a higher proportion of expenditures committed to capital goods than in developing countries, where substantially more is spent on consumer goods. The structural differences with regard to expenditures among nations can be explained by a theory propounded by the German statistician Ernst Engel in 1857. The Law of Consumption (Engel's law) states that poorer families and societies spend a greater proportion of their incomes on food than "well-to-do people." The Engle's law describes that the people generally spend a smaller share of their budget on food as their income rises. The reason is that food is a necessity, which poor people have to buy. As people get richer they can afford better-quality food, so their food spending may increase, but they can also afford luxuries beyond the budgets of poor people. Hence, the share of food in total spending falls as income grows. Developing countries like the Philippines and Sri Lanka spend a larger percentage on food than countries like the USA (Rajagopal 2007).

Microeconomic factors are found within a company's business environment and they guide the company in managing its competitiveness in the destination market. The microeconomic factors are largely woven around the marketing-mix followed by the company. Globalization has altered the conventional marketing-mix largely and now the elements of marketing-mix possess 11Ps comprising the conventional 4Ps including product, price, place, and promotion. In addition 5Ps including packaging, pace (competitive dynamics), people (front liners in marketing), performance, and psychodynamics (peer-to-peer, word or mouth, or the grapevine effect) constitute the extended operational factors of marketing-mix. The additional 2Ps known as corporate factors involve posture (corporate image) and proliferation (product and market diversification). This new marketing-mix concept has become an essential part of marketing practices of multinational companies. The integration of 11Ps in a marketing-mix strategy is both effective and simple. Interconnecting the marketing-mix elements such as product, price, packaging, and promotion with psychodynamics and posture, companies may gain a sustainable competitive advantage like Samsung in the consumer electronics product markets and Walmart in the global retailing sector. By applying marketing-mix, companies can attain consistency, integration, and advantage in a marketing program to fit the needs of the marketplace (Rajagopal 2011).

However, the political intervention may affect the marketing-mix functions of a firm in the host country in several ways. The political directions may also govern the functions related to transfer pricing, price ceiling and price floor, price contracts, price paid for local raw materials and price paid for imported raw materials to be used in production in the host country. Besides, the activities of distribution and product retailing may also be subject to political interventions in many developing countries. Advertising and communication are another important area of a multinational firm affected by political interference in a country. Of these, local production of commercials, local artists, type of message, type of copy, availability of media, and time restrictions on the use of certain media are significant political interventions faced by a foreign firm.

The globalization effects and the shifting marketing strategies of multinational companies have opened many avenues for future research. New research studies can be explored in the area of cognitive dimensions affecting shopping arousal, marketplace attractions, interpersonal influences, and sales promotions driving the behavior of urban shoppers. Research can also be directed in the related areas of the changing market taxonomy, shopping ambiance and impact of customer-centric marketing strategies on consumer behavior. Future research could examine issues related to the customer perceptions of quality, and retailer or dealer performance. Identifying the variables that have an intervening effect on the quality–performance relationship may provide both academics and managers with potentially compelling answers to the question of why customer-oriented quality improvement programs sometimes do not succeed (Rajagopal 2009). The market orientation of a firm has significant influence on the behavior and attitudes of its sales force, which can be studied in relation to the cognitive and economic factors related to a business firm.

Today, competition is increasing in the markets. It has therefore become necessary to understand the internal and external dynamics that consist of an inter-product and inter-organization marketing-mix strategy in optimizing profit and the volume of sales. The consumer-oriented factors constitute the external dynamics of marketing. A marketing manager has to explore all possibilities of developing an effective plan for launching and sustaining the product in the market. To do so he needs a clear perspective based on the information analyzed. This necessary step of information collection for important decision-making variables and an explorative analysis forms the core of marketing research. It is a tool used in formulating marketing strategies and for reforming plans based on the extensive feedbacks. Marketing research, hence, may be defined as a systematic gathering, recording and analyzing of data on the variables of marketing goods and services. Global concern for business development has led to a close competition of product standards, and to administer customer-oriented strategies for accrediting the product and the company with the welfare business theory. In an attempt to establish such theories, one of the important factors to be considered is evolving an efficient marketing-mix system, which is a complex and important parameter that determines growth in business. Thus, monitoring and evaluation studies have a vital role to play in reconciling the business administrative tasks within a competitive environment. The marketing-mix factors comprising product, price, place, promotion, packaging, pace (market dynamics), people (sales force), performance and psychodynamics (buying appeals) are developed interlinking each factor. The common goals of the foreign firms seeking business in the host country are oriented towards stability, growth, profits, and returns on investment. Most multinational companies develop differentiated products efficiently, make their manufacturing processes flexible, and achieve higher market share.

These firms attain higher product-marketing strength in the market as they focus on developing one product at a time and share components and production processes across a platform of products.

Managing Distribution

There are two forms of international distribution - direct and indirect, practiced by the multinational firms. The direct distribution channel may appear to be more effective, in practice it is better only if the customers are geographically homogeneous, have similar buying habits, and are limited in number. Indirect channel is used by the companies preferably in the regions where customers segments and their buying habits are heterogeneous (Bruce 1989). A foreign company may go through either one or multiple agents or merchant intermediaries in a host country. The major difference between these intermediaries may be described in terms of the legal ownership of goods. An agent, without taking title to the goods, distributes them on behalf of the principal, the manufacturer. Merchant intermediaries do business in their own names and hold title to the goods they deal in. The different types of indirect distributors, who operate in the overseas market include:

- Export management company
- Manufacturer's export agent
- Foreign freight forwarders
- Commission agents, and
- Country-controlled buying agents.

Besides these categories of intermediaries, the export merchants, cooperating exporters and export vendors are the merchant middleman involved in the operation of distribution of goods and services. The above types of intermediaries do not take the title, they do take possession of goods. However, they have different duties with respect to continuation of relationship with the principal (long-term versus temporary); degree of control maintained by the principal (complete versus slight versus none); pricing authority accorded to the agent (full versus partial versus advisory), affiliation with buyer or seller; number of principals served at a time (few versus many); involvement or noninvolvement with shipping or handling of competitive lines; provision of promotional support (continuous versus one-time versus none); extension of credit to the principal (regularly versus occasionally versus rarely versus never); and provision of market information (good versus fair versus poor).

Indirect Distribution Channels

An *export management company* (EMC) may be defined as an independent export organization that serves different companies in their export endeavors. The relationship of EMC with exporter is a client and not of an employer. The EMC operates under the client's name for all international communications. However, the scale of the operations of EMCs would vary in different countries. An EMC may appear just as a person or an organization and manage all export activities of the client overseas. The large export management firms often maintain international offices in strategic locations. The export management companies generate their income either from commissions or from discounts on goods they buy for resale overseas, as they also undertake exporting more effectively, and generally at a lower cost than other channels. The *Manufacturer's Export Agent* (MEA) is another type of indirect distributor, who provides services similar to those of EMC, but the MEA covers limited markets and the contractual relationship is short-term. An exporter may offer MEA a contract for performing a particular transaction, and the MEA would act using own name while following the procedural requirements and receive a commission for its services. A *Webb-Pomerene Association* (*WPA*) may be described as one of the organizations undertaking international distribution services indirectly in the USA. This association is formed among competing US manufacturers especially and exclusively for the purpose of exports according to the Act of 1918 of USA. The members of the WPA can engage in different international marketing activities to their mutual advantage. These members can determine prices, combine shipments, jointly undertake marketing research, or share information with each other, and allocate orders among different members of the association within the operational area as stipulated by the US law. The *foreign freight forwarder* specializes in handling overseas shipping arrangements and their services can be utilized for handling goods from the port of exporters' location to the foreign port of entry. A foreign freight forwarder receives a discount or fees from the shipping company. However, freight forwarders undertake extra services such as packing at an additional cost.

Commission agents also anchor as the distribution channel in the overseas markets. Foreign customers interested in buying overseas products are represented by commission agents. They serve as so-called finders of desired goods at the lowest price for their principals. The commission agents receive their commission from their overseas clients. The *country-controlled buying agent* may be defined as a procurement operator of a foreign government, seeking to buy designated goods for his country. Many developing countries have entrusted these agents with the task of procuring different goods for them. There is another channel for distribution of products and services overseas described as *export merchants*. They buy directly from manufacturers according to their specifications, taking title to the goods. These merchants generally have contacts with the overseas agents through whom the goods are sold either to the wholesalers or retailers. The export merchants assume all possible risks associated with the products they purchase from the manufacturers and sell them in their own names. Their compensation consists of a markup percentage based on market conditions. In general, export merchants may be considered alike domestic wholesalers. On the contrary, the *export vendors* are the organizations, which specialize in buying inferior quality and overproduced goods in a country for distribution in overseas markets. These companies procure the sub-standard goods outright, taking title to them and ship the goods to one or more countries for selling therein through their established contacts.

Many companies develop an alliance with other companies to establish the distribution network or form a joint venture with other companies in order to manage the distribution of their products and services in international markets. For example, the Colgate-Palmolive company distributed Wilkinson Sword men's toiletries in selected overseas markets, Whirlpool used Sony in Japan and Breck Shampoo used Schick in Germany to be the distributor for their product. This system of distribution is known as a *cooperative exporter*. A cooperative exporter may be any company that has an established system of handling exports for its own goods and distributes products overseas for other manufacturers on a contract basis. These cooperative arrangements are also termed as *piggybacking*. The piggybacking consists of two players—the carrier and the rider. The firm actually engaged in exporting is usually the larger firm with established export facilities and foreign distribution and it may be described as the carrier. The rider is the company using the exporting company to carry its products to the foreign countries by piggybacking, companies can please foreign distributors by giving them a complete line of products. This distribution channel also intends to offer extra customer convenience by providing related products. For example, Singer sells fabrics, patterns, and sewing accessories in addition to sewing machines. Finally, firms with seasonal sales may piggyback to keep their export operation working at full capacity throughout the year. However, piggybacking is a sale of know-how and services rather than a sale of products from the point of view of the carrier firm. The Schick Company for its safety razors tried piggybacking after encountering difficulty in the distribution in the German market and established a temporary alliance with another consumer goods company. Later the company set up its own sales subsidiary in Germany to distribute the wide range of its products. However, in some international markets where distribution is complex or customer requirements are highly personalized, the company might choose to engage in a distribution alliance with a competitor. The Ricoh Company of Japan which is original equipment manufacturer of photocopier machines allowed its competitor, the Savin Company to sell their copies in the USA in order to gain quick market penetration.

Direct Distribution Channels

The manufacturing company overseas performs the international marketing largely by proxy, wherein the products are distributed through another firm that carries its products overseas. The overseas manufacturing companies gain international marketing know-how and achieve the sales targets through indirect approaches. A firm can commit to its performance in the host country by direct exporting in which the manufacturer firm undertakes the export task rather than delegating it to others. The manufacturing company then takes up the tasks of market contact, market research, physical distribution, export documentation, pricing, promotion and other strategic functions. It has been observed that direct exporting activity generally generate more sales than indirect exporting. The advantages of direct distribution are reflected not only in augmenting the sales but also in exercising increased control, better market information, and development of expertise in international marketing. The direct exporting may have higher costs as they are borne by the manufacturing or exporting firm, whereas they are shared in the process of indirect exports. A Firm may choose direct distribution for its products through agents, which include sales representatives, purchasing agents and export broker.

The sales representative may be described as a person in-charge of distributing the products and services of a manufacturing company. A manufacturer supplies the sales representatives with literature and samples to conduct sales in a pre-designated territory. These representatives usually work in reference to time, target, and territory. They largely undertake no risk or responsibility and operate in reference to a stipulated contract for a fixed tenure. They may also choose to operate on either exclusive or non-exclusive basis and serve as a good source of market information. The purchasing agent is also referred to as a buyer for export or an export commission house. Such agents operate in may developed countries including in North America, seeking goods of interest to their foreign principals. Their product quality and price demand are determined according to the requirements of their principal business houses. The *export brokers* are another form of direct agents who play a significant role when firms choose to get their products distributed in overseas markets. An export broker brings the home country seller and foreign buyer together on the negotiating platform. The export brokers receive a commission from the seller for their services. In the process of transaction, the brokers take neither title nor possession of goods and assume no financial responsibility relative to the export transaction. Export brokers who are popularly engaged in the international transaction of agricultural products like grains, cotton etc. are rarely involved in the export of manufactured goods.

Another type of distribution process through direct export agent firms involve *foreign merchant intermediaries*, who generally take title to the goods and arrange to sell them under their own name. The foreign merchant intermediaries offer services similar to a domestic wholesaler. The important types of foreign merchant intermediaries include export distributors, foreign retailers, export jobbers, and trading companies. Of these, an *export distributor* procures products from a manufacturer in the home country at the greatest possible discount and resells them for a pre-determined profit by him. Such intermediaries get active in distributing products that require periodic servicing as they are committed to provide adequate service to the customers through carrying a sufficient quantity of spares and parts, maintaining facilities, and providing technicians to perform all normal servicing operations. Export distributors procure the products in their own names and usually maintain an ongoing relationship with the exporter in the home country. They acquire exclusive sales rights in a host country or a region and receive easy terms of payback from exporters. However, sometimes the manufacturers of a home country prefer to deal directly with *foreign retailers*, particularly in the case of consumer goods like cookies and other confectionary products. In some countries, reputed and large retailers dealing in general merchandise or a specific range of products like textile, photo goods, electronics etc. perform dual roles in terms of selling the products directly to consumers through their own outlets and also distributing imported goods to smaller retailers. Thus, it is observed that exports handled by the retailer generally receive wide coverage. On the contrary, the *export jobbers* determine customer needs overseas and provide them by making purchases in the home country. Some jobbers reverse the process, catering to the needs of home country customers by supplying imported products. The jobbers mainly deal in staple groceries and freely traded products under open general license for which brand names have little importance.

Operations and Logistics

Managing operations and logistics in the international trade is complex per se but has now become friendly to the companies due to the process networking and digitization. The operations and logistics management has turned more applied base on the geo-demographic and techno-economic platforms than merely following the theoretical development. Accordingly, since the mid-twentieth century, many business practices have evolved, and logistics currently costs between 10 and 25% of the total cost of international distributions. In international destinations, material management and physical distribution are time bound to make the products and services always available at the outlets using the cost effective measures. The use of distribution technology like radio frequency identification (RFID) in operations and logistics management help the companies stay abreast of current demand and inventories at international destinations. Information technology has increased the capability to efficiently manage logistical operations to the latest possible time and then accomplish rapid delivery of required inventory. Most companies achieve the efficiency in logistics and operations management by applying network design, information analytics of demand and inventory, transportation, inventory and warehousing, material handling, and packaging technology. Such planning in operations and logistics help companies in the elimination of excessive inventories traditionally stocked in anticipation of customer requirements. Rapid response capability shifts operational emphasis from an anticipatory posture based on forecasting and inventory stocking to responding to customer requirements on a shipment-to-shipment basis.

The network design requirement is to determine the number and location of all types of facilities required to perform logistics work. It is also necessary to determine the inventory stock requirements in reference to demand and supply balance, and cost, at each facility. The operations plan of the companies to serve the overseas markets also works closely with the 3-T parameters, which include streamlining the time, target, and territory requirements to assign customer orders for shipment. The network of facilities forms a structure for performing logistical operations at the delivery hubs and outlets. Thus, the network plans incorporate information and transportation capabilities to processing customer orders, maintaining inventory, and improve material handling within the 3-T network design framework. Most companies try to develop operations and logistics plans in the overseas markets with a minimum variance that involves maintaining the delivery commitments in reference to time and volume of merchandise. The managerial commitment in the logistics leads to the financial value of inventory deployed throughout the 3-T networking system. Turn velocity involves the rate of delivery of inventory over time while the high turn rates, coupled with inventory availability, indicates that assets devoted to inventory are being effectively utilized. Most companies aim at reducing inventory deployment to the lowest level consistent with customer service goals to achieve the lowest overall total logistics cost. Concepts like zero inventories have become increasingly as managers seek to reduce inventory deployment. The business process and logistics reengineering are followed by companies as a system enhancement approach to identify the operational defects do not become apparent until inventories are reduced. While the goal of maintaining zero inventory is attractive and economical as most North American companies have adapted after the economic recession of 2007–2010, adequate inventory facilitate companies to gain some benefits in a logistics system. Inventories can provide an improved return on investment when they result in economies of scale in manufacturing or procurement.

In addition to inventory management, forecasting and order management are two distinct areas of logistics tasks that depend on chronological database of the company and dynamic market information. The logistics forecast is an effort to estimate future requirements and needs to be analyzed in reference to clusters and categories of products and services. The forecast guides the positioning of inventory to satisfy anticipated customer requirements. Therefore, one of the main reasons managers use the information to achieve positive control of logistical operations is their desire to replace forecasting inaccuracy with faster response to customer requirements. Control concepts such as just in time, zero inventory, quick response, and continuous replenishment represent approaches to positive logistical control that can be administered using various information technology platforms. In developing the logistics design, a fine balance must be maintained between transportation cost and quality of service. In some circumstances, low-cost, slow transportation will be satisfactory, while under different destination requirements, faster service may be essential to achieve operating goals. Developing and managing the desired transportation-mix depends on the 3-T matrix in reference to estimated costs and profit.

The objective of operations and logistics planning is to make the product available to the consumers at a more convenient outlet. The distribution planning for products should be considered with prime importance to withstand the market competition. It is because, if a competitive product is available at approachable outlets or at a low price, there are all chances of foregoing the sale. Therefore, to deal with such competitive market situation, a systematic planning for delivering the product to the consumers through different distribution channels is required. The time and distance factor for the delivery of goods normally influences the buying decisions where the manufacturing of products is subject to consumer order, occasional demands, and door to door delivery promises. In this regard, the planning needs to be done evolving different methods for efficient product distribution through identified channels. In this process, there is a need to look into the infrastructure factors viz. transport, road, and communication in support of the channel efficiency. In fact, the consumer is only interested in getting the product, but a lot of responsibility lies with the marketing personnel in delivering the product at appropriate time and place.

Inventory planning may invariably be based on the market survey carried out at the time of preparing the business plan. The distribution planning should be done to make the products available to larger number of consumers at lower marketing costs. To reduce the cost of marketing it is required to determine the most feasible channel. The product characteristics and the operational area are the major factors to be considered while selecting a distribution channel. In a different channel, distribution approach can be adopted to get the products more economically to the ultimate user. An important factor to be assessed in this process is the cost effectiveness. It is observed that longer the chain of intermediaries in product distribution, higher is the cost of marketing. Since cost is one of the determinants of profit, it should also be viewed from the angle of product distribution. The exclusive distribution approach is always confined to an area. Such distribution plan can be useful in the markets where the demand concentration for the product is low. In urban areas where market competition for the product is high and the retailing is at large scale, selective distribution policy would be more useful. However, retailers and consumers in areas, where the purchasing power of consumers is low but a large number of retailers are in business fray, feel the need for extensive distribution of products. In other words, such approach would help the market condition.

Managing International Brands

Building brands is a complex process influenced by the internal and external drivers. Internal brand drivers include competence and capability of the company in managing the new brand, allocation of resources to cater the brand in the destination markets, and ability to develop appropriate marketing strategies to promote the brand. Best Buy Inc., the largest retailer of consumer electronics in the USA has acquired Five Star, the third largest retailer of appliances and consumer electronics in China in May 2006. The management of Best Buy had undergone a challenging debate within the company on a branding option discussing how to integrate the new brand into its brand basket. The dilemma that steered the company was whether Best Buy should retain the Five Star brand and let the two brands compete with each other in the Chinese market, or should allow Five Star to lose its identity in the Chinese market. The option had a sense of precedence when it had faced such dilemma at the time of acquiring Future Shop, the largest consumer electronics retailer in Canada, in 2002. The company had then decided in favor of dual brand strategy, which had worked. One of the major threats to the company was cannibalization of brands within the brand basket of the company by agreeing to the dual branding strategy. However, no evidence of cannibalization appeared thereafter with the company. Best Buy and Future Shop had both grown together as independent brands in Canada (Dawar and Ramsastry 2009).

Over the twentieth century, global companies were obsessed with achieving sustainable competitive advantage and secure a position within an industry by introducing multiband strategies that allowed them to be the business leaders for the long term. Some organizations like General Electric Company, Colgate-Palmolive, and Unilever have succeeded with this approach. However, in the current competitive market and politico-economic edge, most companies with tactical strategies do not last long to rule the global branding in the marketplace. Brands are being architected and grown locally considering the consumer preference and the influence of social media on disseminating brands among consumers. The forces driving the brands in the global marketplace today include innovation, technology, consumer value, digital revolution, and regional trade agreements that relax the barriers to entry like North American Free Trade Agreement (NAFTA) between USA, Mexico, and Canada, inforce since 1994.

The "voice of a brand" is part of the promise and experience of a brand. Customers hear the voice in automated service systems, at retail, in the media and elsewhere. The tone, content, and nuances of the brand voice are critical. The meaning or user understanding on the product is also an important source of brand personality creation in the advertisement or any type of media communication. The communication represents the product's meaning—the claimed image of the product. Although the definition of advertising from a semiotic perspective states that the advertisement represents the actual product image, the advertisement represents the product only when there is harmony between the actual and the claimed image of the product. The representative or anchor in advertising provides the most direct way to build this relationship with consumers and to bridge the brand and the mind of the consumer. This consumer–brand fusion process leads to the brand behavior in the market in the short-run and long-run dynamics. The key function of advertising is to communicate the brand and the promise that can be delivered to the customers. The advertisement of a product has two dimensions representing the core promise of the product and creating the consumer personality by transferring the personality traits. This process enhances the customer–brand relationship. The personification of brand through advertisement or market communication is actualized when there is a match between the personality of the advertised product and of the customer.

The social media comprising various digital platforms has become one of the most popular sources of peer communication and a potential channel for brand awareness. Social media platforms enhance the power of social communities by establishing continuous relationships with brands, products and services, and the companies operating at the global marketplace. Social media also facilitates companies to understand consumer perceptions on brands. Most companies use social media as a strong and sustainable driver for disseminating existing brands and building new competitive brands. The social media channels like Facebook, Twitter, and blogs by consumer segments enable robust filtering of information and improving the brand attributes of the company. With the growing use of information and communication technology, consumers stay connected with brands in several new ways ranging from the Internet to digital marketing channels and through the print media. Companies are redesigning the traditional brand communication strategies to develop the brand relationships from the competing perspectives. Positive advertising and communication help in building and nurturing the brand personality in the competitive situation in a market. The intimacy theory of communication builds the brand personality more effectively across varied consumer situations than exchange or seduction theory. Drawing concepts from psychology and social psychology, it can be stated that the five C's of communication, caring, commitment, comfort, and conflict resolution, play a vital role in developing a brand personality. The concept of the sensitivity of communication is that the consumers perceive the brand personality when the advertisement is positive to their own personality and endorses the intimacy attributes with the communication.

Brand literacy is one of the principal drivers in the global marketplace to educate, acquire, and retain consumers, which require companies to strengthen their organizational competencies, capabilities, and focused customer services. Managers need to improve the brand manifestation scenarios to develop brand literacy through verbal and nonverbal communications, and disseminate a 360-degree view of a brand among consumers in the marketplace to drive brand knowledge-led buying behavior. Managers should enhance the attractiveness of consumer brands and link them to brand literacy campaigns for new products. New interactive capabilities such as a brand information call center and online brand–customer interfaces designed to deepen consumers' connection to the brand need to be built by the companies in order to uphold the brand value. The successful global brands offer rich brand experience and build sustainable brand knowledge across premium, upper mass, mass, lower mass, and bottom-of-the-pyramid consumer segments. Though, brand expressions invariably drive the cognitive behavior of consumers, flexible and open-minded managers can propagate brand insights with a universal brand literacy campaign to stimulate knowledge flow through the social network.

Effective brand literacy requires driving a brand stronger towards communicating to consumers through ethnic, family, and peer psychodynamics. Continuous brand literacy delivers consumers comprehension, competitive appraisal on brands, conviction towards brands, and setting up actions towards getting associated with the brands. Brand literacy can also be reinforced by improving and demonstrating the brand attributes that ensure innovation in product design, manufacturing, and merchandising and ensuring relevance in user and usage imagery. Another critical consideration managers can make in reinforcing brands with sensitive expressions is the consistency of the cognitive support that the brand delivers, both in terms of the value for money and perceived use value to the consumers. Managers should look into the two general approaches of brand literacy—firstly diffusion of knowledge through the community and secondly sharing brand knowledge through the family catchments to improve the brand recall and recognition. Brand literacy campaign can also be planned through the Internet modules and social networks. Successful web-based marketing campaigns have an appealing message that delivers brand fantasy, fun and divulgence prompts visibility and leverages the convergence of technology. The multinational companies to expand their consumer outreach and gain competitive advantage have approached globalization, urbanization, and cosmopolitanism from a multitude of perspectives. Cultural knowledge provides an innovative tool for the companies to address the possibilities and complexities in acquiring consumers for preferred brands. These ideas constitute an ontological shift about developing consumer literacy towards brands and its consequences (Johnson 2014).

Many factors determine the nature of brand competition, including not only rivals, but also the attributes of new entrants, the bargaining power of customers and suppliers, and the threat of substitute services or products. A strategic plan of action based on this might include positioning the brand so that its capabilities provide the best defense against the competitive forces, influencing the balance of forces through strategic moves and anticipating shifts in the factors underlying competitive forces (Porter 1979). In outwitting the competing brands, the companies must detect the changes in the strategy game in reference to the market players' status in gaining more knowledge, networking, entrepreneurship and increasing ambitions. The driving forces of competing firms, their organization, and microeconomic environment need to be studied carefully by the company planning to overtake competitors in the business. Further, in the process of winning the battle of rivals, it would be helpful for a company to understand the changing stakes of the competitors and the forces after such developments. A company can outmaneuver the rival brand by being more skillful in particular tasks and reshaping the stakes in one or more business arenas. Outmaneuvering the rival brands is the core of changing the rules of the marketplace. The strategy for outperforming the competitor is largely based on two basic issues—the performance parameters and assessment criteria of the performance. However, the critical parameters may include a probe for the following information on rival brands:

- Creating new customer needs that do not exist
- Developing and establishing the new attributes of the product
- Establishing new channels to reach all the existing and potential customers
- Reinventing stakes to make others confined to play catch-up roles
- Creating new capabilities as the source of new products and customer needs
- Creating knowledge base for driving the capabilities for the new goods and services
- Establishing new relationships with the channels, institutions, and customers
- Winning or losing in the business battle
- Establishing new chain of customer delight
- Leading the product
- Dominating the price–value relationship.

The parameters and assessments of the above actions would help in focusing both the thinking and strategy building process for sailing through the competition successfully. The current and future strategy of competitors must be considered by any company planning to outwit, outmaneuver and outperform them.

Brand strategies can be planned specific to the different stages of the product life cycle. Brand strategies at the introductory stage may be backed by the price (high or low), promotion (unique and competitive), and non-price factors including quality, technology, services, and customer value. In the introductory stage when the brand is new to the market, it should be backed by the attractive promotional schemes. The high price might push the brand into the premium niche. However, if the brand promotion strategies are ineffective, the life cycle of the brands turns shorter due to low attractiveness in the marketplace. The brand segmentation strategy also needs to be built by the company in the introductory stage of the brand. Companies launch many brands with too few priorities and too little advantages in the competitive marketplace to exhibit omnipresence of the company. Brands significantly contribute to market proliferation and developing portfolios across the consumer segments. Developing a brand portfolio strategy involves making the decision to add or eliminate brands, assign roles and establish priorities, and determine how to leverage the strategic brands (Aaker 2008).

In order to identify new brand segments and make them attractive, most companies are exploring high-technology and high-value brands in a less crowded market destinations, which allow the brands to grow sales without tough market competition. Companies have used perceptual mapping strategy to understand how consumers feel about their brands in comparison to those of competitor's and to find weaknesses of the competing brands in the marketplace. Such strategy has also helped the companies to develop customer-centric brand positions and add value to the brands by making them attractive to the consumers. However, as consumer perceptions are volatile and influenced by the tactical moves of the competitors, the business value of perceptional mapping strategy is limited. Often the developing brand strategies based on the perceptions of consumers are arbitrary and fail to link a brand's market position to business performance metrics such as pricing, promotion, and sales. Companies should also consider the role of the operational factors measure such as market share, growth rate, and profitability while developing the brand strategy. Large companies like Toyota and General Electrics, which pioneer in experimenting new brand strategies are leaning towards using consumer perception that links a brand's position to competitors according to its perceived centrality and distinctiveness. The centrality factor explains how such brand strategy is representative of the company while distinctiveness differentiates the brand of the company from competing brands. Using such strategic tool, companies can determine a brand's current and desired position, predict its marketplace performance and devise and track marketing strategy and execution (Dawar and Bagga 2015).

Pricing in International Markets

The pricing structure is largely affected by the strategies of profit and cost centers immensely pushed by the firms to gain an advantage over the competitors tactically. One of the pertinent problems in the profit-center structure is that it makes it impossible for the firm to consider a product's revenues and costs separately. Another is the cost accounting system, which is not good for identifying the actual expense of generating additional offerings. Managers can push profit responsibility up, push revenue and cost responsibilities down to separate groups, and step back from the cost accounting system in order to overcome these challenges. They may find pricing flexibility they didn't realize they had (Bryce et al. 2011). There are many price equilibrium states that firms may achieve over the time in the market competition. Different price structures may be constructed based on various states of price equilibrium. Firms may engage in Stackelberg competition[1] if a firm has some sort of advantage enabling it to move first. More generally, the leader must have commitment power. Moving observably first is the most obvious means of commitment as once the leader has made its move; it is committed to that action. Moving first may be possible if the leader has been the incumbent monopoly of the industry and the follower is a new entrant.

Globalization and growing competition have driven e-commerce with new opportunities and encouraged the application of differentiated pricing. Firms engaged in e-commerce today determine pricing by creating customer switching barriers and differentiating by consumer segment in order to optimize profits. The competitive pricing strategies throw a challenge to managers towards for integrating the customer price search technologies with marketing strategies of the firm. Such integration sometimes may be affected by the market rumors on pricing that are provoked by social media. It has been observed that consumers may not have an accurate sense of what the price should be for most of the items they buy. Research shows that consumers' knowledge of the market is often discrete, and they rely on retailers to tell them whether a good price is being offered to them. In subtle ways, retailers send signals to customers, conveying that a given price relatively offers a competitive advantage. Pricing cues are powerful tools for guiding customers' purchasing decisions, but they must be applied judiciously. Used inappropriately, the cues may breach customers' trust, reduce brand equity, and give rise to lawsuits. Technology led management has set apart the conventional pricing methods in the firm. However, deciding what prices to be charged to the end users represents one of the critical decision variables confronting managers. Though prices indicate clear messages about customer value, purchase intentions, and objectives of the firm, pricing has been one of the least emphasized strategic issues in the management today. A strategic perspective on pricing includes price objectives, price strategy, price structure, price levels, and price promotions. Firms may combine an integrated framework for the analysis of strategic pricing analyzing various strategic frameworks such as market-based versus cost-based, proactive versus reactive, risk assumptive versus risk aversive, and flexible versus standardized dimensions of pricing (Schindehutte and Morris 2001).

In order to develop a right pricing, structure firms need to look into existing market competition and observe whether the competitor's prices are affecting the target market. Also, it is essential to understand what type of value the competitors are providing for the prices offered. Next, firms should strategically harness the local resources in collecting the prince information pertaining to the market and competitors. If a particular consumer segment has been offered a pricing standard for the specific products and services, these resources need to be critically appraised and analyzed by the firms. Further, firms should obtain feedback from the customers. One of the ways to find out about pricing structure is to conduct a survey to the consumers to know their perceptions and values associated with the prices offered by the firms. In addition, firms should evaluate the supply and demand of products or services. If firms are selling a low supply, high-demand product, probably the price structure would touch the higher end compared to when the operational situations are in reverse. Firms may decide to conduct market research in order to broaden the pricing focus. However, firms should decide on price offerings on fixed and variable costs to determine the profitable price structure. In the current market, competition firms seem to follow a hierarchy of pricing objectives where their focus is on the maintenance of the existing customers and the attraction of new ones, in order to ensure their long-term position in the market (Avlonitis and Indounas 2004).

In a competitive marketplace, many companies attempt to take advantage of their customers in order to maximize the value of price through every transaction. However, consumers fight back by rooting out and disseminating pricing policies that seem unfair, using the social media as their strategic tool. One of the major problems in administering the market-oriented prices is that with such pricing strategy customer value is not fixed, as it neither originates with nor belongs solely to the firm. The core principle of pricing is that it should be customer centered. Without a willing customer, there is no value to the price offerings. Hence, firms should view customers as partners in value creation to the prices offered through a collaboration that increases customers' engagement and taps their insights about the value they seek and how the firms could deliver it. Such strategy of pricing may result in generating new revenue streams, increasing customer satisfaction and loyalty, boosting positive word of mouth, and driving the efforts on cost savings (Bertini and Gourville 2012).

In general, firms develop the pricing structure for their products and services in different stages of their life cycles. Firms adapt initial pricing strategy as an introductory price to acquire new customers, play tactically the competition, and gain competitive advantage. To select the best tactics for the situation a firm faces in determining the price in a competitive marketplace, it needs to explore whether existing resources are relevant to play (increase or decrease) with the price in the market or not. In case of an affirmative answer, the firm can look into the internal requirements like cost, resources, technology etc. available for setting the pricing structure. In determining the introductory price most companies enter into the price war with their rivals. Successful price warriors in the global marketplace are attempting to shift the nature of competition by employing several tactics that include focusing on just one or a few (micro) consumer segments, delivering the basic product or providing one benefit better than rivals do, and backing low prices with superefficient operations. However, entering price wars will destruct the pricing structure for sustainable growth (Kumar 2006). Cutting prices usually lowers profits for incumbents without driving the low-cost entrants out of business. Hence, firms should take alternate approaches to competing against cut-price players, may be by differentiate their products or discriminating the price in different market segments.

The quality of price is referred also as value for money from the perspective of consumers. Unwarranted increase in the prices often lowers down the value for money perceptions of buyers and chances of quitting the price for the brand increases. Under such circumstances, competitors tend to decrease the price of the substitutes to acquire the defected brand customers. So, the price war begins in the market. Firms need to go beyond refining cost-cutting capabilities to develop expertise in cost innovation in order to reduce the price and enhance the value for money perception of consumers (Williamson and Zeng 2009). Large and international firms from emerging markets, who have long experience with value-conscious customers, are proceeding ahead with cost-innovation capabilities to unlock mass markets in the global marketplace. Some firms have learned to sell high-tech products profitably at mass-market prices through a combination of lower labor costs and manufacturing innovations.

The life cycles of products and customer value originate with product awareness. Low customer value at the introductory stages drive the firms to penetrate in the mass-market segments offering low prices to acquire customers. At this level of the price life cycle, the prices are set below the level of competition in order to drive the sales and market share of products against competing products. Firms keep close track of the sales of substitute products at the introductory stage that might nip the products of the firm from business growth. Despite the brand value of competing products in the market, there will always be scope for both low-cost and value-added players. However, the extent of scope that the low-end price products would generate depends not only on the competitive advantage experienced by the customers but also on the strategies that the competing firms intend to deploy (Rajagopal 2013).

As the life cycles of product, price, and consumer value move to the growth stage, the influence of substitute products on buying decisions of consumers' increases, because the differences on product attributes, quality, and price tend to get narrowed. Such scenario appears in the market as the market competition intensifies among the firms within the product categories. Consequently, firms adapt to follow tactical approaches for gaining short-run profits. It has been observed that the firms leaning more towards the tactical pricing approaches lead to the price wars in the long run as lowering pricing to retain customers becomes a principal catalyst factor in consumer buying decisions. Such pricing structure of firms stays volatile in the competitive marketplace that consequently creates instability in the customer values. Most firms do not know how pricing influences the demand for a product, but a few of them realize how it affects the consumption of a product. The extent to which a customer uses a product often determines whether he or she will buy the product again. So, pricing tactics encourage repeat buying among consumers that helps firms in building long-term relationships. In the growth stage, a product price turns volatile due to tactical price cuts. Firms initiate price cuts anticipating the long-term strategic consequences. However, they need to meticulously weigh them against the short-term benefits. A pricing decision should be taken not simply to make the next sale or meet some short-term sales objective, but to enhance the firm's long-term ability to operate profitably (Cressman and Nagle 2002).

Generally, price offerings on products and services have prolonged brand impacts that help in building consumer loyalty. Accordingly, the life cycles for products, price, and customer value turn sustainable against market competition and develop a specific posture of the firm or brand in the market. The social media and interactive platforms among the customers and market players would help in building the customer value. Firms will make effort for developing price leadership in the market by setting the price parity across the segments and controlling the price fluctuations for short-term gains. In the stage of maturity, the market competition becomes predictable so firms rely on strategy planning to gain long-term benefits. Hence, firms reduce the tactical approaches in determining prices to win the competitive moves instantaneously. The operational factors influencing supplies, price, sales, customer value and the like become measurable, and the likelihood of buying, consumer preference, and timing of competitive and market events turn predictable. At this stage firms drive their resources on developing long-term plans for a timed sequence of conditional moves to manage competition that provides an offensive rather than a reactive way of sustaining in the market. Corporate awareness at this stage affects decisions on marketing factors such as pricing, product identity, and sales and distribution networks (Levitt 1965).

Price quality is the key factor to determine the unit price. Firms need to assess the quality of price in reference to the perceived value of customers towards the unit price paid for the product or service, and the extent of competitive advantage derived. Determining the right unit price to fix the consumer price is a critical issue. Firms should meticulously observe the unit of product or service that offers maximum value to the consumer and the unit price to be fixed accordingly. With the right pricing tools, firms can communicate the value (price quality) to customers, and deal with their competitive tactics by negotiating the price offer. Price is considered as the corridor of the mass that identifies what price will unlock the greatest number of customers. Firms may develop the business model consider the market competition, profitability, and customer value and offer a framework for figuring out whether and how a firm can profitably deliver the new idea at the targeted price (Kim and Mauborgne 2000).

It is important to realize that price is the key factor that drives consumers to get involved in the buying process. If the price metrics were unique for a firm, it would add value to its profitability and provide higher competitive advantage. Firms commonly offer low-price, low-margin, and high-volume strategy for pursuing business in the mass market and at the bottom of the economic pyramid market. In order to cover the built-in costs of doing business among low-income customers scattered in rural villages and urban slums, price penetration rates must be at the low end as demand governs unit price of a product or service over other attributes that are woven around the added user advantages (Simanis 2012). How firms can make prices more attractive to the consumers and hence the switching attitude are sensitive strategies that need to be derived by analyzing the competitive market environment. Developing a competitive defense strategy that minimizes both the self-inflicted and competitor-inflicted damages of price competition depends on several factors ranging from organizational culture to profitability goals. Before acting to defend market share or initiate price cuts, managers must anticipate the long-term strategic consequences and weigh them against the short-term benefits. A pricing decision should be made not simply to make the next sale or meet some short-term sales objective, but also to enhance the firm's long-term ability to operate profitably (Cressman and Nagle 2002).

Consumers' rising power and retailers' enhanced ability to serve consumers through multi-channel store formats in international destinations affect shopping perceptions. Needs of consumers are found to be increasingly manifested into a propensity to shop which prompts consumers to look for alternate channels of shopping in order to strike the best bargain across the available routes to shopping. Globalization in retailing sector has evolved empowered consumer behavior in developed countries, which determines the choice of store format and quality of business–consumer relationship. Customers buy products because they perceive that the benefits it confers outweigh the price premium they must pay, and as long as customers focus on the benefits side of the equation, superior suppliers can sustain the premium. In an intensive market competition, firms often end up with price wars in order to attract customers as well as augment their market share. However, such dynamic pricing strategy of firms tends to upset the customer price-benefit balance. As firms play out, suppliers place increasing emphasis on price, storming customers with price rather than value enhancement messages. Under such price battles in the market, the inevitable result is that customers become more and more price-sensitive, and less and less benefit-sensitive, narrowing consumers' value streams and buying options. For instance, such price war is observed in the mobile phone industry. Despite a steady stream of quantum performance improvements, evidence is growing that demand for new mobile phones may collapse as soon as prices stop falling at their current dramatic rate (Garda and Marn 1993).

Successful firms in the competitive marketplace always try to gain a distinct place among competing firms and focus on acquiring new customers and retaining the existing ones. Repeat buying behavior of customers is largely determined by the values acquired on the product. The attributes, awareness, trial, availability, and repeat (AATAR) factors influence the customers towards making re-buying decisions in reference to the marketing strategies of the firm. The perception on repeat buying is affected by the level of satisfaction derived from the buying experience of customers (Rajagopal 2008). Among growing competition in retailing consumer products, innovative point of sales promotions offered by supermarkets are aimed at boosting sales and augmenting the store brand value. Purchase acceleration and product trial are found to be the two most influential variables of retail point of sales promotions. Analysis of five essential qualities of customer value judgment in terms of *interest, subjectivity, exclusivity, thoughtfulness, and internality,* need to be carried out in order to make the firm customer-centric and its strategies touching the bottom of the pyramid (Dobson 2007).

Competitive Differentiation

Product differentiation has become one of the pre-requisites for the companies to stay competitive in the growing global and local marketplaces. Most companies are engaged in meticulously designing and positioning the product differentiations as a continuous strategy and invest enormous resources including financial, intellectual, and technological to keep abreast with the market demand. Five major drivers that actively catalyze the product differentiation process consist of market, competitive, cost, technology, and advertising and communication drivers. In introducing the product differentiations, large firms often face tough challenge with local firms to match ethnic values and consumer orientation. Local enterprises that operate in niche compete with large firms as their markets are firmly based in the local culture. Some local firms move from their ethnic strengths, and develop an understanding of global production and consumption dynamics in due course to turn capable of challenging the innovation and technology of large companies. Large firms can offer product differentiations in products and services by ways of standardization, price competitiveness, convenience, and sustainability in the market as against the products available in the local markets. However, large companies need to develop an ethnic innovative perspective, a local business vision, prevention against disruptive and counterfeiting products in local markets, develop partnerships and alliances at the destination market, and drive a supportive consumer ambience (Ger 1999).

The market drivers of product differentiation and new products development comprise the needs of common customers, global customers, global channels and transferable marketing. The customers' needs become a compelling factor for the multinational companies, when customers of the different countries have the same needs in a product category. The free trade and unrestricted travel have created homogenous groups of customers across the countries in reference to specific industries. However, some markets that typically deal with the culture-bound behavior and resistance of consumers towards adoption of differentiated products, seek companies to offer customized products to consumers within niche. The global channels, distribution and logistics companies offer seamless transport, storage, and delivery services. Companies can expand internationally provided the channel infrastructure is met with the distribution needs of the company. Hence their integrated networks thrive to bring new products and technologies close to the global distributors, and retail stores like supermarkets and departmental stores in order to generate systems effect. Transferability in technology marketing is applied in congruence with the marketing ideas on brand names, packaging, advertising and other components of marketing-mix in different countries. Nike's campaign anchoring the basketball champion Michael Jordan pulled up the brand associated with technology led new products in many countries. This is how the good ideas of multinationals get the new technology and innovative products leveraged in the global markets.

The competitive drivers of product differentiation support the companies for matching their technology development and marketing strategies in accordance with the consumer preferences. The existence of global competitors indicates whether a new technology or products is ready for international business operations. Firms need to develop market infrastructure for the new technologies and products to be able to explore the scope of expansion. The competitive efforts put pressure on companies to globalize their marketing activities and derive optimum performance of the new products by interpreting appropriately the competitor signals.

The cost drivers of technology and new products are largely based on the scale of economies that involve the cost of production functions in large and complex industries, cost of outsourcing, diffusion and adaptation of technology, tariffs and taxes, and costs associated with the basic and advanced marketing functions. The macroeconomic factors of the neighboring countries also govern the cost drivers. When a new automobile plant is set up, it aims at designing, manufacturing or assembling, and delivering a particular model by penetrating into the neighboring markets to gain the advantages of economies of scale. The high market share multi-domestic companies derive gains from spreading their production activities across multiple product lines or diversified business lines to achieve advantage through the scope of economies. Developing new technologies, products, manufacturing and marketing activities of Proctor and Gamble, Unilever, and Colgate-Palmolive may illustrate this global attribute that is explained by the cost drivers. The other cost drivers include global sourcing advantages, low global communications, and automation processes. The location of strategic resources to the production plants, cost differences across the countries, and transport costs are also some important considerations of the cost drivers.

The lowering of trade barriers has made globalization of markets and production a theoretical possibility, and technological change has made it a tangible reality. The technology drivers play a significant role in global business. Global expansion of the multinational companies has been highly stimulated by the technological advancements in the designing, manufacturing and marketing of consumer and industrial products. The services have also been improved by many technological breakthroughs. The internet revolution has triggered the e-commerce as open access channel that acts as a strong driving force for global business in the consumer and industry segments. Improved transport and communication now makes it possible to be in continuous contact with producers anywhere in the world. This makes it easier for companies to split production of a single good over any distance. Storage and preservation techniques have revolutionized the food industry for example, so that the idea of seasonal vegetables is no longer relevant today as anything can be exported all the year round from anywhere. Technological upgrading in the form of introduction of new machinery and improvement of technological capabilities, provides a firm with the means to be successful in competition. In the process of introducing better technologies, new lower cost methods become available, which allow the firm to increase labor productivity, i.e., the efficiency with which it converts resources into value. Information and communication technologies, optical technologies, production technologies, materials technologies, biotechnologies, nanotechnologies, microsystems technologies and innovative services are considered the drivers of innovations and differentiation—above all in the areas of application such as automotive engineering, medical technology, mechanical engineering and logistics. Developments in these key technologies provide solutions for the challenges of our time. The dynamic differentiation and product innovations have created high product attractiveness. Increased involvement of consumers and market player in new product development has led to the co-creation strategies and demand for intelligent products and services. Flexible differentiation architectures and application frameworks tie all new products, technologies, and users together. Rapidly changing consumer markets in many industries have called for strategies to expedite support services for technologies and product development. However, an unplanned or ad hoc technology in the market makes the managerial tasks of forecasting, marketing and its user values indistinct and erratic. Fast-cycle decision-making for induction of new technology and products should be based on rethinking of the decision-making model, where managerial intuition replaces extensive analysis as the main driver of decisions (Prewitt 1998). The development and marketing of new or improved technology led products with competitive performance is currently receiving more attention in the business-to-consumers and business-to-business industries. A more innovative strategy to push the technology products in the market has proven to be successful to the industries operating in mature markets. It is also important to be cost-competitive to develop and launch new technologies, which depends on an efficient production process. The technology drivers that move the technology as well as new products towards success also include measuring the performance for management of technology. It is recognized that success at project level does not necessarily mean success at company level (Lager and Horte 2002).

Firms adopt these newer methods of production if they are more profitable than the older ones. The ability of a firm to take advantage of technical progress is also enhanced if the firm improves its entrepreneurial and technological capabilities through two competitive strategies namely learning and adaptation, and innovation strategies. The latter is a process of searching for, finding, developing, imitating, adapting, and adopting new products, new processes, and new organizational arrangements. Because rivals do not stand still, the firm's capacity to develop these capabilities, as well as its ability to compete, depends on the firm's maintaining a steady pace of innovation (Asian Development Bank 2003). Containerization has revolutionized the transportation business, significantly lowering the costs of shipping goods over long distances. Before the advent of containerization, moving goods from one mode of transport to another was very labor-intensive, lengthy, and costly. It could take days to unload a ship and reload goods onto trucks and trains. The efficiency gains associated with containerization, transportation costs have plummeted, making it much more economical to ship goods around the world, thereby helping to drive the globalization of markets and production. The government drivers for the globalization include diplomatic trade relations, custom unions or common markets. The government drivers add favorable trade policies, foreign investment regulations, bilateral or regional trade treaties and common market regulations.

Market competition and growth of innovation and technology have always featured the unpredictable, the surprising, and the unexpected in the global marketplace. However, the increasing deployment of information technology in the firms has developed hyper-connectivity on one hand and complexity in business management on the other. Market competition and growth of technology are now intertwined and interdependent as the market need has become the principal driver of innovation and technology. The new products are embryonic to the consumer need and market demand and are grown largely on predicting outcomes. There are too many continuously changing interactive elements in play that create complexities in managing the marketing of technology led innovative products in different market segments. Managers looking to handle these difficulties need to adopt strategic rather than tactical approaches for sustainable results, and to overcome conventional wisdom by using the models that simulate the behavior of the market players including consumers in order to make the technology led new products sustainable. They should also make sure that their strategies are future-oriented and can manage the market risk. Firms introducing new products rapidly in the marketplace should minimize the need to rely on predictions and work with the user-oriented product design and applications. They can list the complexity factors in a system and build resistant production systems to minimize the consequences of failures in the business system, develop strategic alliances to share the unforeseen risks in the innovation and technologies led products, and enhance organizational capabilities and competencies (Sargut and McGrath 2011).

Administrative complexities play a significant role in explaining new technology drive. Process simplification, zero defect products, cost and profit and overall governance of new products development have many odds to be either eliminated or managed within the organizational system. Most managers are not involved in setting up business thinking about managing probable odds and complexities during the innovation process, and tend to withdraw their role if complexity occurs. Such behavior is also significantly affected by the perception of administrative complexity (van Stel and Stunnenberg 2006). Firms engaged in the rapid development of new products find the gap between diffusion and adoption. It is expensive for companies to manage over piled inventory of obsolete products unless they can be improved and reverted to the active demand. Expensive downtime for production-line changeovers, and merchandise languishing on retailers' shelves or in their showrooms also cause serious concerns to the firms engaged in developing new products. For service companies, though, complexity is much harder to spot and root out, largely due to the ease with which new products can be created and marketed (Gottfredson and Schwedel 2008).

There are four possible complexity areas the companies would meet while introducing the differentiations in products and strategies in the competitive marketplace. The companies observe these complexity areas in internal and external fits. The complexities in the internal fit consist of possible problems a company may face while developing and implementing the strategic and tactical approaches in introducing the differentiations. Besides administrative complexities, most companies are unable to build strong competitive intelligence for collecting the market information and sharing knowledge within the company. Such internal difficulties would drive the companies less competitive in the market in driving the co-creation of differentiated products, seeking consumer cooperation, and understanding the market behavior. Every company expects to enjoy a temporary monopoly on the differentiation of products and services for a while until the disruptive or competitive products appear in the marketplace. The complexities in implementing tactical differentiation might arise for a short term, but cause long-term effects for companies to manage their business in the competitive marketplace. Often the tactical complexities are observed when companies enter into price wars, competitive promotions and go-to-market (GTM) strategies involving salesforce and consumers towards selling and buying of differentiated products. The companies might observe another complexity in the market when the competitive congruence grows in the marketplace. This situation may occur when competitors follow the identical strategies for introducing their innovative differentiations in products and services to grid the consumer decisions.

Notes

1. Firm in the competitive Marketplace tend to engage in playing with price for their products and services to get the first mover advantage. This offers the first firm to gain an advantage over the price of its competing company. If the second firm is going to respond to the price move by choosing the appropriate time and target, it has no choice but to choose the pricing strategy of the first firm. This form of competition is called Stackelberg competition and the firm moving first is called the Stackelberg leader.

References

Aaker, D. (2008). *Prioritize brands in the portfolio: Developing a brand portfolio strategy in a silo environment*. Cambridge, MA: Harvard Business School Press.

Asian Development Bank. (2003). Drivers of change, globalization, technology and competition, section III. *Competitiveness in Developing Asia*. Asian Development Outlook, 2003.

Avlonitis, G. J., & Indounas, K. A. (2004). The impact of market structure on pricing objectives of service firms. *Journal of Product and Brand Management, 13*(5), 343–358.

Bertini, M., & Gourville, J. T. (2012). Pricing to create share value. *Harvard Business Review*, (In press).

Bruce, S., & Ford, J. (1989). Export distribution channels. *Columbia Journal of World Business, 24* (2), 15–22.

Bryce, D. J., Dyer, J. H., & Hatch, N. W. (2011). Competing against free. *Harvard Business Review, 89*(6), 104–110.

Chung, J., Jin, B., & Sternquist, B. (2007). The role of market orientation in channel relationships when channel power is imbalanced. *International Review of Retail, Distribution and Consumer Research, 17*(2), 159–176.

Cressman, G. E., & Nagle, T. T. (2002). How to manage an aggressive competitor. *Business Horizons, 45*(2), 23–30.

Dawar, N., & Ramasastry, C. S. (2009). *Best Buy Inc.-Dual Brand Building in China*. Cambridge, MA: Harvard Business School Press.

Dawar, N., & Bagga, C. (2015). A better way to map brand strategy. *Harvard Business Review, 93*(6), 90–97.

Dobson, J. (2007). Aesthetics as a foundation for business activity. *Journal of Business Ethics, 72*(1), 41–46.

Ferraro, F., & Cassiman, B. (2014). Three trends that will change how you manage: Globalization. *Digitization and Politicization, IESE-Insight Magazine, 23*(4), 23–30.

Garda, R. A., & Marn, M. V. (1993). *Price wars, Mckinsey Quarterly, August*. Retrieved June 21, 2012, from https://www.mckinseyquarterly.com/Price_wars_23.

Ger, G. (1999). Localizing in the global village: Local firms competing in global markets. *California Management Review, 41*(4), 64–83.

Gottfredson, M., & Schwedel, A. (2008, August, 01). Cut complexity and costs. *Harvard Business Publishing Newsletter*.

Johnson, P. C. (2014). Cultural literacy, cosmopolitanism and tourism research. *Annals of Tourism Research, 44*(1), 255–269.

Kim, W. C., & Mauborgne, R. A. (2000). Knowing a winning business idea when you see one. *Harvard Business Review, 78*(5), 129–138.

Kumar, N. (2006). Strategy to fight low cost rivals. *Harvard Business Review, 84*(12), 104–111.
Lager, T., & Hörte, S. Å. (2002). Success factors for improvement and innovation of process technology in process industry. *Integrated Manufacturing Systems, 13*(3), 158–164.
Levitt, T. (1965). Exploit the life cycle. *Harvard Business Review, 43*(6), 81–94.
Porter, M. E. (1979). How competitive forces shape strategy? *Harvard Business Review, 57*(2), 137–145.
Prewitt, E. (1998, August, 01). Fast cycle decision making. *Harvard Business Publishing Newsletters*. Cambridge, MA: Harvard Business School Publications.
Rajagopal. (2007). *International marketing: Global environment, corporate strategy, and case studies*. New Delhi: Vikas Publishing House.
Rajagopal. (2008). Consumer response and cyclicality in new product management. *Journal of Customer Behaviour, 7*(2), 165–180.
Rajagopal. (2009). Effects of customer services efficiency and market effectiveness on dealer performance. *International Journal of Services and Operations Management, 5*(5), 575–594.
Rajagopal. (2011). The symphony paradigm: Strategy for managing market competition. *Journal of Transnational Management, 16*(3), 181–199.
Rajagopal. (2013). *Marketing Decision making and the management of pricing: Successful business tools*. Hershey, PA: IGI Global.
Sargut, G., & McGrath, R. G. (2011). Learning to live with complexity. *Harvard Business Review, 89*(9), 68–76.
Schindehutte, M., & Morris, M. H. (2001). Pricing as entrepreneurial behavior. *Business Horizons, 44*(4), 41–48.
Simanis, E. (2012). Reality check at the bottom of the pyramid. *Harvard Business Review, 90*(6), 120–125.
van Stel, A., & Stunnenberg, V. (2006). Linking business ownership and perceived administrative complexity. *Journal of Small Business and Enterprise Development, 13*(1), 7–22.
Williamson, P. J., & Zeng, M. (2009). Value-for-money strategies for recessionary times. *Harvard Business Review, 87*(3), 66–74.
Yip, G. S., & Johansson, J. K. (1994). *Global marketing strategies of US and Japanese business* (Rep. No. 93–102). Cambridge, USA: Marketing Science Institute.

PART III

Rethinking Future Strategies

CHAPTER 9

Opportunities in International Trade Development

The local market competition is targeted toward the customers, and the competitors strive to win the customer, temporarily or permanently. However, in the business-to-business process, the competition may turn tactical and strategic in order to outperform the rivals firms. In this way, competition can be seen as regulated struggle. This chapter addresses the new opportunities in international trade by cooperating with the local industries in the trade region. Restructuring the contract manufacturing policies, updating investment and joint venture strategies, mergers and acquisition (M&A), and building strategic alliances have been categorically discussed in this chapter. Companies need to work out the process of diagnosing, designing, implementing, and evaluating an effective method of resolving conflicts in the business projects as well as within an organization. This chapter critically examines the drivers and attributes of market chaos, complexities in technology growth, and dynamics of organizational work culture that affect the building and implementation of business projects.

The growing technology and its impact on the competitive advantage of the firm also prompt the brands of the company to cannibalize the existing brands in the market. The ability to keep up with the changing technology is critical for a company's long-term survival. However, companies need to balance the risk of rushing into new areas and potentially cannibalizing their existing business against the risk of dropping down their market share in the emerging markets. It has been observed that when new entrants penetrate into prevailing market niches, they pose

Rajagopal and V. Zlatev, *Business Dynamics in North America*,
DOI 10.1007/978-3-319-57606-0_9

higher threats to cannibalize the products of competing firms. Such crash entries of new firms pose threats to the existing firms irrespective of their sizes, and this may continue as a contagious process. New entrant firms in the market are more likely to respond to innovations in their industry at par with their counterparts. However, the threat of cannibalization appears more critical for the firms that are similar in size and resources in a given market (Debruyne and Reibstein 2005). It is difficult to develop sustainable strategies to enter new markets, or to decide to do business. Most companies emerging out of the regional base and intending to go global operate on a cost-effective pattern by managing the business tasks within small resources. Emerging markets are still not equipped with business operations infrastructure and lack specialized intermediaries, regulatory systems, and contract-enforcing methods that hinder their mobility in the overseas markets. Consequently, multinational companies find it difficult to operate in emerging markets, which has resulted in resistance in investing by many companies. If multinational companies are unable to develop appropriate strategic directions to engage with emerging markets, they are unlikely to remain competitive and penetrate their brand in the destination markets. Many firms choose the international destinations tactically, based on the short-term goals, but fail to sustain in the market due to the behaviors of rivals (Khanna et al. 2005). As the global competition tends to increase continuously, the global face of the customer-centric industry is changing dramatically in the twenty-first century, and emerging markets continue to observe manifold growth in regard to innovation, product differentiation, consumer preferences, retailing strategies of the companies, and per capita spending.

As the competition in the global marketplace is increasing continuously, most companies are also penetrating the low-end competition in order to avoid congestions of firms in the urban areas and exploring the alternative markets to secure the path of market leader. There are many industries in fray in the global market to acquire customers and retain the existing ones. In this competitive dynamics, every firm lives in fear of the low-end competition, wherein a company might lean toward offering much lower prices for an apparently similar product. The majority of such low-end firms fall into the categories of strippers, predators, reformers, or transformers in sustaining the market competition. Such categories of firms are defined by the functionality of the product and the convenience of purchase. Stripper firms, for instance, typically enter a market with skeletal offerings, limited functions, and usually offer convenience services. Large firms have significant advantages for combating low-end competition, but they often hesitate because they are afraid their actions will adversely affect their current profit margins. Thus, the new and growing firms in the competitive market environment need to find the response that is most likely to restore market calm in the least disruptive way. The market leader firms could choose to ride out the challenge by ignoring, blocking, or acquiring the low-end competitor or decide to strengthen its own value proposition by adding new price points, increasing its level of benefits, or dropping its prices (Potter 2004).

Modes of Entry

Many companies begin their internationalization opportunistically through a variety of arrangements that may be described as *piggybacking*. It involves taking advantage of a channel to an international market rather than selecting the country-market in a more conventional manner. Piggybacking is an interesting development, in which organizations with little exporting skill may use the services of one that has. Another form is the consolidation of orders by a number of companies in order to take advantage of bulk buying. Normally, these would be geographically adjacent or able to be served, say, on an air route. The fertilizer manufacturers of Zimbabwe, for example, could piggyback with the South Africans who both import potassium from outside their respective countries. American breakfast cereal products like Post from the owners of the leading US brand entered the Mexican market via their subsidiary Kraft rather than direct from the USA, thus leading to the rather bizarre situation of packs of breakfast cereals with English language packaging covered with stickers in Spanish. The most common form of piggybacking is to internationalize by serving a customer who is more international than the vendor firm. Thus, a customer requests an order, delivery, or service in more than one country, and the supplier starts selling internationally in order to retain the customer and increases its penetration of the account. This is particularly common in the case of business-to-business companies and technology-oriented start-ups (Arnold 2003). The innovative concept of market entry strategy is based on moving with *consumer space*, which indicates that foreign firms enter the destination market by developing adequate consumer awareness on the products and services prior to launch. This strategy is followed largely by the fast-moving consumer goods manufacturing companies and is termed as go-to-market strategy. The go-to-market planning enables the firm to achieve higher margins, accelerated revenue growth and increased customer satisfaction through existing sales channels. An effective go-to-market strategy aligns products and services, processes, and partners with customers and markets to deliver brand promise, the desired customer experience, and tangible value. The go-to-market strategy services help technology suppliers overcome market challenges.

Some aggressive firms have clearly defined plans and strategy, including product, price, promotion, and distribution and research elements. Passiveness versus aggressiveness depends on the motivation to export. In countries like Tanzania and Zambia, which have embarked on structural adjustment programs, organizations are being encouraged to export, motivated by foreign exchange earnings potential, saturated domestic markets, growth and expansion objectives, and the need to repay debts incurred by the borrowings to finance the programs. The type of export response is dependent on how the pressures are perceived by the decision maker. The degree of involvement in foreign operations depends on "endogenous versus exogenous" motivating factors, that is, whether the motivations were a result of active or aggressive behavior based on the firm's internal situation or a result of reactive environmental changes (Piercy 1982). There is certainly no single strategy that fits all firms, products, and markets. The competitive strategy for an established firm to start a new venture and launch a new product must be shaped by the characteristics of the firm, the market, and other environmental factors. Market entry through expansion of the company draws many challenges to firms considering new business options. Capitalizing on overseas markets often opens doors to new levels of top and bottom line growth. Moreover, introducing a new product or service into a new market is an even bigger strategic challenge. A successful entry strategy may conceptualize and implement well-structured entry processes to drive future growth, explore diversified stream of revenues, and augment profit margins. It also addresses new competitors, customers, partners, suppliers, and other market dynamics. However, there are five major modes a foreign firm may apply to enter in the international markets, as listed below:

- Exporting
- Contractual agreement

- Licensing
- Franchising
- Joint venture
- Strategic alliance
- Wholly owned subsidiaries

Exporting is a low risk-low investment strategy wherein a company may minimize the risk of dealing internationally by exporting domestically manufactured products either by minimal response to inquiries or by systematic development of demand in foreign markets. Exporting activity requires small capital for a quick start. Exporting is also a good way to gain international experience. A major part of the overseas involvement of large firms is through export trade managed by the various channels involved in the process.

There are several types of contractual agreements including patent licensing agreement, turnkey operation, coproduction agreement, management contract, and licensing. Patent licensing agreement is based on either a fixed fee or a royalty-based agreement and on delivering managerial training on manufacturing and quality control process. The plant construction, personnel training, and initial production run on a fixed fee, or cost plus arrangement are be covered under turnkey operation agreement. Coproduction agreement was one of the popular practices among the Soviet-bloc countries, where plants were built and then paid for with part of the output. In the Middle East, management contract requires that an MNC provides key personnel to operate the foreign enterprise for a fee until local people acquire the ability to manage the business independently. Technology licensing is a contractual arrangement in which the licensor's trademarks, copyrights, or other intellectual property may be sold or made available to a licensee against a compensation negotiated in advance between the parties. This is one of the common tools of franchising a firm to set quality and operational control standards. In the past, multinational companies used licensing for many reasons. One of the major reasons may be the use of a trademark of the company.

Licensing may be understood as one of the many varieties of contractual agreements whereby a multinational firm makes available intangible assets such as patents, trade secrets, knowledge, trademarks, and company name to foreign companies in return for royalties or other forms of payment. Transfer of these assets is usually accompanied by technical services to ensure their proper use. It also helps in regulating the import and export operations of firms in countries or regions where trade restrictions prohibit the movement of products. A technology licensing agreement usually enables a firm to enter a foreign market quickly and poses fewer financial and legal risks than owning and operating a foreign manufacturing facility or participating in an overseas joint venture. In considering the licensing of technology, it is important to remember that foreign licensees may attempt to use the licensed technology to manufacture products in direct competition with the licensor or its other licensees. During the mid-twentieth century, most industrial firms focused on applying technology assets in their own products and services. As globalization became the key for business growth in the late twentieth century and encouraged open innovation, many firms started to actively license out the technology. These firms consider technology licensing as a strategic advantage, which may yield on technology assets and drive the growth of the firm in a competitive marketplace (Lichtenthaler 2007).

Franchising is not a business itself, but a way of doing business. It is essentially a marketing concept introducing an innovative method of manufacturing and distributing goods and services. Franchising is a business relationship in which the franchisor (the owner of the business providing the product or service) assigns to independent entrepreneur (the franchisee) legal rights to manufacture, market, and distribute the franchisor's goods or service using the brand name for an agreed period of time. The International Franchise Association defines franchising as a continuing relationship in which the franchisor provides a licensed privilege to do business, plus assistance in organizing training, merchandising, and management in return for a predetermined fee from the franchisee. Franchising has become popular because it allows a much greater degree of control over the marketing efforts in the foreign country. In franchising, two important features from a marketing perspective, namely, product lines and customer service, are standardized, though cultural differences might require adaptation. Franchising can offer people willing to be self-employed a greater chance of success than starting their own businesses, but it is a path many people are not aware is open to them. A franchisor's main ongoing commitment to his franchisees is to provide support. The support program should be well-defined prior to joining a given franchise group and is likely to cover areas such as staff issues, marketing, and system compliance. There are four possible models of franchising as discussed below:

- Manufacturer–Retailer: Where the retailer as franchisee sells the franchisor's product directly to the public (e.g., automobile dealerships).
- Manufacturer–Wholesaler: Where the franchisee under license manufactures and distributes the franchisor's product (e.g., soft drink bottling arrangements).
- Wholesaler–Retailer: Where the retailer as franchisee purchases products for retail sale from a franchisor wholesaler (e.g., hardware equipment and automotive product stores).
- Retailer–Retailer: Where the franchisor markets a service, or a product, under a common name and standardized system, through a network of franchisees.

The first two categories cited above are often referred to as product and trade name franchises. These include arrangements in which franchisees are granted the right to distribute a manufacturer's product within a specified territory or at a specific location, generally with the use of the manufacturer's identifying name or trademark, in exchange for fees or royalties. The business format franchise, however, differs from product and trade name franchises through the use of a format or a comprehensive system for conducting of the business including business planning, management system, location, appearance and image, and quality of goods.

One of the challenges in franchising is the need for meticulous and continuous quality control. Such close supervision of the various aspects of distant operations requires well-developed global management systems and labor-intensive monitoring. Inevitably, the relationship between the franchisor and franchisee must involve the imposition of controls. These controls regulate the quality of the service or products to be provided or sold by the franchisee to the consumer. As the effective managerial skills are required, international franchising has become successful largely among these enterprises having long experience with franchising at home before venturing out into international markets. Though franchise system in international business has spread over the three-fourth of the global retailing share by the end of the twentieth century, yet, prospective franchisors need to consider carefully whether to expand a business by franchising or by opening company-owned outlets. Franchising the business not only enables a firm to overcome resource constraints of limited capital and putting a large number of experienced managers onto the corporate role but also provides a means of trading off certain functions cost effectively and relatively quickly (Tikko 1996).

A joint venture involves a partnership between two or more business firms interested in pooling their resources and expertise to achieve a common goal. The risks and rewards of the enterprise are also shared. The reasons for forming a joint venture may include business expansion, development of new products, or moving into new markets, particularly overseas. The joint venture may offer more resources, increased capacity of production, enhanced technical expertise, and established markets and distribution channels. Entry into an international market would be possible either as a wholly owned subsidiary of any firm or as a joint venture. Joint ventures provide the best partner-like manner of obtaining foreign trade income when the firm chooses to begin a business relationship with a firm in the host country. These two partners could agree upon a contract setting out the terms and conditions of how this will work. Alternatively, joint ventures may be set up as a separate joint venture business, possibly a new company. A joint venture company can be a very flexible option wherein partners own substantial resources in the company and agree on a managing strategy. Firms of any size can use joint ventures to strengthen long-term relationships or to collaborate on short-term projects.

The parent ventures managed by wholly owned subsidiaries are more successful than shared management ventures, where both companies—parent and subsidiary—contribute on operational strategies. Problems often arise in shared situations because managers of international ventures have communication problems and different attitudes regarding time, job performance, and the desirability of change (Killing 1982). Firms become multinational by setting up manufacturing or marketing subsidiaries overseas and transferring knowledge, which embodies its advantage, from one country to another. That is, knowledge flows from headquarters to overseas subsidiaries. Venturing is serious business requiring skill, patience, and entrepreneurial flair. Most new ventures involve entering unfamiliar markets, employing unfamiliar technology, and implementing an unfamiliar organizational structure. An approach of particular promise is the new-style joint venture, in which a small company with vigor, flexibility, and advanced technology joins forces with a large company with capital, marketing strength, and distribution channels (Rajagopal 2006). In order to determine the fit between the parent company and its subsidiaries, corporate strategists should evaluate the operational areas, which includes the critical success factors of the business, the parenting opportunities in the business, organizational attributes of the parent company, and the financial results (Campbell et al. 1995).

Competitiveness is industry sector-specific and depends heavily on each company's ability to bring value to an alliance with other companies to form a competitive value chain for the customer. Products that are labor intensive, high volume, and non-complex are more likely to be offshored from the high-wage countries, such as the USA and Canada, to the low-wage regions, such as Mexico and Asia. In North America, Mexico has the competitive advantage in many labor categories, which explains why the production of many parts suppliers migrated south. Advanced technology products, complex products, and products restricted by national security tend to be developed and produced in the advanced countries, but there is no guarantee that this generalization will last as developing countries increase their capabilities and cost differentials converge. Small companies typically have been more vulnerable to the effects of global competition than the large multinational companies that have the resources to move production, engineering/research and development (R&D), and other operations to the location where they yield the strongest advantage.

It is difficult for the companies to develop a geo-demographic monopoly in business as it is unusual to get a large homogenous consumer segment in an overseas destination. As overseas firms enter the destination markets, there are chances of collisions with the local or other multinational companies dealing with similar or identical products and services. As the competition grows in the destination markets, product differentiation turns more complex, as companies may not be able to stick to the same price line with innovative products and services. To survive in a competitive marketplace, it is important for the firms to have an obvious sense of advantage and to drive the business to achieve its predefined objective. Defining the objective, scope, and advantage requires them to manage the trade-offs amid market competition. If a firm pursues growth or size, profitability will be jeopardized, which may ignore retail customers in case the firm chooses to serve institutional clients. Hence, the trade-offs in the marketplace will bounce if the appropriate decision is not taken by the firms. On the contrary, a firm may derive its competitive advantage from economies of scale, and it may not be able to accommodate idiosyncratic customer needs. Accordingly, the growth of local firms may emerge with high brand equity in niche amid the threats of large firms while large firms can follow a combination of long-run and short-run strategies to outwit regional firms. The winning combination will be one that can provide the "best" total value chain combining innovation, production, sales, and service for the final customers. Traditionally, the ability to closely integrate product development and production has allowed companies to explore advances in product design and production efficiency, thus pushing the envelope in terms of innovation and productivity. If the production portion of the value chain loses its luster in North America, it remains to be seen whether manufacturers in the region can hold on to their lead in global innovation and continue to march up the value chain to higher value-added, and more profitable, products and services.

There appear to be seven key dimensions of competitive capabilities, with positive benefits from NAFTA perceived across all: opening new markets; overall performance; top-line growth; creating a platform for global growth; financial management; structural cost; and talent management. Interestingly, executives indicated that the primary impact on their business was improved access and growth into new markets. This was one of NAFTA's primary goals, and it appears that, at least for a majority of these executives, it has been successful. Key infrastructure elements (financial management, structural cost, and talent management) were not affected significantly. In order to encourage the joint ventures and strategic alliances among the North American companies, tax policy and government bureaucracy should be brought down to reduce the barriers to competitiveness. The North American tax policies must be made more competitive and government bureaucracy, which is often manifested through increased compliance costs and introduced as part of regulation around employee health, safety, environmental protection, and manufacturing safety.

International Collaborating Strategies

The soundness of the economy of a country largely governs the consumer confidence, which further determines the buying plans of the consumers. A favorable economic environment helps consumers optimize their buying decisions and augment propensity to spend money. The opposite occurs when economic conditions are unfavorable. The economic environment in Brazil was not encouraging for the various segments of consumers during period 1998–1999 though the inflation was under control. The credit restrictions had a negative impact on consumption during the above referred period. However, after the country exercised appropriate economic measures to stabilize the economy of the country in the recent past, it has been observed that foreign business corporations consider Brazil to be Latin America's most attractive investment target. International marketers should examine the extent to which their business is vulnerable to economic conditions. For example, in a booming economy, consumers tend to buy durable goods; on the contrary, in a recession, they avoid spending money.

As global competition is growing rapidly since the mid-twentieth century, companies are shifting their strategies to survive in the marketplace through cooperation with the competitors instead of investing resources in outperforming, outwitting, or outmaneuvering competitors. Business partnerships and alliances have become a common corporate strategy as they yield substantially in a win-win business environment and deliver better results than struggling in the competition on their own. However, establishing business partnerships are also risk averse as they can fail if the partners have a mismatch of expectations. Companies should examine the partnership conditions meticulously and facilitate the business cooperation, and choose the right options to implement the partnerships in business (Lambert and Knemeyer 2004). The partnership strategies in the twenty-first century have proved effective from Ben Cohen and Jerry Greenfield (Ben & Jerry) to Google cofounders Larry Page and Sergey Brin as each partnership has led to the development of pioneering products and services as well as some of the most successful businesses of recent times. The business partnerships of successful companies have helped emerging companies in determining the most appropriate type of partnership in business.

There are many areas in emerging markets as listed below which attract business partnering opportunities with developed countries.

- Turnkey projects
- Process consultancy
- Consortium production and marketing
- Cooperative ventures
- Strategic alliances
- Buyback agreements
- Corporate chains—technology, retail, and consultancy

- Custom hiring—production and branding.
- Technology diffusion—creating demand
- Green marketing

The companies to provide built-in solutions to revive the sick industries in overseas destination and make them as revived partners in doing business handle turnkey projects. Overseas turnkey projects are initiated with the political will and approval to the revival business partners on the win-win terms of business. The concept of turnkey projects is not only economic but also has socio-political motives. In turn, in key project, the solution provider company undertakes the entire responsibility from design through completion and architecting the right solution, and shares the business responsibilities. The implementation of the turnkey project is generally oriented toward new goals and is managed as a dynamic system. The owners of the Novotel Suvarnabhumi Airport Hotel planned a grand star hotel in a prime location near the airport terminal. There were some administrative and operational problems in the construction of this hotel, which was built on a turnkey basis by the management consultancy group. The management group spent the first few months grappling with those challenges and seeking solutions (Goodwin and Smith 2007).

Process consultancy for a client is carried out by professional consultancy services to improve the existing manufacturing, marketing, distribution, logistics, or services process. In process consultancy, the service providers not only offer research recommendations but also work with the client organization to see that all recommended strategies are properly implemented. Process consultants work with the client toward offering a larger change process through facilitative interventions. Process consulting is a powerful tool, which is used to enhance organizational effectiveness, shorten administrative loops on task management, resolve conflict, and optimize the resource use. It helps teams to work together more effectively, and its effects can last long after the consultants have departed from the client organization. In organizational development, a process consultancy task may be determined as a specialized type of consultation designed to facilitate the organizational teams to deal with issues involving production, business operations, or task administration. Process consultant acts as a coach or guide for the organization in implementing the recommendations of a market research project.

Consortium production strategies have become popular among multinational companies since the 1990s in order to stay cost effective and reduce the corporate liabilities in carrying business at overseas destinations. This strategy is similar to contract manufacturing but is implemented within an agglomeration of small and medium firms at the destination country or across the firms in the neighborhood. In the consortium production strategy, the parent company holds product designing, control of manufacturing process, quality control, marketing strategies, and customer relations management while the associated firms in the consortium are engaged only in production activities. The consortium firms receive required training, transfer of technology, and knowledge, and are connected through common information and communication networks. Such manufacturing process is often appreciated by the multinational companies in India, South Korea, Thailand, and other Asian countries. The consortium production through interactions between public and private companies to boost cooperation in the semiconductor industry has become increasingly international. In Japan and South Korea, the consortium production of semiconductors is supported by the government in promoting or inhibiting cooperation and eliminating the lingering rivalries in the industry that impede truly global dynamics of such a high-technology industry (Ham et al. 1998).

Cooperative ventures and strategic alliances among the companies are built around the similar corporate dynamics. Cooperative ventures involve political moves between countries to establish manufacturing and marketing operations either in public sector with the involvement of state or in cooperative enterprises engaging members of the society in carrying business activities. Governments of home and destination countries support the cooperative ventures with companies that want to explore international trade without taking on the full responsibilities of cross-border business transactions with a foreign partner. International investors entering into a joint venture minimize the risk associated with the outright acquisition of a business. Commonly, strategic alliances are held in the following four major business areas:

- Production alliance
- Distribution alliance
- Financial alliance
- Technology alliance

Strategic alliances are established commonly in partnering supply chains in destination markets to support international marketing of products. Such relationships require special care and handling. During negotiations with a highly valued partner, companies must balance the need to get the lowest price possible and the need to maintain and enhance the alliance. The contemporary global trend shows that the most successful strategic alliances are in companies involved in production, distribution, and technology. Companies such as Hewlett-Packard, Oracle, Eli Lilly, and Parke Davis, who excel at generating value from alliances, have a dedicated strategic alliance function. Companies with a dedicated function could solve problems related to the four key alliance management elements comprising knowledge management, external visibility, internal coordination, and accountability. However, alliances are subject to some ambiguities concerning partnerships, interaction, and evaluation that are important at different stages of evolution of strategic alliances. Partner-related ambiguity is most prevalent at the formation stage of the alliance, and interaction ambiguity is often found at the operational stage, while evaluative ambiguity may encounter the companies at the outcome stage (Kumar 2014).

Some parent companies sell raw material and technology to other companies to manufacture products according to the standards of parent companies and enter into an agreement to buy back the manufactured products. For example, PepsiCo India Holdings Pvt. Ltd (Pepsi) entered an agreement with BASIX (a non-governmental organization engaged in microfinance) for promoting contract farming of potatoes in Jharkhand, an eastern state of India. As per the agreement, Pepsi would supply seedlings and receive an assured supply of chips grade quality potatoes. BASIX was to provide microfinance to the farmers and render training and consultancy for package of practices (POP). Farmers were to get assured buyback of the produce and also an opportunity to learn modern farming practices. The collaboration was successful in the first year, and the project witnessed a very high growth in the second year (Bajaj and Bhullar 2013).

Cross-Border Foreign Direct Investment

The global competition is observed on both aggressive and defensive dimensions in the market. The companies that are capable of managing appropriate diffusion of technology and adaptation process among the customer segments are found to be highly successful. Competition among multinationals these days is likely to be a three-dimensional strategic game wherein the moves of an organization in one market are designed to achieve goals in another market in ways that are not immediately apparent to rivals. There is growing consensus among international trade negotiators and policy makers that a prime area for future multilateral discussion is competition policy. Competition policy includes antitrust policy (including merger regulation and control) but is often extended to include international trade measures and other policies that affect the structure, conduct, and performance of individual industries. The leading alliances between the major multinational enterprises may be seen in reference to production, finance, and technology and supply chain along with other complementary activities. To compete in the major global markets, the multinational companies manage with substantial financial resources. Logistics and the supply chain management is an art of management of the flow of materials and products from the source of production to the end user. The function of distribution is the combination of activities associated with advertising, sales, and physical transfer of the goods and services to the retail and wholesale delivery points as is being observed by the global companies in order to establish their competitive strength in the market. Logistics management is an important function handled by such business companies in the marketing process, and effective logistics management improves both cost and customer service performance of the company. Globalization of distribution is particularly important for companies using Internet for e-commerce as they can operate on economies of scale with a wider reach of customers.

Government investment policies such as foreign direct investment (FDI) and joint venture programs (JV) with the benefits of tax flexibility, low interest rates, and flexible policies of repatriation of funds including profits attract foreign companies toward such destinations. Developing countries encourage FDIs in selected sectors and allow foreign companies to participate through JVs in manufacturing and business operations in the consumer sector. FDI and JV opportunities are offered by both the developed and developing countries, and as the globalization is rapidly growing, bidirectional movements of companies in carrying investments in both types of destinations are seen. The outward FDI of China is steadily increasing and is targeting the USA as a beneficial destination for investments in potential manufacturing sectors such as consumer electronics, automobile parts, consumer durables, and mass consumer products. However, Chinese FDI in the USA faces challenges in cultural, marketing, and technological aspects besides the fitness of politico-business ideologies (He and Lyles 2008). Technology and managerial know-how elements are also important determinants of comparative advantage for the companies to choose the right overseas destination for manufacturing and business operations. Destination markets that have low cost for accessing technology like information and communication technologies for use of Internet and mobile communications and offer low charges for online banking and insurance services, and encourage seamless office operations, appear to be the right choice for multinational companies for doing business. In some countries, governments restrict the import of technology in the generic areas such as food, textile, etc., if any threat is foreseen toward the disruption of the local economy.

Most companies aim at going global and choose to invest extensively through joint ventures, subsidiaries, or making FDIs in potential destinations. The objective of corporate venturing is to gain a competitive advantage by responding quickly to changes in markets and managing local threats. The customer-centric investments in destination countries earn attractive returns. During their first 3 years as public companies, firms backed by corporate venture funds show better stock price performance than those companies backed by traditional venture capital. Most companies meticulously align their goals with the investment so that they can focus on right portfolios. Many companies streamline their decision process to optimize the returns. The market niche also helps in encouraging the FDI with a specific focus on the product and services. FDI is to some extent firm-specific as each firm specializes in a particular niche of the market.

Opportunities for Business in North America

Beyond NAFTA, the future possibilities of doing business in North America largely depend on the international trade policies among the triadic power countries—the USA, Canada, and Mexico—as the political agenda and public diplomacy among these countries are tending to shift. The new governance in the USA is heading toward the domestic manufacturing and trade policies, as against the production sharing. Although there are many opportunities for the companies to explore the business in new sectors in North America, the major driver of the business appears to be the political clearance to move ahead with the business strategies.

The most promising sectors for manufacturing, business collaborations, exporting, and research and development can be identified as listed below:

Oil and gas	Exploration, drilling, and refineries and distribution
Mining	Precious metals, stones, and geo-physical substance exploration
Renewable energy	Solar, wind, and biofuel energy process, products, services, and distribution industry
Industrial and plastics	chemicals Fertilizers, pesticides, insecticides, rubber, high- and low-density polyethylene products
Automobile parts	
Agriculture	Processed and semi-processed products
Pharmaceuticals	Organic and over-the-counter-products, research and development
Consumer products	Green products, food and beverages, electronics, and leather products

The plastics industry, for example, valued at more than $20 billion per year, has averaged 13.4% growth in exports over the past 5 years. Additionally, Mexico's small but burgeoning aerospace industry has grown even faster in recent years. The city of Queretaro is an aerospace cluster, representing 36% of Mexico's aerospace manufacturing, and home to companies such as Bombardier, General Electric, and Textron. Canada is the second largest trading partner of the USA after China, and its economy is closely linked to the economic health of the USA. Since 2009, Canadian exports to the USA increased by more than 50%, reaching a record high in 2014. This demand has bolstered Canadian industrial production by more than 18% since the economic recovery has begun (Kushman and Wakefield 2015). With the low Canadian dollar enhancing the value of goods and services, the US demand for Canadian exports has increased during 2015 and 2016.

Manufacturing is a predetermined industry sector in the region, and it always attracts new investments, collaborations, and markets to make companies grow internationally competitive. There is potential for growth in the domestic market through import substitution and a greater opportunity to increase export sales to national and international markets. The North American Free Trade Agreement, the emergence of the European Economic Community as a major trading block, and the changes in the Eastern European nations are all attractive measures of the trend in the North America in general and Canada in particular toward more open markets and increased trading in manufactured goods. Though the innovative technology sector overlaps with the information technology sector, the manufacturing sector offers enormous business opportunities for investing in the research and development to support the performance of export industries. Expertise already exists in the fields of marine and cold ocean technology, biotechnology, electronic and electrical products, food production technology, and computer hardware and software. Atlantic region firms have been involved in technology related to the marine, defense, aeronautics, information, communication, and space industries. These areas may be customized for global markets or business-to-business deals through the geomatics and global positioning tools.

The North American countries are showing deep concerns on investment in the green and environment-friendly industries as the environment has become more of a public concern, processes, products, and services that reduce, reuse, and recycle to grow internationally along the societal philosophy. Some companies are already engaged in the environmental industries sector including those in environmental consulting, oil spill cleanup, recycling, waste management, environmental assessment, geomatics, and environmental technology development. The growth in this sector is expected to grow in four main areas as listed below:[1]

- Conservation: Information services, planning, and management systems design,
- Environmental assessment: Impact assessment and assessing ways to reduce and avoid air, water, and noise pollution,
- Environmental mitigation: Treating polluted water, air and soil resources, and the cleanup of damaged sites, and
- Environmental information: Monitoring of ice and icebergs, weather forecasting, mapping and geomatics activities, forestry, wildlife population management, and the protection of rare and endangered species and their habitats.

Some of the opportunity areas include basic scientific research, biotechnology, clinical trials, diagnostic services and kits, export services, equipment and supplies, health care delivery research and consulting, home care services, and marketing and distribution of family health care products. The demand for Canadian goods and services is found in such areas as information and communications technologies, transportation services and equipment, environmental equipment and services, engineering and construction, agro-food, and resource industries.

Mergers and Acquisitions

The life cycle of international markets has only the forward dynamics that moves from the initial stage of exporting and ends up in a loop while exploring the new markets as the competition intensifies in the destination country and pulls down the market share of the company. Exporting from home market to destination market works initially out cost effective for the firms in the first stage (Entry) of a firm's business moves to the international destination. As the brand is established in the overseas market in the second stage (Growth) of their internationalization life cycle, companies prefer to reduce their export costs to stay competitive in the destination markets, and firms start manufacturing process in the destination countries. This strategy prompts companies to explore the M&A options at the destination markets.

The M&A activity for USA targets totaled US$2.3 trillion during 2015, an increase of 64% compared to the level of activity seen during 2014 and the strongest period for US M&A since records began in 1980. With US$1.1 trillion in announced deals during 2015, Asia Pacific M&A also registered the strongest period for deal making in the region since records began, topping US$1.0 trillion. The strategic rationale makes use of the merger or acquisition in achieving a set of strategic objectives. As discussed above, a merger to secure control of capacity in the chosen sector is an example. M&As are usually central in the achievement of strategic objectives, though there are usually other alternatives available. One way of overcoming this may be to acquire a company that already has a record of accomplishment of success in the new market. The alternative might be to develop a research and development division in the new market products in an attempt to catch up and overtake the more established players. In the past, it has only really been achieved successfully where the company wishing to enter the new market already produces goods or has expertise in a related area. The M&A in the North America has grown by 30.2% in the USA over 2014 in terms of

Table 9.1 Completed mergers and acquisitions in North American region during 2014–2015 (in million US dollars)

Countries	*2014*		*2015*		*Change in percent*
	Value	*No. of deals*	*Value*	*No. of deals*	
USA	1,154,166.5	8652	1,503,075.9	8579	+30.2
Canada	106,617.8	1344	90,289.0	1176	−15.3
Mexico	11,661.5	148	12,608.1	141	+8.1
North America	1,260,784.3	9996	1,593,364.9	9755	+26.4

Source Thomson Reuters (2015), mergers and acquisitions review, full year review (http://share.thomsonreuters.com/general/PR/MA-4Q15-(E).pdf Retrieved on March 10, 2017)

total value of deals. Table 9.1 exhibits successfully completed M&A deals in NAFTA countries.

Table 9.1 reveals that in the North American region during 2014–2015, there was an increase in the growth of M&A among the USA industries. This situation also supports the inflows of foreign investment and suggests that the USA has been an attractive manufacturing location relative to other high-income countries in recent years. In 2014, 67% of FDI coming into the USA went into the manufacturing sector. Of this, some 43% involved the acquisition of pharmaceutical manufacturers.

Most companies aim at going global and choose to invest extensively through joint ventures, subsidiaries, or making FDIs in potential destinations. The objective of corporate venturing is to gain a competitive advantage by responding quickly to changes in markets and managing local threats. Customer-centric investments in destination countries earn attractive returns. During their first 3 years as public companies, firms backed by corporate venture funds show better stock price performance than those companies backed by traditional venture capital. Most companies meticulously align their goals with the investment so that they can focus on right portfolios. Most companies streamline their decision process to optimize the returns.

Companies need to invest as much in learning from their start-ups as in making and overseeing deals (Lerner 2013). Some companies have seen their venture initiatives fail, and even firms with successful funds have struggled to make use of the knowledge gained from start-up investments. The multinational company must follow the guidelines given below while drafting and pursuing the investment proposals with the governments or organizations of the host countries:

- Focus the investment proposal specific to the requirements of the country or region.
- Develop necessary convergence with the macropolicies of the country.
- Delineate the approval points and schedules.
- Check with all the people whose approval is needed.
- Define alternative goals and approaches.
- Determine the key indicators for all business proposal.
- Prospect for selling the proposal at reasonable bid to optimize long-term gains.
- Establish priorities and develop activity schedule accordingly.
- Be on the competitive edge along with participating bidders and draw defense for the project in terms of project execution and achievements.
- Identify any potential competitors of the project and any points of potential resistance, and then establish strategies, or at least mental contingency plans to deal with them.
- Measure the proposal against all stated corporate policy objectives.
- Write the proposal in the prescribed format with the required information only.
- Prepare strong defense for all possible objections on the investment project.
- Try to keep the project moving forward at a deliberate speed. Don't let it get stalled by excessive reviewing.

The systematic appraisal and professional management of all capital projects help to ensure that the best choices are made and the best value for money is obtained. It is not enough to be satisfied that the investment is justified; it is also necessary to ensure that it produces its planned benefits at minimum costs. These costs include the ongoing current costs generated by the use of the capital asset, as well as the initial capital cost. The appraisal stage involves two separate tasks: preliminary appraisal and detailed appraisal. The preliminary appraisal aims to establish if there is a sufficiently good prima facie case for considering a project in depth. It leads to the recommendation, whether or not to proceed to the detailed appraisal stage. A detailed appraisal should only be carried out if justified by the outcome of the preliminary appraisal, and it leads to a recommendation on whether or not to proceed further with the project in principle. However, it is necessary for the multinational companies to carefully review their investment proposals before the appraisal at the government or sponsor's level.

The financial objectives of the multinational companies are aimed at measuring the performance of the capital employed. Capital employed is the sum of all assets along with the accumulated reserves for depreciation. The multinational companies may recognize that not all operations are directly comparable. They may realize that while setting targets and state that targets for area profit centers and operations, the nature of the operations and performance plans must be taken into account. Emphasis on asset management by the multinational company at all levels is laid in reference to annual targets for cash generation, capital expenditures, and balance sheet items including inventory and receivables management. The finance managers of the company pay special attention to the differences between actual cash-generating capacity and book results. Each production group and profit center of product categories develops the net cash-generating capacity for its own requirements and also pools up sufficient funds for the company to meet its high-priority investment commitments and opportunities. Financial objectives constitute the foundation for making financial decisions for a company. The companies should be able to integrate the financial objectives for both domestic and international business. For example, in order to protect against exchange rate fluctuations, a firm might require managers in the overseas subsidiaries to regularly forecast the exchange rates month by month. Based on these forecasts, corporate funds in a currency are likely to be substantially depreciated and would be utilized before funds in stronger currencies.

M&A in destination markets is largely governed by the economic and financial situations of the country where the merger or acquisition takes place. The economic indicators are the variables that are used to measure the soundness of a country's economy such as GDP per head, the rate of unemployment, or the rate of inflation. Such statistics are often subject to huge revisions in the months and years after they are first published, thus causing difficulties and embarrassment for the economic policy makers who rely on them. The analysis of factors of production is an important consideration in the international marketing to optimize the comparative advantages over natural resources, labor, capital, and entrepreneurship. Entrepreneurs thus play an important role in enabling the economy to adapt to changing conditions and to new possibilities for material improvements by creating new production organizations, and even to whole new industries. Because of its essential role in initiating the process of production, entrepreneurship is identified by some economists as a "fourth factor of production," alongside land, labor, and capital. It may thus be explained that the higher the productivity of a factor of production, the higher may be the income that accrues to its providers. On the other hand, anything that rises above the expected levels of productivity within a society is responsible for the increase in the overall prosperity of the society.

The price indicators in the international markets broadly include export and import price indices, consumer prices, wholesale prices, and industrial producer prices. The export and import price indices can be used to determine the impact of exchange rate movements on the prices of exports and imports. International price data have been useful for both multilateral and bilateral trade agreements, as the countries often utilize these statistics to negotiate trade agreements for some of the important industrial and consumer products such as construction material, plantation crop products like tea and coffee, cotton textiles, oil, airfreight services, etc. A primary reason for measuring import prices is to track the impact they have on domestic inflation. Movement in import prices can often be an indicator of future inflation since some inputs to domestic production, as well as consumption, are imported. The export and import price indices are essential for assessing the impact of international trade on the domestic economy. Among their most important uses are analyzing developments in the trade balance, measuring foreign prices' contribution to domestic inflation, and deflating nominal values of exports and imports for estimating the volume of gross domestic product (Dridi and Zieschang 2004). The producer price index (PPI) is a family of indices that measures the average change over time in selling prices received by domestic producers of goods and services. PPIs measure price change from the perspective of the seller. This contrasts with other measures, such as the consumer price index (CPI), that measure price change from the purchaser's perspective. Sellers' and purchasers' prices may differ due to government subsidies, sales and excise taxes, and distribution costs. It is difficult for a marketer to access information about and review all of these indicators from each country. However, at any given time, the choice of economic indicators may be identified to determine the entry strategies of a firm. These indicators may reflect on the marketer's domestic operations and the potential business in the host country.

The financial indicators related to the international marketing consist of corporate bond yield, factor income, the value of a local currency with reference to US dollars, and money supply. Besides, the extent of FDI in a country also reveals its financial strength. A foreign investment is classified as a direct investment if the foreign investor holds at least 10% of the ordinary shares or voting rights in an enterprise and exerts some influence over its management. The higher yields of the corporate bonds indicate the soundness of the financial conditions in a country. Corporate bond interest rates and associated yield spreads are core topics in financial economics. The factors that affect the level of changes in these variables are important to many financial analysts. An examination of these variables and the relationships between them, as well as possible linkages between yield spreads and stock market behavior, is the focus of major financial analysis. In particular, changes in yield spreads between high- and medium-quality corporate bonds and Treasury bonds are examined, as are changes in the spread between the differing quality corporate bonds. Variations in the interest rates are given in financial market history and are taken for the financial analysis as the guideposts. Changes in macroeconomic factors such as inflation and the business cycle cause these fluctuations. Investor perception of risk, of course, affects both interest rates and stock market valuations. Interest rates tend to move together due to common influences, such as inflation. Although this is true, the difference between corporate and government bond interest rates, and between corporate bonds rates on different quality bonds, is not constant. Other vital financial indicators include the exchange rate, stock trends, and long-term interest rates. The sensitivity of longer-term interest rates to expectations about future short rates is also operative in a short term. This phenomenon is well illustrated by the rise in Japanese long-term rates during the summer of 1996 when financial markets began to anticipate that monetary policy would be tightened in response to recently published information on growth. In addition, the interdependencies among financial markets have certainly increased with globalization; consequently, the foreign exchange markets and bond markets abroad collectively have become much more sensitive to changes in financial conditions in partner countries. However, the long-term interest rates are not fully protected from the influence of external factors even in the developing countries.

Note

1. For details, see Business Development Bank of Canada, From ideas to Business opportunities, Government of Canada, 1995 (http://publications.gc.ca/collections/Collection/C89-4-25-1995E.pdf Retrieved on March 10, 2017).

References

Arnold, D. (2003). *The mirage of global marketing: How globalizing companies can succeed as markets localize*. Upper Saddle River, NJ: Hall.

Bajaj, G., & Bhullar, N. (2013). *Pepsi-Basix Partnership*. Ontario: Ivey Publishing, Richard Ivey Business School.

Campbell, A., Gold, M., & Alexander, M. (1995). Corporate strategy-the quest for parenting advantage. *Harvard Business Review, 73*(2), 120–132.

Dridi, J. & Zieschang, K. (2004). Export and import price indices, *IMF Staff Working Papers, 51* (1), 1–9.

Debruyne, M., & Reibstein, D. J. (2005). Competitor see, competitor do: Incumbent entry in new market niches. *Marketing Science, 24*(1), 55–66.

Goodwin, N., & Smith, R.A. (2007). *Novotel Suvarnabhumi Airport Hotel: Aligning development with operation*. Singapore: Nanyang Technological University, Asian Business Case Centre.

Ham, R. M., Linden, Greg, & Appleyard, M. M. (1998). Evolving role of semi-conductor consortia in the United States and Japan. *California Management Review, 41*(1), 137–163.

He, W., & Lyles, M. (2008). China's outward foreign direct investment. *Business Horizons, 51*(6), 485–491.

Khanna, T., Palepu, K. G., & Sinha, J. (2005). Strategies that fil emerging markets. *Harvard Business Review, 83*(6), 63–76.

Killing, P. J. (1982). How to make a global joint venture work. *Harvard Business Review, 60* (3), 120–127.

Kumar, R. (2014). Managing ambiguity in strategic alliances. *California Management Review, 56*(4), 82–102.

Kushman and Wakefield. (2015). Manufacturing in North America, Cushman and Wakefield Special Report, New York.

Lambert, D. M., & Knemeyer, A. M. (2004). We're in this together. *Harvard Business Review, 82*(12), 114–122.

Lerner, J. (2013). Corporate venturing. *Harvard Business Review, 91*(10), 86–94.

Lichtenthaler, U. (2007). Drivers of technology licensing: An industry comparison. *California Management Review, 49*(4), 67–89.

Piercy, N. (1982). Company internationalization: Active and reactive exporting. *European Journal of Marketing, 15*(3), 26–40.

Potter, D. (2004). Confronting low end competition. *Sloan Management Review, 45*(3), 41–49.

Rajagopal (2006). Innovation and business growth through corporate venturing in Latin America: Analysis of strategic fit, *Management Decision, 44* (5), 703–718.

Tikko, S. (1996). Assessing the franchise option. *Business Horizons, 39*(3), 78–82.

CHAPTER 10

Globalization and Challenges Ahead

Globalization promotes transformations in the business environment, and consumer culture along the dimensions of economic geography can be evidenced with the growth in the urban areas and shorter travel distances, as businesses migrate closer to denser population and generate competition among firms to take advantage of scale and trade in specialized products. The chapter demonstrates that multinational firms have been slow to understand consumers in the developing world, and as a result, they have been vulnerable to local competitors that know how their shoppers think, what they crave, and how they buy. This chapter examines critical shifts in political ideology, reengineering bilateral business, business process engineering for higher growth and profit, and corporate dynamics among the US–Mexico firms for mutual growth.

In the protectionist era until the mid-twentieth century, markets in most countries were operating on conventional platforms with less focus on international trade and regional customer-centric approaches. Market operations of the companies across various industries were viewed as simply the convergence of regional supply and demand to develop regional trade and economy and enhance domestic employment. Over 1950, international conscience about trade liberalization geared up with the participation of the developed countries in the General Agreement on Tariffs and Trade (GATT) and later with the World Trade Organization. Accordingly, political ideologies toward

Rajagopal and V. Zlatev, *Business Dynamics in North America*,
DOI 10.1007/978-3-319-57606-0_10

international trade have been shifted toward encouraging free trade agreements and open market access to industries, companies, and customers in the global marketplace. As the benefits of globalizations were revealed, they could attract a sufficient number of buyers and sellers, map clearly the consumer preferences, acquire new customers, and overcome market congestion by improving the infrastructure and opening more routes to market. In the recent past, industrialization, population growth, the "revolution of rising expectations" in the less-developed countries, and international tensions have affected the political thinking largely. However, the political instability generally occurs when the distribution of wealth fails to correspond with the distribution of political power. This situation may be described in reference to the classical school of political thought as the political stability in a country is largely based on a large middle class in a country. Such market-oriented strategies helped the competing firms to find solutions to the challenges of increasing market competition (Routh 2007).

The political situation of a country can be explained in terms of economic growth, which is reflected in the gross domestic product, economic stability, and social security. The political environment of a country also contributes in building the social position of individuals. A sense of insecurity and uncertainty for the future and an aggravation of the relationships among social classes also result in the politico-economic conflicts in a country. A severe political crisis develops distrust in the economic system of the country, triggers an outbreak of revolutions in the political systems, and declines the prospects of business growth. The political unrest in a country spurs several experimental conditions for the stability of the political system in extremely revealing ways that often induce either change in the political leadership or the restructuring of the political governance system. Since the quality of the political leadership is often decisive, those systems that provide methods of selecting able leaders and replacing them possess important advantages toward internal and global political concerns. The unstable political systems are vulnerable to social and economic crises that break down into various forms of civil warfare damaging the business and social sustainability. The fundamental causes of such failures appear to be the lack of a widespread sense of the legitimacy of state authority and the absence of some general agreement on appropriate forms of political ideology and action.

Shifts in Political Ideology

Despite the support of several nations on globalization, though with the delayed decision, some powerful nations like the USA and UK have undergone significant internal turmoil in endorsing the public diplomacy. The American political ideology has been swinging over the end of twentieth century across the board liberal or conservative views. Americans continue to express a mix of liberal and conservative attitudes. Yet, those who express ideologically consistent conservative and protectionist views have a proportionate influence on the current political thinking, which may discourage the liberal trade ideologies and tend to renegotiate the international trade agreements. One of the major concerns is that the NAFTA may be renegotiated affecting the current trade and investment arrangements.

The emerging regionalization of markets has opened up alternative possibilities and new challenges for tourism development, especially in the northern peripheries of Europe, which often consist of national borderlands. Emerging forms of global governance have produced significant challenges to conventional conceptions of international relations. Educational multilateralism is an area that has been significantly affected by such challenges, but to date, there have not been many efforts by education scholars to sum up the relative impact and total effect of the various clusters of change affecting educational multilateralism (Mundy 2007). Initially, most developing countries had shown resistance to globalization assuming that internationalization would jeopardize the growth the native industries. However, after the Chilean political ideology countering such protectionist thinking in 1980, Mexico stepped in opening its closed economy focused on reforming its import substitution policies in the mid-1980s. Further reforms were made in 1986 when Mexico became a member of the General Agreement on Tariffs and Trade (GATT). Upon joining the GATT, Mexico agreed to lower its maximum tariff rates to 50%. Mexico went further by reducing its highest tariff rate from 100 to 20%. In reference to Mexico, an FTA with the USA opened a way back to the reforms of internal and external trade policies, and transformed the Mexico's formerly statist economy after the devastating debt crisis (Tequila effect) of the mid-90s.

Market orientation requires a different competitive mind-set and a systematic way of looking for opportunities. Instead of looking within the conventional boundaries that define how an industry competes, managers can look methodically across them. In the process of market orientation, firms can find scope for real value enhancement than looking at competitors within their own industry (Kim and Mauborgne 1999). Accordingly, firms with a customer-oriented business culture have shown to facilitate innovativeness in customer services to improve the overall business system and develop a positive perception among the customers, which is expected to yield long-term loyalty. Customer-focused firms, which also have market orientation, rely on developing strategies toward increasing customer satisfaction and loyalty through improved service quality. It is commonly perceived by the marketing managers that market-oriented campaign is expensive, but it can lower the operating costs and increase the market share yielding high sales. It is more profitable for a retailing firm to establish long-term customer relationships than to adopt a short-term transaction-oriented approach. The customer-centric strategies in a firm should go beyond customer relationship and cater to the cross-functional integration of processes, people, operations, and marketing capabilities, which is enabled through information, technology, and applications (Payne and Frow 2005).

Most economists and political analysts argue that NAFTA was unusual in global terms because it was the first time that an FTA linked two wealthy, developed countries with a low-income developing country. This might drive more advantages on costs and prices for the developed countries than an upthrust of international trade and economy for the developing and emerging country. This agreement has lived with this dichotomy of views since its inception in 1994. For this reason, the agreement received considerable attention by US policy makers, manufacturers, service providers, agriculture producers, labor unions, non-government organizations, and academics. Proponents argued that the agreement would help generate thousands of jobs and reduce income disparity between Mexico and its northern neighbors. Opponents warned that the agreement would create huge job losses in the USA as companies moved production to Mexico at lower costs (Villareal and Ferguson 2017).

During the 1980s and 1990s, the prevailing view in academic and policy circles was that trade openness had a positive impact on income growth and industrialization. Multilateral institutions, such as the World Bank and the International Monetary Fund, regularly promoted trade liberalization and even linked development assistance to the undertaking of liberalizing reforms. However, the evidence, on which this view was built, is controversial, partly because researchers and policy advisers often mistake trade volume for trade policy (Rodríguez and Rodrik 2001). The trade liberalization encouraged cost-effective manufacturing to gain a competitive advantage in the global marketplace in reference to the price, innovative differentiation, quality, and technology. However, the protectionist ideologies argued over the demerits of globalization as replacement of native workforce with the low-cost quality labor. This argument repeatedly reached the prime concern of the political agenda over the years in the developed countries and often caused unusual swings in the political ideology. Several factors have contributed to these transformations, including advances in technology that enable effective management of production networks involving multiple locations, the ongoing push toward trade and investment liberalization, and a shift in corporate strategy to one that emphasizes the cost savings and flexibility afforded by outsourcing (UNCTAD 2016).

The world markets are changing rapidly promoting new emerging markets across the countries. In this century, China, India, South Africa, Mexico, and other Latin America based economies promise new opportunities for global trade. The Pacific region had shown a significant leap in Asian population participated in the rapid transition in response to the global movement of trade and services since 1980. Asia may be portrayed as the fastest-growing market for the top brands of Western companies, and at the same time, the Asian companies began penetrating in the Western markets at low-price, high-quality strategy. While the luxury and fashion goods are dominating the Asian and Far East markets, the specialized products such as electronics and automobiles from Asian markets are trying to capture considerable market share in Europe and North American countries. In the emerging markets, the technology has homogenized with the world markets for a variety of customer and industrial needs, and the reduction in the tariff barriers, duties, and liberalization process worldwide has further given a stimulus to the international marketing across the regional boundaries.

Most bilateral negotiations and FTAs are on the edge of strategic renegotiations in the current period (2016 onward) in view of the critical trade and economic analysis and changing political ideologies. Accordingly, many countries are re-negotiating within their trade blocs about eliminating or reducing the non-tariff and investment barriers. However, the protectionist political ideologies are recommending increasing the tariff barriers in international trade to develop their native markets. Such steps might dichotomize the global trade concerns, liberal trade, and economy policies of the countries that were established in the mid-twentieth century and coordinated by the World Trade Organization. The trade-related negotiations among the Latin America and East Asian countries should also focus on the technical norms and standards; rules of origin, anti-dumping, subsidies, countervailing measures; other liberalization and deregulation measures (privatization); sub-regional, regional, and hemispheric integration processes; and convergence and divergence between regional integration and multilateral trade regimes. The negotiations should also be dealt on simplifying the customs rules and procedures including non-transparent and inefficient infrastructures; differing customs; and improper application of rules of origin, customs valuation, pre-shipment inspection, and import licensing. Customs problems can be especially difficult for small and medium enterprises that have less experience and fewer resources for handling these problems.

Bi-regional multilateral trade needs to be encouraged among the Latin America and East Asian countries which would enable them to promote liberalization which is conducive to increasing the traditional trade flows among the participating countries. The bi-regional diplomatic negotiations should be evolved toward developing an action plan aiming at reducing non-tariff barriers and transaction costs, as well as promoting trade and investment opportunities between the two regions. Such a trade development policy could provide concrete goals to be achieved in identified priority areas such as (a) customs procedures, standards, testing, certification, and accreditation; (b) public procurement; (c) quarantine and sanitary and phytosanitary procedures; (d) intellectual property rights; and (e) mobility of business people. Sanitary or phytosanitary measures which conform to international standards, guidelines, or recommendations shall be deemed to be necessary to protect human, animal, or plant life or health, and presumed to be consistent with the relevant provisions of this Agreement and of GATT 1994.

In view of the changing political concerns, most countries have set off structural reforms as growth drivers toward macroeconomic activities, international trade, financial markets, generation and use of public resources, governance, and labor markets. The macroeconomic policies adopted during the reforms process in these countries intend to maximize growth-curbing rise in inflation and unemployment. Most common form of economic reforms includes process of trade liberalization and reducing financial barriers required for investment and production operations to support the international trade movements. Trade liberalization process has also triggered off the opportunities in the countries of Central and Eastern Europe, Asia, and Latin America to look for new business collaborating countries and expand their international trade relations. The trade relationships need to be based on fundamental principles and shared values, which in turn can be translated into clear political messages and a general sustained process of dialogue and cooperation for sustainable trade development among the partnering countries. The negotiations should also be dealt on simplifying the customs rules and procedures and enhancing the coverage of products and services under international trade. New markets, lower production costs, and higher profit rates have been the main motivators in investing to the transition countries.

Cross-Cultural Shifts in Global Marketplace

Global enterprises are increasingly concerned about the effects of international expansion on their corporate culture. The multinational companies nurture a set of enterprise-wide mind-sets which can maintain a unity of purpose while at the same time successfully adapt practices to diverse local economic and cultural conditions (Bellin and Pham 2007). It has been observed that adequately balanced, individualism–collectivism may be a good source of intercultural fit while building shared leadership protecting mutual values. Such managerial outlook would help in reconfiguring individual and cultural orientations and styles of persons of different origin in the design of management teams to build high levels of social effectiveness in the work environment (Rodriguez 2005). However, managing the cross-cultural challenges in the workplace may be made easy by developing a strategic fit of values in the organization with flexibility in individual values and shared personality traits. In the low-trust cultures, the inter-personal relationship remains obscure, and business dealings are largely bureaucratized and tagged with evidences. Such negotiation approaches slow down the process of getting the work done and may cause retrenchment from the business scenario over time. Thus, it is necessary to identify the right and responsive people who could be relied upon as well as qualify on organizational parameters to build future relationship continuum (Bridgewater et al. 2004). In order to compete in an aggressively interactive competition, firms need to shift their corporate culture from the narrow focus on accelerating transactions to optimizing customer lifetime value. It indicates that products and brands must be made acquiescent to the customer and nurtured through the value-based customer relationships. Accordingly, the corporate culture of the emerging firms facing the market competition should develop stronger customer relationships rather than pushing products, adopt new performance metrics, and think of building a customer-focused culture within marketing umbrella (Rust et al. 2010).

Social institutions play a significant role in nurturing the cultural heritage, which is reflected in the individual behavior. Such institutions include family, education, political structures, and the media, and they affect the ways in which people relate to one another, organize their activities to live in harmony with one another, teach acceptable behavior to succeeding generations, and govern themselves. The status of gender in society, the family, social classes, group behavior, age groups, and how societies define decency and civility are interpreted differently within every culture. Social institutions are a system of regulatory norms and rules of governing actions in pursuit of immediate ends in terms of their conformity with the ultimate common value system of a community. Urban and ethnic marketing strategies integrate consumer marketing solutions including Internet and technology aspects within the cultural environment of the host country. An international marketer should evaluate the psychographic and demographic profiles that indicate the target market of urban and ethnic groups. The firm may choose to provide the marketing communication to the target segments close to their lifestyle. The General Motors (GM) Company has made significant contributions to the cultural event on "America on the Move" to exhibit at the Smithsonian's National Museum of American History. GM has appeared to be the largest single donor ever contributed to a cultural group. This promotional strategy has won the car company naming rights and a prominent place in all promotions.

Consumers' buying preferences become more diversified as the extent of retail stores increases within a confined area. Thus, the market size reaches a threshold, and the consumers' preferences of shopping are jeopardized due to indecisiveness in shopping. However, shopping centers and hypermarkets became important elements in the urban landscape, though the lack of planning and vision led to chaotic development and congestion of marketplaces affecting the growth retailers (Kok 2007). A larger shopping center can facilitate a greater variety of shops and create a more pleasant environment for the shoppers, thus enticing shoppers to visit and stay longer. This proposition leads to one of the challenges faced by the managers of shopping malls located outside the traditional shopping belt, which is how to attract shoppers to patronize their malls (Ooi and Sim 2007).

The process of suburbanization has gone beyond purely government-initiated relocation of households and polluting industries in emerging markets such as India, China, Brazil, and Mexico. In order to reduce the shopping area congestion, a new round of suburbanization has been driven by the development of large suburban shopping malls and retail parks. It is observed that large and recreational shopping malls attract the regular shoppers and tourists toward frequent shopping. Accordingly, most of the growing cities are patronizing their suburban shopping malls and power centers, rather than downtown marketplaces. Major attributes of shopping mall attractiveness include comfort, entertainment, diversity, mall essence, convenience, and luxury from the perspective of shoppers. Such shopping mall attractiveness may be designed in reference to the three broad segments of shoppers that include stress-free shoppers, demanding shoppers, and pragmatic shoppers. This enables mall managers to develop appropriate retailing strategies to satisfy each segment (El-Adly 2007).

Business Collaboration and Market Competition

Globalization has also induced regional growth of markets as a springboard for firms to go global. In this process, firms grow out of their niche with the support of technology and customer relation strategies. Many firms serving the niche move to the regional marketplace as the Internet and related technologies vastly expand the variety of products that can be produced, promoted, and purchased. Although this revolution is based on a simple set of economic and technological drivers, its implications are far-reaching for managers, consumers, and the economy as a whole. In this process, customers derive value from an important characteristic of Internet markets and the ability of online merchants to help consumers locate, evaluate, and purchase a far wider range of products (Brynjolfsson et al. 2006). Developing new competencies in the niche firms requires constant experimentation. However, the innovation–imitation–equilibrium cycle suggests that industry leaders teach customers what to demand by defining the current state of the art in performance, price, service, and other dimensions; firms learn to judge competitive offerings against these standards, and the learning effect is cumulative (Werther and Kerr 1995).

A strong market-oriented strategy of the firm alleviates the possibility of using coercive influence strategies by the competitors and offers an advantage to the customers over competitive market forces. Market orientation is an organization-wide concept that helps to explain sustained competitive advantage. Since many manufacturing firms have linked their marketing strategies with services delivery attributes, the concept of market orientation is expanding as a system in global corporate settings. The process of market orientation contributes to continuous learning and knowledge accumulation by an organization, which continuously collects information about customers and competitors and uses it to create superior customer value and competitive advantage (Slater and Narver 1995). It is important for the company to consider how well competition satisfies the needs of potential customers in the selected markets, as well as to determine the best fit of the firm's strategies in the determined market segment or niche. Should the firm offer a better location, convenience, better price, later hours, better quality, and better service, may be the further interest of the firm to gain the competitive advantage.

The business partnership strategies should be developed keeping in view the heterogeneity in economic development, culture, and institutional modalities that exist in both regions, while seeking globally balanced relations. The relationship should be based on fundamental shared principles and values, which in turn can be translated into clear political messages and a general sustained process of dialogue and cooperation. Relationships can be deepened at the bi-regional, regional, or bilateral levels, taking advantages of the special circumstances of country groupings. Building relationships should proceed at different levels and speeds among the countries of the region. Considering the multiplicity of forums, it is necessary to focus the trade partnering negotiations at bilateral and multilateral levels and avoid overlap between distinct dialogues and similar initiatives taken at other forums. Bilateral negotiations should be strategically pursued in removing/reducing the non-tariff and investment barriers. The trade-related negotiations among the Latin America–East Asian countries should also focus on the technical norms and standards; rules of origin, anti-dumping, subsidies, and countervailing measures; other liberalization and deregulation measures (privatization); sub-regional, regional, and hemispheric integration processes; and convergence and divergence between regional integration and multilateral trade regimes. The negotiations should also be dealt on simplifying the customs rules and procedures, including non-transparent and inefficient infrastructures; differing customs; and improper application of rules of origin, customs valuation, pre-shipment inspection, and import licensing. Customs problems can be especially difficult for small and medium enterprises that have less experience and fewer resources for handling these problems.

Regional or bilateral agreements may bring faster results than the multilateral process, may enable parties to conclude levels of liberalization beyond the multilateral consensus, and may be able to address specific issues that do not register on the multilateral menu. The resulting achievements in trade liberalization can be substantial complements to the WTO system, and they can be the important building blocks for future multilateral liberalization. The most powerful economic arguments against regional and bilateral trade agreements are that they can cause trade diversion and trade distortions and ultimately undermine the multilateral system because of their discriminatory nature. In some cases, preferential rules of origin have proven to stifle technological developments, networks and joint manufacturing, and to unduly restrict third-country sourcing, leading to trade diversion. Moreover, they can create obstacles to trade facilitation by increasing administrative complexity at customs. One specific example is the proliferation of different preferential rules of origin a prominent source of trade costs and complexity in today's global marketplace in which companies depend on the rapid delivery of products and components from multiple overseas sources. Such effects are costly to business and detrimental to the regional trading areas. Harmonization and simplification of preferential rules of origin and the accumulation of origin could alleviate some of these obstacles to trade facilitation.[1]

Route to market is the multi-channel retailing strategy that caters to the wide preferences of shopping of the customers at a varied price, delivery, and services options. A company may set more than one routes for its products and services to facilitate consumer convenience in buying. It is necessary that sales people should know these routes to markets and prospect consumers at their most convenient route. In multi-channel selling strategy, salespeople can prospect consumers for offering superior products, typically accompanied by superior service outputs, to be sold at higher prices for premium market segment while low-price strategy is followed for mass-market retail locations (Jindal et al. 2007). However, luxury goods are not commonly sold through catalogs, e-bays, or call centers, and differentiated products usually need relatively more intermediary support to be delivered satisfactorily to the end customer. However, urban shoppers incur higher search costs when searching for a product across retailing channels and gathering information on prices as the urban shoppers are more guided by the value for money considerations in shopping. It is observed that price-sensitive customers always intend to strike a beneficial deal over the costs they incur during searching for such bargain through various channel options (Rajagopal 2008). A route to market is a distinct sales process followed by salespeople toward prospecting customers for a selected product or service through a specific market channel. Agents of call centers, representatives of e-bay, and personal selling representatives engaged in prospecting consumers may be assigned to manage sales in different routes to market. Globalization and innovative selling practices have introduced multiple channel selling strategies to improve customer satisfaction and strengthen customer–retailer dyadic loyalty (Wallace et al. 2004).

The markets today not only provide the multiple goods and services to the customers but also expose their behavior to the cross-cultural differences and innovations. The specialization of the production process has also brought such cultural changes by business penetrations in the low production skill regions across the countries. The apparel from Asian countries like Indonesia and Korea and all types of consumer goods from China, electronics from Japan, and perfumery from France may be some good examples to explain the specialization and cross-cultural sharing of consumer behavior. Conducting business is a creative enterprise and doing it out of one's own country is more demanding. The industry structure varies dramatically across countries in the world, and a global enterprise to strive against odds requires strong adaptation behavior. In the international business, a company needs to best prepare itself to achieve competitive advantage in the marketplace. The international alliances in reference to production technology, co-branding, distribution, and retailing may bring a high success to the companies of home country in increasing the market share in the region as well as augmenting the customer value for mutual benefit.

Technology Drivers Ahead in Marketing

One of the growing concerns in the global marketplace is that new firms from emerging markets are becoming significant global players boosting the market competition at regional and global levels. However, there exists the scope for a large number of follower firms to catch up with emerging firms at different levels of markets. The firms from emerging markets can be best understood in terms of intensity of technology application and research and development. Broadly, the emerging firms may be categorized as regional challengers, global exporters and importers, original equipment manufacturers, original design manufacturers, value-added reseller firms as technology followers, and regional exporters and importers (Tsai and Eisingerich 2010).

Technology is associated as one of the principal factors of production and economic growth of a country or development sector as an agent of growth and prosperity. However, retailing sector, which is part of the distribution side of the economy, has also contributed significantly to advances in technology, economic growth, and the betterment of society. Technology and retailing have been inextricably linked in terms of both their development and their ability to deliver unique benefits to consumers (Tamilia and Reid 2007). Increasing globalization and competitiveness in the retail environment is thrusting retail firms to reach high levels of consistent experimentation of new technology in store management, product information, and customer services. Technology management can be used to help retailers test new ideas and implement the most successful ones. However, human behavior is particularly important in the retail setting, where projects are generally focused on testing new concepts, increasing collaboration, and implementing new technologies (Thomas et al. 2008).

In the scenario of growing competition, retailer firms can also establish how a customer relationship management and monitoring system ensures the buying decision-making process with joint project teams and facilitating technology. Development and innovative applications of e-commerce transactions, as well as the integration of available technology, can provide an organization with a unique opportunity to remain competitive within today's global business environment. Although technology plays an important role in gaining a competitive advantage for organizations worldwide, information technology professionals, consumers, and e-retailers ensure proper security measures to overcome the harmful impact of the misuse of these same technologies (Medlin and Romaniello 2008).

The technological changes are the main impetus behind new market opportunities. The extent of such change may be explained from super-technologies to the appropriate and intermediate technologies. The strategic choices have wide-ranging ripple effects through the organization that determine the key success factors and growth performance. Some companies would be making right strategic choices by improving the implementation process of competitive advantages. These companies are guided by the shared strategic vision and are driven by the responsive attitude toward the market requirements. They emphasize the continuous strive to satisfy the consumers. A strategic vision in managing markets may be understood as the guiding theme that explains the nature of the business and the future projections thereof. These projections or business intentions depend on the collective analysis of the environment that determines the need for new developments or diversifications. The vision should be commissioned on a concrete understanding of the business and the ability to foresee the impact of market forces on the growth of the business. The vision will motivate the organization for collaborative business planning and implementation. The powerful visions are also the statements of intent that create an obsession with winning the organization. The business strategy broadly incorporates the following dimensions:

- Consumer needs
- Consumer segments
- Technology and resources
- Activities in the value-added chain.

Strategic thrust has a significant magnitude and direction in sailing the business through the turbulent situation. The factors associated with the competitive advantage and business investments uphold the strategic thrust to achieve the business objectives through the positive channel efforts. The competitive advantage may be assessed in reference to the superior consumer value and the lowest delivered cost. Such combination of the strategies may be termed as competitive superiority that explains the cost-effective delivery strategy to enhance the consumer value. An overall edge is gained by performing most of the activities at a lower cost than competitors. This would enable the company to optimize its cost of delivery of the new products and simultaneously enhance the consumer value to uphold the strategic thrust of the company.

It is observed in many research studies that logistics and information technology strategies are developed and implemented in a parallel way by both manufacturers and multiple retailers. Applying improved technology suggests that multinational firms possess greater operational efficiency at both secondary and in-store distribution operations as compared to the firms using conventional practices, which is largely attributed to their integration of logistics and information technology operations (Bourlakis and Bourlakis 2006). As the market competition is increasing in the global marketplace, emerging firms tend to apply technology assets in their own products and services securing them through the property rights protection. In view of the upcoming trend toward open innovation, however, many firms have begun to actively license out the technology. These firms consider technology licensing a strategic activity, which may include all technology assets and goes far beyond the marginal activity of commercializing residual technologies. The strategic drivers strengthen the interdependencies in both internally and externally commercializing technology (Lichtenthaler 2007).

The role of marketing strategies in fostering controlled consumer empowerment is reflected in the development of information-based consumer-centric marketing strategies that seek to enable and control delegation. In designing such strategies, consumers' familiarity with the use of information and communication technologies are both strengthened and widened, emphasizing the uncontrolled nature of the consumer empowerment process. There is a need to regain control over the marketing process, that is, to manage the technological empowerment of consumers, or to devise new strategies cognizant of the possibility that such technological empowerment cannot be managed. The valuation of consumer loyalty in this environment rises significantly (Pires et al. 2006).

In developing countries, the business opportunities may be explored for the two prominent reasons. First, a large number of developing countries are pursuing a growth path. Most recently, India and Eastern European countries have also opened up the gates to globalization in consonance with the neoliberalism concepts. The developing world is beginning to rely on the international market mechanism to attract investment and technology and become industrialized. Such change proneness has given scope to the increasing demand for the technological and environmental products world over. An example of organic products marketing may be appropriately discussed in this context. Most major markets offer good prospects for suppliers of organic products that are not produced domestically, such as coffee, tea, cocoa, spices, tropical fruits and vegetables, and citrus fruits. These opportunities stem from the simple fact that rapidly growing demand in most markets cannot be met by local supply, at least in the short and medium terms. Developing countries produce a wide range of organic products and many are exporting them successfully. Second, opportunities in developing countries should be even more closely examined than those in advanced countries as the government plays a significant role in business decisions in developing countries. This necessitates dealing with the procedural issues therein in foreign investment with considerable sophistication and confidence.

Notes

1. International Chamber of Commerce: Regional Trade Agreements and the Multilateral Trading System, Document# 103, 2002.

References

Bellin, J. B., & Pham, C. T. (2007). Global expansion: Balancing a uniform performance culture with local conditions. *Strategy and Leadership, 35*(6), 44–50.

Bourlakis, M., & Bourlakis, C. (2006). Integrating logistics and information technology strategies for sustainable competitive advantage. *Journal of Enterprise Information Management, 19*(4), 389–402.

Bridgewater, S., Bridgette, S. T., Mattsson, J. R., & Bruce. J. E. (2004). The internationalization process and the role of learning in small service firms. In F. McDonald, M. E Mayer, & T. Buck (Eds.), *The Process of Internationalization: Strategic, Cultural and Policy Perspectives.* New York: Palgrave MacMillan.

Brynjolfsson, E., Hu, Y. J., Smith, M., & Smith, M. (2006). From niches to riches: Anatomy of the long tail. *Sloan Management Review, 47*(4), 67–71.

El-Adly, M. I. (2007). Shopping malls attractiveness: A segmentation approach. *International Journal of Retail & Distribution Management, 35*(11), 936–950.

Jindal, R. P., Reinartz, W., Krafft, M., & Hoyer, W. D. (2007). Determinants of the variety of routes to market. *International Journal of Research in Marketing, 24*(1), 17–29.

Kim, W. C., & Mauborgne, R. (1999). Creating new market space. *Harvard Business Review, 27*(1), 83–93.

Kok, H. (2007). Restructuring retail property markets in Central Europe: Impacts on urban space. *Journal of Housing and the Built Environment, 22*(1), 107–126.

Lichtenthaler, U. (2007). Drivers of technology licensing: An industry comparison. *California Management Review, 49*(4), 67–89.

Medlin, B. D., & Romaniello, A. (2008). The cost of electronic retailing: Prevalent security threats and their results. *International Journal of Electronic Marketing and Retailing, 2*(1), 80–96.

Mundy, K. (2007). Global governance, educational change. *Comparative Education, 43*(3), 339–357.

Ooi, J. T. L., & Sim, L. L. (2007). The magnetism of suburban shopping centers: Do size and Cineplex matter? *Journal of Property Investment and Finance, 25*(2), 111–135.

Payne, A., & Frow, P. (2005). Strategic framework for customer relationship management. *Journal of Marketing, 69*(4), 167–176.

Pires, G. D., Stanton, J., & Rita, P. (2006). The internet, consumer empowerment and marketing strategies. *European Journal of Marketing, 40*(9–10), 936–949.

Rajagopal, (2008). Point of sales promotions and buying stimulation in retail stores. *Journal of Database Marketing and Customer Strategy Management, 15*(4), 249–266.

Rodrigues, F., & Rodrik, D. (2001). Trade Policy and Economic Growth: A Skeptic's Guide to the Cross-National Evidence. In Ben S. Bernanke and Kenneth Rogoff, (Eds.). *NBER Macroeconomics Annual* 2000, *15*, Cambridge, MA: MIT Press.

Rodríguez, C. M. (2005, January). Emergence of a third culture—shared leadership in international strategic alliance. *International Marketing Review, 22* (1), 67–95

Routh, A. E. (2007). Art of designing markets. *Harvard Business Review, 85*(10), 118–126.

Rust, R. T., Moorman, C., & Bhalla, G. (2010). Rethinking marketing. *Harvard Business Review, 88*(1), 94–101.

Slater, S., & Narver, J. (1995). Market orientation and the learning organization. *Journal of Marketing, 59*(3), 63–74.

Tamilia, R. D., & Reid, S. E. (2007). Technological innovation and the rise of the department store in the 19th century. *International Journal of Technology Marketing, 2*(2), 119–139.

Thomas, R., Tillmann, W., & Fawcett, S. (2008). Project management in retailing: Integrating the behavioral dimension. *The International Review of Retail, Distribution and Consumer Research, 18*(3), 325–341.

Tsai, H., & Eisingerich, A. B. (2010). Internationalization strategies of emerging markets firms. *California Management Review, 53*(1), 114–135.

UNCTAD. (2016). Trade and Development Report-2016. In *United Nations Conference on Trade and Development*. Geneva: United Nations.

Villareal, M. A., & Ferguson, I. F. (2017). *The North American Free Trade Agreement (NAFTA)*, CRS Report, Congressional Research Service, Report #7–5700, Washington, DC.

Wallace, D. W., Giese, J. L., & Johnson, J. L. (2004). Customer retailer loyalty in the context of multiple channel strategies. *Journal of Retailing, 80*(4), 249–263.

Werther, W. B., & Kerr, J. L. (1995). Shifting sands of competitive advantage. *Business Horizons, 38*(3), 11–17.

Index

Rajagopal and V. Zlatev, *Business Dynamics in North America*,
DOI 10.1007/978-3-319-57606-0

I

J

K

L

M

Year	*Canada*			*Mexico*			*NAFTA*		
	Exports	*Imports*	*Trade balance*	*Exports*	*Imports*	*Trade balance*	*Exports*	*Imports*	*Trade balance*
2001	163.4 (24.7)	216.3 (17.8)	−52.8 (6.9)	101.3 (16.7)	131.3 (10.9)	−30.0 (5.8)	264.7 (41.4)	347.6 (28.7)	−82.9 (12.7)
2005	211.9 (32.8)	290.4 (22.6)	−78.5 (10.2)	120.2 (22.5)	170.1 (14.4)	−49.9 (8.1)	332.1 (55.3)	460.5 (37.0)	−128.3 (18.3)
2010	249.3 (53.1)	277.6 (27.4)	−28.4 (25.7)	163.7 (24.6)	230.0 (14.0)	−66.3 (10.6)	412.9 (77.7)	507.6 (41.4)	−94.7 (36.3)
2015	280.6 (56.4)	296.2 (29.0)	−15.5 (27.4)	235.7 (31.5)	296.4 (21.9)	−60.7 (9.6)	516.4 (87.9)	592.6 (50.9)	−76.2 (37.0)

The manufacturer's authorised representative in the EU is Springer Nature Customer Service Centre GmbH, Europaplatz 3, 69115 Heidelberg, Germany. If you have any concerns regarding our products, please contact ProductSafety@springernature.com

Printed and bound by CPI Group (UK) Ltd, Croydon, CR0 4YY
30/09/2026
02225216-0011